NAHC

Wild Game Cookbook

edited by
Bill Miller, Ron Larsen
Colleen Ferguson

designed by
Dean Peters

Published by the North American Hunting Club
Minneapolis, Minnesota 55343

We would like to thank the following for their help:

NAHC Members, past and present, for being the source of more than 350 wild game recipes for this special anniversary 1992 NAHC Wild Game Cookbook. The recipes in this book are considered the *best* of the best. They are recommended from your fellow members and are the heart of this cookbook.

NAHC Staff Members, for their long hours in seeing that this project became a reality, Publisher Mark LaBarbera; Editor Bill Miller; Associate Editors Dan Dietrich and Ron Larsen; Art Director Dean Peters; Editorial Assistant Colleen Ferguson; Vice President of Products Marketing Mike Vail, Marketing Manager Linda Kalinowski and Marketing Project Coordinator Laura Resnik.

Cover photo by Dan Dietrich.

*Address reprint requests
and orders for additional books to:*
NAHC Cookbook Editor,
P.O. Box 3401
Minneapolis, MN 55343

Library of Congress Catalog Card Number 84-649847
ISBN 0-914697-36-6
Copyright 1991, North American Hunting Club

Contents

Paul S. Burke, Jr.

Introduction

When Christopher Columbus was trying to raise money for a second voyage to the New World, the story goes, he was making his case to a council of royal ministers. Perhaps because of jealousy of Columbus' success, the ministers were reluctant to provide him with funds. "All you did," said one of them, "was sail westward until you struck land. Anyone could do that."

On the table was a bowl filled with fruit and hard-boiled eggs. Columbus took an egg from the bowl, and asked, "Can anyone balance this egg on its end?"

Several of the ministers tried without success. Columbus took the egg, tapped it on the table until the shell cracked slightly, then stood the egg up on the small flat spot he had created.

"Why," said one of the ministers, "anyone can do that."

"Yes," said Columbus. "Anyone can do it—*after they have been shown how.*"

The same holds true for cooking wild game. The secret, most North American Hunting Club members have discovered, is finding the right combination of ingredients to make a wild game recipe work. That is the tough part. Certain spices work with certain wild game and juices to flavor the meat the way we like it best. As Columbus said, "Anyone can do it—*after they have been shown how.*"

This NAHC Cookbook shows you how to serve up satisfying wild game meals to your family and friends. It is the Christopher Columbus of your new world of preparing mouth-watering wild game meals. The tough part is done. We've sifted through and explored every original game recipe submitted by NAHC members during the past decade and selected only the best. The result is this special edition.

We're hunters and wild game cooks like you. We understand what you're looking for in a cookbook. We believe in the old Indian saying that, "No man should criticize his neighbor before he has walked a mile in his moccasins."

Well, we've walked hundreds of miles in your moccasins because we're hunters, too, plus we pay close attention to what you have told us.

We took all of this information and used it like a bright lantern in the wilderness of cookbooks and recipes, and it guided us to this special edition. Your comments about earlier, highly successful NAHC game cookbooks allowed us to fine-tune the design and content so this NAHC Cookbook could zero in, right on target, to fulfill your needs when faced with a thawing piece of wild game.

At my home in Minneapolis, Minnesota, I'm always amazed at how quiet it gets around our dining room table when my wife, Irene, serves a wild game dinner. No one wastes time talking when they could be digging into venison tenderloins or roast pheasant. I don't blame them, and Irene recognizes silent compliments. When you prepare wild game with the recipes found on the following pages, expect the same satisfying silence as your table guests savor these great dishes.

While most every hunter looks forward to a meal of wild game, some people are actually afraid of eating the meat once they know it is wild game. You'll find that if they hadn't known what it was before they tasted it, they would not hesitate to admit how good the meat really tastes.

There are also people who are afraid to cook wild game. These same people, who regularly prepare farm-raised chickens, turkey, beef and pork, worry unnecessarily that they won't be able to cover up the "wild game taste" of meals harvested from the wilds. What a mistake they're making! Why should elk, deer and moose taste like beef when they have a delicious taste of their own? The recipes in this cookbook will enhance, not hide, the real flavor of each meal.

While hunting success is not measured solely by the amount of game taken, converting that success to tablefare is a vital tradition dating back to man's earliest history. A delicious wild game meal is the final satisfying reward a hunter has before only memories are left. This cookbook will help you carry on that tradition and heighten your enjoyment of wild game.

Best afield and in the kitchen.

Paul S. Burke, Jr.
Chairman of the Board

Steven F. Burke

Ten Great Years

Thinking back on hunting trips I've been lucky enough to enjoy, it would be difficult to pick the best. No, let's make that impossible to pick the best.

If pressed, I could probably come up with a list of favorites, but even that would number in the teens, maybe the twenties. In musical parlance, it would require a four-album set to cover "the best of" my personal hunting trips.

My guess is that such is the case for every NAHC member. We all certainly have a few hunts that stick out as the greatest among the greats, but by examining our scrap books a bit more closely, I think we'd all find that nearly every moment spent afield becomes a favorite in one way or another. Some hunts produce trophies. Some hunts are special because of the people who shared them. Some hunts didn't seem so enjoyable at the time, but produce smiles and chuckles when viewed through the perspective of passing years.

It was with that "best of" attitude that the NAHC staff used to set out to create the cookbook you have in your hands. We dug deep into the club's historical files to gather recipes, hunting tips, favorite campfire yarns and woods lore dating way back to the first *NAHC Wild Game Cookbook* which was published more than a decade ago.

In doing so what we discovered was that just like trying to sort hunting trips into mental "best of" ranks, there was no way we could label any material from previous cookbooks as the cut and dried "best of". Each tip, each recipe and each story proved a jewel all its own. Not only because the information they provide is great, but because each represents a shared moment among NAHC members. Each is a reminder of the camaraderie which non-hunters will never know.

In the NAHC's 13-year history it is that willingness to share, that dedication to our common cause and that kindred spirit among the ever-growing membership that has made our organization what it is today. Those things are also what make my job as president of the NAHC so gratifying.

So what we've instead decided to call this tenth edition of the *NAHC Wild Game Cookbook* is a celebration of 10 years of great recipes. In a large part, it's made up of the recipes which NAHC members have been generous enough to share over the years. It also contains recipes from the most prestigious of our celebrity chefs. We're especially honored to include recipes from the late Fred Bear and Roy Weatherby, the loss of whom we all mourn.

All totaled, this 1992 celebration cookbook includes nearly *twice* as many mouth-watering recipes as any of our previous editions! That's what you'd expect of a true celebration; that's what you get in this jam-packed edition.

You'll be glad to see that we've also included the field tips, meat handling information and kitchen cutlery pointers which

Members have told us have been of great importance in preparing the highest quality wild game meals. All this information is provided in simple, easy-to-follow language which will keep you coming back to this special book time and time again.

All of this is spiced with brand new information on basic cooking solutions that you can use in making your hunting buddies believe that you're the greatest chef in the world! Just try these great new techniques and you'll see!

Being forced to pick favorites could quickly become an unpleasant task. But preparing for you this Celebration of 10 Years of Great Wild Game Recipes has been a pleasure. It's given us the opportunity to reminisce over a wonderful decade, and, even better, plan for the day when we'll put together a collection of 20 years of great wild game cooking and NAHC camaraderie.

Good hunting and good eating.

Steven F. Burke
President

COOKBOOK ABBREVIATIONS

tsp.	=	teaspoon
T.	=	tablespoon
pt.	=	pint
oz.	=	ounce
lb.	=	pound
pkg.	=	package
qt.	=	quart

MEASUREMENT CONVERSIONS

1 pinch	=	less than ⅛ tsp.
1 T.	=	3 tsp.
2 T.	=	1 oz.
4 T.	=	¼ cup
5 T. + 1 tsp.	=	⅓ cup
8 T.	=	½ cup
10 T. + 2 tsp.	=	⅔ cup
12 T.	=	¾ cup
16 T.	=	1 cup

1 cup	=	8 oz.
1 pint	=	16 oz.
1 quart	=	32 oz.
1 gallon	=	128 oz.

1 cup	=	½ pint
2 cups	=	1 pint
4 cups	=	1 quart
2 pints	=	1 quart
4 pints	=	½ gallon
8 pints	=	1 gallon
4 quarts	=	1 gallon
8 gallons	=	1 bushel

Venison

Deer are the most popular big game animals in North America. By that virtue alone, you can understand why they rate such a large section in this collection of all-time great NAHC recipes. In fact, in the pages that follow you'll find an amazing 130 ways to prepare your prized harvest of venison.

All choice cuts of venison, which by broad definition can include the meat from deer, elk and caribou, can be prepared in the same manner you would cook beef. Other non-choice cuts can be marinated and then cooked as beef.

An important thing to remember, although some hunters still disagree, is a freshly taken animal should be bled completely. Where it's legal, cutting the head off of the game is most desirable if you do the job right. In other places, it will be sufficient to cut the jugular.

After dressing the animal and bringing it back to camp or home, skin, cool and hang or freeze it as quickly as possible.

Be careful not to cut glands in the lower belly region of these game animals because the result will be tainted meat.

It's best to remove the fat because it can turn rancid. Keep loose hair from the flesh because the oils in the hair can give the meat an "off" flavor. All the blood from wounds should be cleaned by scraping or washing with salt water.

If you are going to save the liver and heart, we suggest cooking and eating it before the end of the day, preferably within four hours for the best results.

Tips On Using Venison

When you encounter bloodshot meat, most of it can be saved by soaking it in cold, salt water. Put about a gallon of water in a three or four gallon bucket or dishpan, add three or four handfuls of salt and put the bloodshot meat into the solution. Let it soak for an hour or two, then wash and scrub the blood off the pieces and use according to the cut of meat. If the blood impregnates the muscles of the meat, trim it out and throw it in the scrap box.

The boning process usually results in lots of steak meat from the deer or elk. If you don't care to bone your own deer but would like to try cooking and eating venison from a boned deer, ask your butcher to help you. Besides the usual service of processing deer, some meat cutters have even cut up deer and put all the parts in a box for the hunter to take home and finish with the trimming, wrapping, marking and freezing.

A venison steak is not like a beef steak. A venison steak is smaller in diameter, without bone or much fat, and can be cut from most of the larger muscles. In other words, the loin, tenderloin and round are not the only sources of steaks from a deer. Muscles from the shoulder blade, rump roast, arm roast and on the rib cage can be isolated and cut into thin venison steaks. They are small, but delicious, and are a favorite breakfast meat for many NAHC families.

Venison steaks from a boned deer are cut differently than domestic meat. Cut all venison steaks thin, except those coming from the loin and tenderloin. Steaks from tenderloin and loin can be cut either thick or thin, depending on your preference. A thin venison steak is about ¼-inch thick and a thick one is about ¾ inch.

The diameter of small steaks can be enlarged by butterflying them. A butterflied steak consists of two steaks laid side by side but connected by tissue on one edge.

The chunks of round from the hind leg make excellent steaks when cut thin. Have the chunk partially thawed by dinner time but cut it into ¼- to ⅜-inch steaks just before frying. Fry in a hot skillet or frying pan. The frying time is about 90 seconds on a side for a steak cut ¼-inch thick. Fry steaks just enough to brown the outside, but leave the center slightly pink. The steaks should be juicy and tender. If the steak is dry and tough, it was cooked too long.

Steaks from the loin are usually cut ¾-inch thick. However, they can be as thin as ¼ inch and as thick as 1½ inches. Fry or broil to suit taste.

If roasting venison is a challenge for you, try this recipe:

Lay out a piece of aluminum foil large enough to double-wrap the roast. Sprinkle one-half package of dehydrated vegetable soup mix on the aluminum foil. Place the thawed roast on top of the vegetable soup mix and pour the rest of the soup mix on top of the roast. Tightly wrap aluminum foil around the roast and place it in an oven preheated to 325-350 degrees. Cook the average two- or three-pound venison roast for 1½ to 2½ hours, depending on how well done you prefer the venison. The meat will be juicy and moist with this method of roasting.

Use your favorite shortening in frying steaks, but bacon and beef fat are favorites. If you have never tried beef fat as shortening for frying steaks, you may be in for a pleasant surprise.

Freezing Venison Properly

Freezing chunks of venison whole helps to preserve moisture and flavor in the meat. Also, it saves time in cutting and wrapping and gives the cook a choice of ways to prepare the meat for the table.

Keep all air out of packages and double wrap them with suitable paper or seal tightly in special plastics or freezer bags. The best way to freeze meat is to have it quick-frozen at extremely cold temperatures and then stored at zero degrees or below. Whatever method of wrapping you use, be sure to label and date the packages for later identification.

Finally, as you sit with your family at the table later in the year, make mental notes about how everyone reacted to the various cuts of meat. Then, next year you can tailor your meat cutting to each individual's preference. Bon appetit!

Weigh Your Deer Without A Scale

You can weigh your deer with nothing more than an ordinary dollar bill. That's right, George, Abe and the more costly greenbacks all work with an amazing degree of accuracy.

Borrowing this technique from the cattle industry and verifying it with university wildlife researchers, experts have found this quick way to weigh your trophy.

Carry along a piece of string, shoelace or drag rope to wrap around the deer's chest behind the front legs. Note the spot on the string that shows its girth, or distance around the deer. Pull out a dollar bill from your wallet and notice it is always six inches long. Use it to measure the length of the string to the girth mark.

Just compare the number of inches to the chart on the next page, which you can copy and carry in your wallet, and you will be able to read across to your deer's live weight, dressed weight and edible meat predictions.

For you doubting Thomases, after you've tried this method, verify its accuracy at a certified scale.

Venison

GIRTH	LIVE WEIGHT	DRESSED	EDIBLE MEAT
20"	49 lb.	32 lb.	23 lb.
22"	56 lb.	38 lb.	26 lb.
24"	65 lb.	45 lb.	30 lb.
26"	74 lb.	53 lb.	34 lb.
28"	85 lb.	62 lb.	38 lb.
30"	97 lb.	73 lb.	44 lb.
32"	111 lb.	85 lb.	50 lb.
34"	127 lb.	99 lb.	57 lb.
36"	145 lb.	114 lb.	65 lb.
38"	166 lb.	132 lb.	74 lb.
40"	191 lb.	153 lb.	85 lb.
42"	218 lb.	177 lb.	97 lb.
44"	250 lb.	204 lb.	110 lb.
46"	286 lb.	234 lb.	126 lb.

Easter Day Venison

Serves: 5
Prep Time: 1 hour

3 **lb. venison roast**
bacon
⅓ **cup soy sauce**
⅔ **cup water**
5 **large potatoes, peeled**
and chunked
5 **carrots, peeled and**
sliced

3 **medium onions,**
quartered
Worcestershire sauce
1 **can vegetable soup**
1 **can water**

Heat covered electric frying pan to 350 degrees. Wrap entire roast in bacon strips and pin in place with toothpicks. Place in frying pan with soy sauce and ⅔ cup water. Cover and allow to cook for 20 minutes. Add a 2-to-1 water/soy sauce mixture as needed to keep liquid in bottom of pan. After 20 minutes add potatoes, carrots, onions and a dash of Worcestershire sauce. Cook for another 40 minutes, turning roast occasionally, stirring vegetables and basting as needed with water/soy sauce. In the last 10 minutes of cooking add soup and 1 can water. To serve, remove bacon strips and slice roast ¼- to ½-inch thick. Pepper to taste and serve with fruit salad for a complete meal.

Bill Miller
Eau Claire, Wisconsin

Opening Day Venison Tenderloin

Serves: 6
Prep Time: 2 hours

1 **whole venison**
tenderloin
¼ **lb. butter**
1 **medium onion, sliced**

Worcestershire sauce
5 **bacon slices, cooked but**
not crisp

In skillet over medium-high heat, melt butter. Saute steaks with sliced onion, sprinkling with Worcestershire sauce. Wrap with bacon slices and serve with toothpicks.

Anonymous

Svickova Venison

Serves: 4-6
Prep Time: 8 days

1 **3-4 lb. venison roast**	**salt, to taste**
8-10 **garlic cloves**	3-4 **T. vinegar**
2-3 **celery ribs, chunked**	1 **large onion, chunked**
1 **large onion, chunked**	**Add to gravy mixture:**
3 **carrots, chunked**	½ **cup flour**
8-10 **whole peppercorns**	1 **tsp. sugar**
2 **qts. water**	1-2 **tsp. vinegar**
2 **bay leaves**	**milk, to taste**

Make slits in top of meat and insert garlic cloves. Bring vegetables and spices to a boil in 2 qts. water and simmer until crisp. Let cool. Add salt and vinegar. Mix well. Place meat in non-aluminum container. Pour water mixture with vegetables over meat, adding water until covered. Marinate meat in cool place 7-8 days turning roast over each day. Bring meat/marinade to a boil on stove, then simmer. Skim foam off as it rises from meat. Simmer 10 minutes. Place meat in roaster. Add onion around meat. Roast 2 hours at 325 degrees. To make gravy, remove vegetables to separate pan and mash. Add about 1 qt. water mixture. Simmer. Mix ½ cup flour with water and add to vegetable mixture to thicken. Strain mixture. Season adding sugar and vinegar. Add milk. Slice meat and serve gravy on top.

Andy Simo
Berwyn, Illinois

Straight Forward Roast Venison

Serves: 6
Prep Time: 2-3 hours

1 **neck roast or rump roast**	**garlic powder**
1 **pkg. onion soup mix**	**parsley flakes**
salt and pepper	**sweet basil**

Season meat with ingredients. Wrap tightly in heavy foil. Roast at 325 degrees for 2-3 hours.

Daniel Hotten
Calvin, North Dakota

Venison Roast

Serves: 6-8
Prep Time: overnight, plus 4 hours

5-6 lb. venison roast
½ cup dry red wine
¼ cup olive oil
1 T. salt
1 T. crushed rosemary
½ tsp. black pepper
¼ tsp. powdered cloves
1 garlic clove, chopped

½ lb. bacon, sliced
1 cup celery, diced
1 cup carrots, diced
1 cup onion, diced
1 10½-oz. can beef consomme
remaining marinade

Combine first seven ingredients after venison roast to make marinade mixture. Marinate roast overnight. Place venison in roasting pan. Make a few slits in meat with knife and spoon mixture over meat. Cover with bacon. In bottom of roasting pan combine remaining ingredients. Roast at 400 degrees for 10 minutes. Reduce heat to 350 degrees and roast 1 hour, 30 minutes, basting every 20 minutes with pan drippings. Remove roast to platter. Strain pan drippings and thicken with flour to make gravy. Roast venison 10-15 minutes per pound.

Edward Almeida
Petaluma, California

Joe's Barbecued Deer

Serves: 4-6
Prep Time: 3 hours

1 venison roast, chunked
2 onions, chopped
salt and pepper
1 qt. barbecue sauce

1 large green pepper, diced
2 cups rice

Stew meat for 2 hours with onions, salt and pepper. Drain stock, leaving 1 cup. Add barbecue sauce and green pepper. Cook on low heat for 1 hour. Cook rice. Pour stew over rice.

Joe Sneed
Gastonia, North Carolina

Crockpot Venison Roast

Serves: 6-12
Prep Time: 3-4 hours

**1 3-5 lb. tenderloin,
 shoulder or hind roast**
¼ cup oil
¼ tsp. pepper
¼ tsp. garlic salt

1 pkg. onion soup mix, dry
**1 can cream of mushroom
 soup**
1 cup water

Pour oil in Crockpot and set on medium heat. Sprinkle pepper and garlic salt on meat and brown on all sides. Combine soups and water and pour over roast. Simmer 3 hours or until done. Remove roast and let stand a few minutes before cutting. Potatoes, carrots or quartered onions may also be added to Crockpot for added flavor.

Mrs. Mark Synan
Hanover, Virginia

Roast Saddle Of Venison

Serves: 4
Prep Time: 1 hour

**1 venison saddle, trim
 bones to loin
 salt
 white pepper**
1 cup white wine

**1 cup bread crumbs,
 finely chopped**
**¾ jar Grey Poupon
 mustard**

Season venison with salt and white pepper. Place in roasting pan and add white wine. Roast at 375 degrees until golden brown. Add bread crumbs to white wine mixture until a heavy paste is formed. Coat entire saddle with the mustard. (The Grey Poupon's tangy zest is well worth the extra money.) Spread on bread crumb mixture. Finish roasting at 375 degrees until top is totally brown. Recommended sauce: Bernaise or Mornay. Serve with wild rice.

Anonymous

Sweet And Tangy Venison Pot Roast

Serves: 4-5
Prep Time: 4 hours

3-4 lb. roast	**2 T. lemon juice**
3 T. lard or drippings	**1½ T. brown sugar**
1 medium onion, sliced	**1½ T. white vinegar**
½ cup catsup	**1½ T. Worcestershire sauce**
½ cup water	**½ bag carrots (cooked**
1 tsp. salt	**separately)**
⅛ tsp. pepper	

Cook meat for 2 hours. In pot, heat lard or drippings and saute onion. Add catsup, water, salt, pepper, lemon juice, brown sugar, white vinegar, and Worcestershire sauce. Stir and add meat. Cover and cook over low to medium heat for 2 hours. Slice carrots and cook carrots separately. Drain carrots and add to sauce during last 15 minutes of cooking time.

Richard Menghi
Lindenhurst, New York

Italian Venison

Serves: 4
Prep Time: 8-10 hours

2-3 lb. venison roast	**1 T. Worcestershire sauce**
1 tsp. oregano	**dash of Tabasco**
1 T. marjoram	**salt and pepper**
1 T. thyme	**1 large onion, diced**
1 T. garlic powder	**1 medium jalapeno pepper**
3 beef bouillon cubes	**1 medium green pepper**
3 cups water	**1 medium red pepper**

Mix first 10 ingredients and put in Crockpot. Cook 8-10 hours or until meat falls apart. Cook onions, hot peppers, green and red mild peppers in water to serve over meat. Serve with baked potatoes and salad.

Gloria Jones
Charleston, Illinois

Venison Dinner "Bag"

Serves: 6-8
Prep Time: 3 hours, 30 minutes

1 **6-10 lb. front shoulder, rump roast or small hind quarter**
1 **large cooking bag**
8 **medium potatoes, quartered**
3 **medium onions, quartered**
5 **carrots, sliced**
5 **celery stalks, sliced**
1 **pkg. onion soup mix, dry**
1 **can golden mushroom soup**

Place venison in cooking bag in oven pan. Surround venison with all vegetables. Sprinkle top of venison with onion soup. Pour mushroom soup on top of venison and spread evenly. Close end of bag and seal with wire wrap. Be sure to puncture top of bag prior to placing in oven. Place in preheated oven at 350 degrees for 2-3 hours. Remove from oven, carefully cut bag top open— enjoy—you have a complete meal in the bag. Season with salt, pepper, garlic powder, bay leaf, basil or whatever spices you prefer.

Pete Cuipenski
Tarpon Springs, Florida

Breaded Venison Chops Or Steak

Serves: 6
Prep Time: 1 hour

6 **chops or equal amount of steak**
1 **egg**
2 **T. water**
1 **cup bread crumbs**
1 **10 ½-oz. can cream of mushroom soup**
½ **cup water**

Beat egg with water. Dip chops (or steak) in egg mixture. Then coat with bread crumbs. Brown 10-15 minutes on each side. Add mushroom soup, thinned with ½ cup water. Simmer for 30 minutes or until done.

Ronald Orr
Ogallala, Nebraska

Buckrubs Crockpot Venison

Serves: 6
Prep Time: 9 hours

3 lbs. venison steak
1 cup flour
2 cans mushroom soup
1 tsp. oregano
1 tsp. dill weed
½ tsp. cayenne
½ tsp. black pepper
1 large onion, chopped
1 large bell pepper, chopped

1 pt. morel mushrooms, if possible
1 8-oz. can peeled tomatoes
6 garlic cloves
2 bay leaves
6 shakes of Tabasco

Remove all fat from steaks, roll in flour and brown. Steaks should be no larger than 2 inches x 2 inches. Add all remaining ingredients to Crockpot. Stir to evenly mix. If steaks are not covered by liquid, water or beer can be added to cover meat. Cook for 8 hours on low heat, don't remove lid as you lose needed heat.

LeRoy Ostlund
Traverse City, Michigan

Venison Picatta

Serves: 4
Prep Time: 30 minutes

8 thin venison steaks
1 cup flour
  salt and black pepper, to taste
1½ cups oil

1 cup dry vermouth
2 shallots, chopped
2 T. parsley, chopped
3 T. capers
¼ cup butter

Season and dredge steaks in flour. Fry quickly in hot oil. Pour off grease. Add the vermouth, shallots, parsley and capers, cook for 5 minutes. Take meat out and swirl butter into sauce. Pour sauce over steaks. Serve with pasta.

Scott Ekenberg
Eden Prairie, Minnesota

Venison Scallopini

Serves: 8
Prep Time: 2 hours

3 lbs. tender venison
butter and olive oil
1 green onions bunch
1 garlic clove
1 parsley bunch
2 rosemary sprigs, fresh

1 pinch marjoram
2 small cans tomato sauce
1 large can sliced
mushrooms, save juice
1 pt. dry sauterne or
sherry

About 45 minutes before preparing venison, start sauce. Heat small skillet, add half butter and half olive oil. After chopping very fine or using blender, add the following mixture and cook on medium heat for about 20 minutes: green onions (tops and all), garlic, parsley (not stems), rosemary (not stems), and marjoram. After 20 minutes, add tomato sauce and mushrooms (save juice for later). Stir well and cook for 10 minutes and simmer on low heat while cooking venison. Cut venison into 3-inch squares. Pound well and shake in seasoned flour (salt and pepper). Brown in hot skillet in half butter and half olive oil, about a minute on both sides. Add sauce and mix thoroughly. Simmer for 15 minutes. During last 4 minutes, add 1 cup sauterne or sherry. During last 2 minutes, add mushroom juice. Serve hot.

Harold Doughty
Napa, California

Teriyaki Venison Steak

Serves: 6
Prep Time: several hours

4-6 venison steaks
¼ cup soy sauce
1 garlic clove, crushed
1 tsp. sugar

½ tsp. monosodium
glutamate (MSG)
1 tsp. ground ginger
1 tsp. powdered AuJus

Mix all ingredients. Marinate several hours. Broil or barbecue steaks to desired doneness.

Nancy and Roger Dundas
Toston, Montana

Rita's German Cheese Schnitzel

Serves: 6
Prep Time: 1 hour, 15 minutes

1½ **lbs. venison round steak**
2 **T. lemon juice**
  salt and pepper, to taste
2 **eggs**
2 **T. cold water**
2 **T. cooking oil**
1½ **cups cracker crumbs**

⅓ **cup Parmesan cheese, grated**
⅓ **cup flour**
6 **T. butter or oleo**
  paprika
6 **thin lemon slices (optional)**

Pound meat to not more than ¼-inch thickness. Cut meat into cutlets if desired. Sprinkle lemon juice on both sides of meat. Let stand at room temperature for 30 minutes. Season meat with salt and pepper. Blend eggs, water and oil. Set aside. Combine cracker crumbs and cheese. Set aside. Coat cutlets with flour, then dip in egg mixture, holding meat up to allow excess egg mixture to drip off. Coat cutlets with cheese mixture. Let stand 15 minutes. Cook cutlets in melted butter being careful not to crowd meat. When meat is brown on one side, about 3 minutes, turn over and brown other side. To serve, sprinkle with cheese and paprika and garnish with lemon slices.

Diane Hodges
Fairbury, Illinois

Fried Venison Steak

Serves: 2-4
Prep Time: 30 minutes

1 **lb. steak**
1½ **cups bread crumbs**
1½ **tsp. parsley flakes**
1 **tsp. garlic salt**

½ **cup Parmesan cheese**
  salt and pepper
1 **egg, beaten**

Combine bread crumbs, parsley, garlic salt, cheese and salt and pepper. Dip steak in egg, then bread mixture. Fry covered for 20-30 minutes.

Ronald Bowers
Sugar Grove, West Virginia

Ranger Chops Modenese

Serves: 2
Prep Time: 1-2 hours

4 venison chops	**¼ cup olive oil**
2 6-oz. cans or 1 12-oz. can	**1 large onion, sliced**
tomato sauce	**4 baked ham slices**
½ tsp. dried basil leaf	**1 lb. whole or sliced fresh**
½ tsp. garlic powder	**mushrooms, sauteed**
½ tsp. dried oregano leaf	**3 oz. sliced mozzarella**
½ tsp. dried rosemary	**cheese**

In saucepan, combine tomato sauce, basil, garlic, oregano and rosemary. Cover and simmer over low heat 45 minutes. Heat oil in large skillet over medium-high heat. Add chops and onion and saute until chops are browned. Remove meat and onion from skillet and place in 2-qt. casserole. Ladle sauce over meat. Top with ham slices. Bake at 350 degrees for 45 minutes. Top with sauteed mushrooms and sliced cheese. Return to oven and continue baking 5 minutes longer.

Anonymous

Sportsman's Supper

Serves: 2
Prep Time: 45 minutes

4 venison chops	**1 16-oz. can small Irish**
salt and pepper	**whole potatoes, sliced**
8 smoked bacon slices	**4 T. butter**
1 large yellow onion,	
quartered	

Salt and pepper chops to taste. Wrap 2 bacon strips around each chop and secure with toothpicks. Place chops on grating over hot coals. Broil each side until medium done. At same time, place onion and potatoes in pot with butter, salt and pepper. Cover and cook over campfire, stirring occasionally. When ready, pour contents into tin platter.

"Montana" Mitch McMillen
Minnetonka, Minnesota

Lou's Venison Cordon Bleu

Serves: 10-12
Prep Time: 1 hour

24 venison cutlets	**¼ lb. butter**
12 mozzarella cheese slices	**2 cups dry white wine**
12 boiled ham slices	**salt and pepper, to taste**

To make cutlets, use a medium-cut slice of venison. Place meat between 2 pieces of waxed paper and pound with flat part of cleaver until flat and thin. Lay 1 cutlet down and place a slice of mozzarella cheese on ham on cutlet. Place another cutlet on top. Proceed to roll up until it looks like an egg roll. Insert toothpicks to hold cutlets intact. Place cutlets in fry pan with butter and just lightly brown. Remove from fry pan and place meat in shallow baking pan. Pour wine over cutlets and place in pan at 350 degrees for about 25 minutes. Remove from pan and serve with plenty of French bread for dipping in white gravy.

Louis Barbanera
Nanuet, New York

Glorified Chops

Serves: 8
Prep Time: 3-4 hours

8 venison chops	**3 cans tomato soup**
2 large onions	**3 soup cans water**
4 green peppers	**salt and pepper**
2 cups cooked rice	

Lay chops on bottom of large roaster. Slice a thick layer of onions on top. Cut green peppers in half and put on top of onion. Fill each green pepper with rice. Mix tomato soup and water. Pour tomato mixture all around and put 2 spoonfuls on top of rice. Bake at 325 degrees for 3-4 hours. Salt and pepper to taste. Serve hot with a tasty, green salad.

Haven Post
Sturgis, Michigan

Italian Venison Rolls

Serves: 4
Prep Time: 1 hour

2 **large venison steaks**	6 **T. Worcestershire sauce**
1 **large onion, sliced**	**garlic powder**
1 **large green pepper, sliced**	8 **oz. mozzarella cheese, shredded**
fresh mushrooms, sliced	1 **jar Ragu Italian sauce**
¼ **lb. butter**	

Saute onion, pepper and mushrooms in butter until completely cooked. Remove from pan to drain. Add butter to pan with Worcestershire sauce and increase heat. When pan is hot, sprinkle steaks with garlic and cook 2 minutes on each side. Remove from pan. Place ⅓ cup of vegetable mix and ¼ cup mozzarella cheese on 1 end of each steak. Roll each steak from that end. Place rolls in lightly greased baking dish. Pour Ragu sauce over steaks. Sprinkle remaining cheese on top. Cover and bake at 350 degrees for 30 minutes. Serve with noodles.

Randy Moore
Fairlee, Vermont

Beer Batter Venison

Serves: 4-6
Prep Time: 1 hour

2 **lbs. venison steaks**	3 **cups flour**
2 **eggs**	1 **can beer**
2 **tsp. salt**	**shortening**
3 **tsp. pepper**	

Cut steaks thin and salt and pepper both sides heavily. Pound each side with meat hammer. Beat eggs, salt and pepper and add to flour, mixing thoroughly. Add beer to flour mixture until batter is soupy. Dip steaks in batter. Fry in shortening on low heat until golden brown.

Don Edwards
Omaha, Texas

Chicken-Fried Venison Steak

Serves: 2
Prep Time: 5 hours

1-2 lbs. venison steaks	**1 egg**
salt and pepper	**cooking oil**
creole seasonings	**flour**
2 cups milk	**milk**

Tenderize steaks using hammer. Add seasonings to meat. Beat milk and egg. Marinate meat in mixture for 3-4 hours. Put cooking oil in skillet and heat. When oil is hot, remove steaks from marinade and dredge in flour. Place in skillet. Brown on each side. Do not overcook—let the telephone ring. Pour off oil and add milk. In separate container, mix flour, salt, pepper, creole seasonings and milk for gravy base. Add to meat, cook and stir until gravy thickens.

Andrew Stevens
Loganberries 4-H

Marinated Venison Steaks

Serves: 4
Prep Time: overnight, plus 30 minutes

4 venison steaks	**1 T. Worcestershire sauce**
1 cup red wine	**salt and pepper**
½ cup brown sugar	**¼ cup onion, minced**
¼ cup catsup	**⅓ cup fresh mushrooms,**
⅛ cup molasses	**minced**

In blender, mix all ingredients except steaks, onion and mushrooms. After ingredients are well mixed, stir in onion and mushrooms. Place meat in container, cover well with marinade. Cover and put in refrigerator overnight, turning meat occasionally. Drain excess marinade from steaks and either broil or grill, brushing steaks on both sides with leftover marinade while cooking.

Valerie Waldron
Minneapolis, Minnesota

Venison Pepper Steak

Serves: 4-6
Prep Time: 2 hours, 30 minutes

1½ lbs. venison, cut into ¼-inch strips
1 T. oil
1 chicken bouillon cube, dissolved in ½ cup hot water
1 garlic clove
3 T. soy sauce
1 large onion, finely chopped
1 3- or 4-oz. can sliced mushrooms
1 T. sugar
⅛ tsp. pepper
1 T. flour
2 T. water
1 green pepper, cut into strips

Brown venison in oil over medium heat in large frying pan with tight cover. Remove all browned venison. Pour bouillon into frying pan. Add garlic and simmer 3-4 minutes. Remove garlic. Stir in soy sauce, onion, mushrooms, sugar and pepper. Blend flour to smooth paste with water in cup. Stir in onion mixture. Add browned venison and cover tightly. Simmer, stirring occasionally, for 20 minutes or until venison is tender when pierced with 2-tine fork. Add green peppers, cover and simmer 10 minutes. Serve with buttered noodles or rice.

Robin-Ann Johnson
Winterville, North Carolina

Ken's Venison Steak

Serves: 5
Prep Time: 30 minutes

3 lbs. steak or loin, boned and tenderized
1 cup flour
½ tsp. salt
½ tsp. pepper
lard or cooking oil

Mix flour, salt and pepper on paper plate. Coat steaks well with mixture. Fry in lard or oil on high heat. This is the secret: fry steaks fast in hot oil until brown.

Ken Vargason
Blairstown, Iowa

Stuffed Venison Steak

Serves: 6
Prep Time: overnight plus 1 hour, 30 minutes

**2 lbs. venison steak, cut
¾-inch thick
1½ cups milk
6 bacon slices
⅓ cup green onion,
chopped**

**salt and pepper
½ cup cold water
¼ cup flour**

Cut steak into 6 serving-size pieces. Place in shallow pan. Pour milk over meat. Cover and refrigerate overnight, turning meat several times. Drain meat, pat dry with paper towels. Cook bacon until crisp. Drain, reserving 2 T. drippings. Crumble bacon and set aside. With sharp knife, carefully cut a pocket in 1 side of each meat piece. Mix bacon and green onion. In 10-inch skillet, brown steaks in reserved bacon drippings. Season with salt and pepper. Add ½ cup water. Cover and simmer over low heat until tender, 45-60 minutes. Remove meat to platter. For gravy, measure pan juices and add enough water to make 1½ cups. Blend ½ cup cold water slowly into flour. Stir into pan juice mixture. Cook, stirring constantly until mixture bubbles and thickens. Season to taste with salt and pepper.

Gayle Heilman
Millbury, Ohio

Venison Broiled Filet Mignon

Serves: 8
Prep Time: 45 minutes

**2 lbs. venison tenderloin
16 bacon strips**

salt and pepper

Cut venison into 1-inch thick pieces. Wrap each meat piece in a bacon strip, fastening ends together with a toothpick. Broil until done. Salt and pepper to taste.

Nancy and Roger Dundas
Tostan, Montana

Lou's Venison Steak Pizzola

Serves: 4
Prep Time: 1 hour, 30 minutes

6 **venison steaks**	1 **bay leaf**
2 **large cans tomato sauce**	4 **T. grated Parmesan**
2 **garlic cloves, minced**	**cheese**
2 **T. oregano**	4 **T. olive oil**
1 **T. parsley**	**salt and pepper**

Place steaks in baking pan. Add all ingredients on top of steaks. Cover pan tightly with aluminum foil. Bake at 350 degrees for 1 hour, 30 minutes. Remove from oven. Serve with mashed potatoes or any favorite pastas that you whipped up while the steaks were baking, and French bread for dipping in the delicious sauce.

Lou Barbanera
Nanuet, New York

Deer Steak In A Package

Serves: 4
Prep Time: 1 hour, 30 minutes

2 **lbs. round steak**	**salt and pepper**
1 **cup catsup**	2 **T. lemon juice or 1**
¼ **cup flour**	**lemon**
1 **large onion, sliced**	

Tear off piece of aluminum foil and fold double. Mix catsup and flour and put half in center of foil. Place steak on catsup mixture and season with salt and pepper. Add remaining catsup mixture and onion. Sprinkle with lemon juice or top with lemon slices. Fold foil over and seal securely. Place on shallow pan and bake at 400 degrees for 1 hour, 30 minutes or until done. This is a camper's delight as it may also be baked on hot, campfire coals, and served with potatoes baked in foil.

Mrs. Leon Kern
New Vienna, Iowa

Venison Chops

Serves: 4-6
Prep Time: 1 hour, 30 minutes

4-6 venison chops **flour** **salt and pepper** **shortening**	**1 can brown mushroom** **soup** **1 can water**

Dip chops in seasoned flour. Brown quickly in shortening on both sides. Drain shortening from meat. Mix soup with 1 can water and pour over chops. Now, let it all simmer 1 hour while you check out that latest hunting video you picked up. Serve with mashed potatoes and green salad.

Dave Keith
Phoenix, Arizona

Dick's Mouth-Watering Venison Chops

Serves: 4
Prep Time: 1 hour

4 venison chops	**¼ cup soy sauce**
1 tsp. salt	**¼ lb. butter**
⅛ tsp. pepper	**1 tsp. brown sugar**
2 T. flour	**½ cup sherry**
1 T. olive oil	**3 lemon slices**
1 small jar of currant jelly	**3 orange slices**

Dredge chops in salt, pepper and flour. Fry in heated oil in skillet over moderate heat to desired degree of doneness. Put in baking dish, cover and keep hot in warm oven. Make sauce by combining jelly, soy sauce, butter, brown sugar, wine and fruits; simmer and stir until jelly and butter melt and blend. Pour sauce over chops and serve. Mashed potatoes, bread stuffing and a green salad complete a dinner that will have your family and friends wanting seconds, or even thirds.

Dick Jacobson
Minneapolis, Minnesota

Mustard Fried Venison

Serves: 4-6
Prep Time: 30 minutes

4-6 venison loin steaks or chops **seasoned salt** **pepper**	**2 T. Dijon style mustard** **1 tsp. horseradish** **¼ cup olive oil**

Season steaks with your own blend of salt and pepper. Combine mustard and horseradish. Spread mixture on each side of steaks so that the steaks are fully covered on both sides. Fry in hot olive oil, being careful to avoid being splattered. Poke with fork and as soon as juices run clear, steaks are done and ready to be served with whatever garnishment you prefer. A baked potato and a green, dinner salad rounds out a delicious meal.

Rex Morgan
Kansas City, Missouri

Venison Tournedos

Serves: 2
Prep Time: 2 days

7 oz. venison tournedos (cut from loin) **2 oz. sherry wine** **2 oz. burgundy** **½ tsp. honey**	**1 bay leaf** **1 medium onion, diced** **1 medium carrot, diced** **¼ oz. arrowroot** **1 oz. clarified butter**

Marinate first eight ingredients for two days being sure to turn the tournedos occasionally to take full advantage of the marinade. In fry pan, heat butter and add marinated venison. Cook to desired temperature and remove. Strain marinade. Add 6 oz. of strained marinade to fry pan. Thicken with arrowroot. Pour over the venison tournedos and serve piping hot as a mouth-watering entree for two.

Anthony Hebert
Patterson, New York

Venison Swiss Steak In Sour Cream

Serves: 6
Prep Time: 1 hour, 30 minutes

2 **lbs. sirloin or round steak, 1-inch thick**	1 **bay leaf**
¼ **cup bacon fat**	8 **peppercorns**
1 **garlic clove, crushed**	1 **tsp. salt**
¼ **cup onions, minced**	1 **T. butter**
2 **cups water**	4 **T. flour**
1 **cup tart fruit juice, cranberry or apple**	¾ **cup sour cream**

Cut venison into 2-inch pieces. Melt fat in heavy skillet. Add meat and garlic. Saute until brown on all sides. Arrange meat in 2-qt. casserole. Put onions in skillet and cook 2 minutes. Add water, juices, bay leaf, peppercorns and salt. Pour mixture over venison in casserole. Bake at 325 degrees for 30-60 minutes or until meat is tender. Melt butter in fry pan, stir in flour. Stir constantly until smooth. Add sour cream and cook at low temperature for 5 minutes. Pour over meat and serve immediately with buttered or plain noodles.

J. Wayne Fears
Helfin, Alabama

Lady Bird Johnson's Pedernales River Special Chili

Serves: 8-10
Prep Time: 1 hour, 30 minutes

4 **lbs. venison or beef chili meat, chopped**	1 **tsp. cumin powder**
1 **large onion, chopped**	2 **T. chili powder**
2 **garlic cloves, minced**	2 **12-oz. cans tomatoes**
1 **tsp. oregano**	**salt**
	2 **cups hot water**

Put meat, onion and garlic into large skillet and sear until lightly browned. Add all other ingredients. Bring to a boil. Lower heat, cover and simmer 1 hour. Skim off grease and serve hot.

Billy's Green Chili Venison Burros

Serves: 4
Prep Time: 2 hours, 30 minutes

3-4 **lbs. venison, diced**
3 **T. butter**
1 **or 2 onions, diced**
¾ **tsp. salt**
½ **tsp. pepper**
½ **tsp. garlic salt**
1 **7-oz. can whole green chilies**

1 **7-oz. can diced green chilies**
1 **12-oz. jar green chili salsa**
1 **8-oz. can tomato sauce**
1 **14½-oz. can stewed tomatoes**

Brown venison in butter. Add diced onions, salt, pepper and garlic salt. Simmer 10 minutes. Add remaining ingredients and cook 1-2 hours. Serve rolled in flour tortillas.

William Boyda
Apache Junction, Arizona

Venison Chili

Serves: 6-10
Prep Time: 3 hours

3 **lbs. boneless venison, finely diced**
¼ **cup beef fat**
2 **large onions, chopped**
½ **lb. beef suet, finely chopped**
2 **garlic cloves**

1 **T. salt**
3 **T. chili powder**
1 **T. ground cumin**
1 **dash hot pepper sauce**
2 **qts. boiling beef stock, or 2 qts. water mixed with 8 bouillon cubes**

In large skillet over medium-high heat, melt fat and saute onion until translucent, about 5 minutes. Reduce heat to low, add suet and cook slowly until suet is rendered and onion is almost melted into fat, about 3 minutes. Add venison, garlic and salt. Brown well, stirring to blend ingredients. Add chili powder, cumin and hot pepper sauce. Cover with boiling stock. Reduce heat to low, cover and simmer 2 hours, 30 minutes. Stir occasionally. Add more salt or chili powder to taste.

Anonymous

Deer Beer Chili

Serves: 8-12
Prep Time: 2-4 hours

4 **cups cubed venison**	1 **large bell pepper**
2 **cans kidney beans**	2 **tomatoes**
1 **2-inch bacon strip**	1 **large can tomato paste**
salt and pepper	1 **bay leaf**
2 **large cans tomato sauce**	½ **cup brown sugar**
1 **large jar chili powder**	3-4 **cans beer**
1 **large onion**	

Soak beans overnight and rinse thoroughly. Put venison cubes in large pot with bacon, salt and pepper. Stir until meat is browned. Remove bacon and add tomato sauce. Spoon in chili powder, stir. Raise heat to medium and cover for 4 minutes. Dice onion and pepper. Peel tomatoes and cut into chunks. Save vegetable seeds and juices. Add onion, peppers, tomatoes, beans, seeds and juices, tomato paste, bay leaf and sugar. Do not saute vegetables before adding to meat. Stir. Add 2 cans beer and stir. Cover and heat, stirring occasionally. Bring to a slow boil, reduce heat to low. Stir and cover for 15 minutes. Season to taste. Add beer if too thick. Cover, heat on low 2-4 hours. Stir hourly. Raise heat again 5 minutes before serving.

Robert Hoague
Dallas, Texas

Quick Venison Chili

Serves: 4-6
Prep Time: 1 hour

1 **lb. ground venison**	1-2 **qt. jars homemade**
mixed with ground beef	**tomato juice or 2 cans**
1 **chili stick**	**tomato juice**
2 **cans kidney beans**	1 **T. chili powder**

Brown venison and ground beef. Mix all other ingredients and add to meat. Cook over low heat to boiling. Simmer 30 minutes.

Lorene Heugel
Leavenworth, Kansas

Chilly Day Chili

Serves: 6
Prep Time: 4 hours

2½ **lbs. ground venison**	2 **jalapeno peppers**
2 **celery stalks**	4 **T. chili powder**
1 **large onion**	½ **tsp. crushed red chili**
1 **large green pepper**	**peppers**
1 **can beer**	1½ **tsp. black pepper**
1 **can chili beans**	1 **T. cumin**
1 **can kidney beans**	1 **tsp. oregano**
1 **large can chopped**	1 **tsp. cayenne pepper**
tomatoes	½ **tsp. ground mustard**
1 **15-oz. can tomato sauce**	1½ **tsp. seasoned salt**
1 **8-oz. can tomato paste**	½ **tsp. garlic powder**

Simmer chopped celery, onion and green pepper in 10-qt. pot with water to cover. Brown meat and drain. Put ingredients in pot and bring to a boil. Reduce heat. Simmer 2-3 hours.

Arthur Hegstrom
Inkster, North Dakota

Cool Water Chili

Serves: 8-10
Prep Time: 3-4 hours

3½ **lbs. ground venison**	3 **cans tomato sauce**
2 **cups celery, chopped**	½ **tsp. garlic powder**
1½ **cups onion, diced**	2 **tsp. beef base**
2 **small cans diced green**	⅓ **tsp. red pepper**
chilies	¼ **cup sugar**
1 **large can whole**	1 **tsp. chili powder**
tomatoes	1 **tsp. cumin**
1 **medium can whole**	**salt and pepper**
tomatoes	**water**

Brown meat and drain fat. Put other ingredients in large kettle; add water to desired consistency. Bring to a boil, reduce heat, simmer 2-3 hours, or cover and bake 3-4 hours at 300 degrees.

Shirley Wilson
Kooskia, Idaho

Crockpot Barbecue

Serves: 6-8
Prep Time: 8-12 hours

3 lbs. venison stew meat
1 cup onion, diced
4-5 garlic cloves, chopped
1 cup red wine vinegar
½ cup Worcestershire sauce
2 tsp. Lawrey's Natural Choice seasoning for meat
2 tsp. seasoned salt
1 lb. bacon
2 cups catsup
½ cup molasses
½ cup brown sugar

Place meat, onion, garlic, vinegar, Worcestershire sauce and seasonings in Crockpot. Cook on high for 1-2 hours until meat is cooked. Fry bacon and crumble or chop. Add bacon, catsup, molasses and brown sugar to Crockpot. Cook on low heat for the rest of the day while you check out new hunting sites. Serve over rice, potatoes or toast.

Barak Capron
Cheyenne, Wyoming

Venison Bar-B-Q

Serves: 2-3
Prep Time: 45 minutes

1 lb. ground venison
1 cup water
½ cup celery
1 T. mustard
1 T. catsup
celery seed
4 oz. chili sauce

Mix venison, water and celery together in a pan and cook until celery is tender. Then add mustard, catsup, celery seed (to taste) and chili sauce to the mixture. Simmer, without lid, for 30 minutes. Serve on hamburger buns.

W. Paul Brandt
Mount Joy, Pennsylvania

Festus' (Ken Curtis) Gunsmoke Chili

Serves: 8-10
Prep Time: 3 hours, 30 minutes

4 **lbs. coarse ground venison or lean beef**	1½ **tsp. basil leaves, crushed by hand**
2 **large onions, minced**	1½ **tsp. oregano leaves, crushed by hand**
2 **tsp. monosodium glutamate (MSG)**	1 **tsp. cayenne**
1½ **tsp. salt**	4 **T. chili powder**
1 **tsp. ground black pepper**	4 **cups bouillon**
2 **T. parsley flakes**	4 **cups tomato sauce**
1 **tsp. Season-All**	

Mince meat fine with fork while browning. Add remaining ingredients in large iron pot. Stir to combine thoroughly and simmer 2-3 hours.

Anonymous

Chickoree Mountain Chili

Serves: 6-8
Prep Time: 2 hours, 30 minutes

2 **lbs. ground venison**	5 **T. chili powder**
2 **large onions**	½ **tsp. oregano**
4 **garlic cloves**	2 **T. bacon drippings**
1 **15-oz. can whole tomatoes**	½ **tsp. sugar**
1 **15-oz. can tomato sauce**	½ **tsp. monosodium glutamate (MSG)**
1 **15-oz. can kidney beans**	1 **T. cumin**
2-4 **jalapeno peppers**	1 **T. vinegar**
1 **T. salt**	1 **16-oz. can squash**

Brown meat in bacon drippings. Slice onions lengthwise and add to meat. Cook 10-15 minutes. Add remaining ingredients and simmer 2 hours.

Nicholas Yurasek
Hollywood, California

Green Chili

Serves: 5-8
Prep Time: 4-10 hours

1½ **lb. venison roast, boneless**	3 **fresh green chilies, seeded**
1½ **lb. beef roast, boneless**	1 **T. chili peppers, crushed**
1 **garlic clove, crushed**	1 **tsp. salt**
2 **medium onions, sliced**	12 **flour tortillas**
1 **large can green chilies, rinsed**	1 **T. cornstarch**

Saute garlic and onions for 3 minutes. Brown meat slightly with garlic and onions, if desired. Add all ingredients to Crockpot, except cornstarch and tortillas. Cook on low heat for 10 hours. Cook until meat can be shredded with a fork. Mix cornstarch in 2 T. cold water. Add to chili. Repeat if necessary until slightly thickened. Put in tortillas and roll.

Nancy Lucius
Idaho Falls, Idaho

Cajun-Flavored Venison Soup

Serves: 8
Prep Time: 3 hours

3-4 **lbs. venison shanks**	1 **T. cajun seasoning**
4 **cups water**	2 **beef bouillon cubes**
1 **28-oz. can crushed tomatoes**	2 **cups cabbage, chopped**
1 **cup celery, chopped**	1 **cup green bell peppers, chopped**
1 **cup onions, chopped**	¼ **cup lemon juice**
1 **tsp. garlic, minced**	2 **cups cooked rice**

Place venison shanks, water, tomatoes, celery, onion, garlic, seasoning and bouillon in large soup pot. Bring to a boil and reduce heat. Cover and simmer 2 hours, stirring occasionally. Remove shanks and cut meat into small pieces. Return meat with cabbage and green peppers and simmer until meat and vegetables are tender. Stir in lemon juice. Serve with rice.

Anonymous

Mild Wild Chili

Serves: 6-8
Prep Time: 1 hour

1-2 lbs. ground game meat
1 tsp. paprika
1 tsp. garlic salt
1 tsp. cumin
1 tsp. chili powder
1 tsp. cayenne pepper
1 T. onion, chopped

1 tsp. dried chilies, crushed
3 celery stalks, chopped
1 can tomato soup
1 8-oz. can tomato sauce
1 8-oz. can dark red kidney beans

Brown meat and drain. Add remaining ingredients. Add water if needed. Simmer 20 minutes.

Allen Hockaday
Casper, Wyoming

Warna's Venison Chili

Serves: 8-10
Prep Time: 3-4 hours

2½ lbs. venison, coarsely ground
2 T. vegetable oil
1 large onion, chopped
3 large garlic cloves, crushed
2 T. Worcestershire sauce
2 T. barbecue sauce
2 T. chili powder
1 T brown sugar
1 T. soy sauce
1 4-oz. jar pimentos, chopped
1 green pepper, diced

¼ cup celery, diced
2 tsp. celery salt
3 T. catsup
1 tsp. ground cumin
1 tsp. salt
1 tsp. pepper
1 tsp. instant minced onion
1 tsp. garlic powder
dash of red cayenne pepper
1 15-oz. can stewed tomatoes
2 T. jalapeno pepper juice (optional)

In 5-qt. saucepot over medium heat, combine ingredients, cook for 3-4 hours. For spicy chili, add 2 T. jalapeno pepper juice.

Warna Miller Reed
Matherville, Illinois

Venison Beans

Serves: 4-6
Prep Time: 30 minutes

1-2 lbs. ground venison	**1 medium onion, chopped**
2 cans pork and beans	**1 medium green pepper,**
1 cup mustard	**chopped**
1 cup catsup	

Brown venison in fry pan. Add remaining ingredients, stir it all up and simmer until well-mixed. Serve hot with bread or whatever strikes your fancy. This dish is guaranteed to remind you of all those hunting campfires past.

Michael Smalley, Sr.
Inman, South Carolina

Courtyard Enchilada Casera

Serves: varies
Prep Time: 1 hour

ground venison	**green chili salsa**
flour tortillas	**Monterey Jack cheese,**
sour cream	**grated**
onion greens, chopped	

Lightly brown ground venison. Steam as many flour tortillas as needed. Spread each tortilla with sour cream and put the following on each one: 2 T. onion greens, 3-4 T. venison and 1-2 T. green chili salsa. Sprinkle 1 T. cheese on meat and a little more green chili salsa if desired. Roll tortillas into enchiladas and hold together with toothpicks. Place in casserole pan. Now, you can add more cheese and chili salsa, spreading it over the rolled tortillas. Place casserole in oven and heat thoroughly. Serve with refried beans or brown rice. This Mexican venison dish is a guaranteed delight!

Casper Greif
Sacramento, California

Venison Taco Salad

Serves: 6
Prep Time: 1 hour, 30 minutes

1 **lb. ground venison**
6 **potatoes**
1 **pkg. taco sauce**
1 **can chilies**
1 **can tomato paste**
6 **oz. mozzarella cheese**

8 **oz. sour cream**
¼ **head lettuce, diced**
2 **tomatoes, diced**
6 **taco shells, crushed into large pieces**

Bake potatoes. Brown venison, adding sauce, chilies and tomato paste. Mix cheese and sour cream together. Cut potatoes into quarters, pour cheese and sour cream over top. Bake at 350 degrees until cheese melts. After cheese melts, put meat mixture over top. Place lettuce, tomatoes and taco shells on top of meat.

Dwylan Reigel
Lebanon, Pennsylvania

Mild Mexican Barbecue

Serves: 20-40
Prep Time: 1 hour

6 **lbs. ground venison**
1½ **cups onion, chopped**
3 **T. margarine**
2 **15-oz. cans tomato puree**
1 **16-oz. can tomato paste**
1 **16-oz. can water**
¾ **cup celery, chopped**

⅓ **cup plus 1 T. lemon juice**
2 **T. plus 1 tsp. wine vinegar**
⅓ **cup packed sugar**
½ **tsp. red cayenne pepper**
½ **tsp. cumin seed**

Brown onion in margarine and add venison. Brown venison, drain and add remaining ingredients, crushing cumin seeds first. Simmer 45 minutes. Serve inside hamburger buns. This is the perfect meal to serve when it's your turn to entertain the neighborhood.

Michael Wagner
Rockport, Illinois

German Venison Stew With Black Forest Mushrooms and Spaetzle

Serves: varies
Prep Time: 1 hour, 30 minutes

venison shoulder meat	½ **bay leaf**
2 **cups flour**	3 **T. red burgundy wine**
bacon slices	**black forest mushrooms**
butter	1 **lb. flour**
1 **large onion, diced**	3 **eggs**
salt, to taste	1 **cup water**
1 **cup beef broth**	**grated cheese**
peppercorns	

Cut well-aged shoulder meat into ½-inch pieces. Roll in flour and pan-fry with bacon slices, butter and onion until golden brown. Add salt, beef broth, whole peppercorns and bay leaf. Cover and simmer for 15-20 minutes. Thicken gravy with flour and wine before serving. Saute mushrooms with bacon bits, diced onion, butter and salt. Garnish with parsley. Spaetzle: Mix 1 lb. flour, eggs, salt, water, grated cheese and browned butter. Blend well, adding flour slowly until slightly foamy. Let sit 30 minutes. Heat 2 pots of saltwater and bring 1 pot to a boil. Press dough through sieve or pasta-maker to form small lumps which drop into boiling water. When they rise to the top they are done. Transfer to other pot with non-boiling water until serving to keep hot. Brown some onions in butter and pour over the Spaetzle when serving.

Wolfgang Harms

Canned Venison

Wash meat and cut up in 1-inch cubes, removing all fat. Pat dry and pack 1-qt. jars until full. Do not add water or salt. Secure lids and process for 90 minutes at 10 lbs. pressure. Venison will make its own juice and a layer of fat will be on top. This will keep for a long time and can be used for several dishes, such as vegetable and venison stew.

Lowell Tinsley
Hamilton, Ohio

Cajun Run Stew

Serves: 4
Prep Time: 2 hours, 15 minutes

1½ **lbs. venison stew meat**
½ **cup seasoned flour**
3 **T. olive oil**
1 **garlic clove, minced**
2 **cups water**
1 **beef bouillon cube**
½ **cup tomato juice**
¼ **cup port wine**
1 **tsp. lemon juice**
1 **tsp. steak sauce**
½ **tsp. thyme**
4 **small onions, chopped**
4 **carrots, chopped**
4 **potatoes, quartered**
1 **cup celery, chopped**
salt and pepper, to taste
flour

Shake stew meat and seasoned flour in plastic bag until meat is coated. Heat oil in large, deep skillet over medium-high heat. Brown meat on all sides. Add garlic and fry 1 minute. Add water, bouillon cube, tomato juice, port wine, lemon juice, steak sauce and thyme. Cover, simmer 1 hour. Add vegetables, simmer 1 hour. Season to taste. Add flour to thicken gravy if necessary.

Herman Guillory
San Antonio, Texas

Deer Burger Stew

Serves: 6
Prep Time: 45 minutes

2 **lbs. venison burger**
2 **potatoes, cubed**
2 **carrots, cubed**
½ **pkg. frozen vegetables**
2 **cups water**
1 **pkg. dry onion soup mix**
2 **beef bouillon cubes**
2 **cups tomatoes**
½ **tsp. garlic**
1 **bay leaf**
½ **tsp. rosemary**
2 **celery stalks, cubed**

Brown venison burger in frying pan. Boil potatoes and carrots in separate kettle. When carrots are half cooked, add frozen vegetables. Add other ingredients to meat and simmer 20 minutes. Add vegetables to meat before serving.

C.E. Husband
Logan, Kansas

Back-Forty Stew

Serves: 4
Prep Time: 3 hours

1	lb. venison, cubed	4-6	carrots, chopped
	flour	4-6	large white potatoes,
½	cup shortening		cubed
4-8	garlic cloves	¼	tsp. basil
2-4	fresh jalapeno peppers	¼	tsp. thyme
½	cup vinegar or dry wine	1	can green sweet peas,
1	cup water		drained
6	medium onions, quartered		

Roll venison cubes in flour. Heat shortening in large Dutch oven or deep cast iron skillet. Saute garlic and peppers. Add venison and brown. Lower heat, add vinegar and 1 cup water. Simmer 30 minutes. Add onions, carrots and potatoes; add water as needed. When potatoes are almost done, add spices and stir well. Remove some potatoes, mash and stir into stew as a thickener. Add peas 15 minutes before serving.

Rudy Goodrich
Newport News, Virginia

Crockpot Stew In Cream Gravy

Serves: 8
Prep Time: 8 hours

3	lbs. stew meat	12	carrots, sliced
¼	cup flour	2	onion slices, thick
2	tsp. salt	1	bay leaf
⅛	tsp. paprika	1	can cream of mushroom
	shortening		soup
8	potatoes, peeled	1	cup sour cream

Combine dry ingredients in paper bag. Shake stew pieces in flour mixture. Brown meat in hot shortening. Remove meat to Crockpot. Add vegetables and soup, cover. Stew on low 8 hours. Stir in sour cream 5 minutes before serving. Serve hot.

Brenda Kuester
Plains, Montana

Shenandoah's Venison Stew

Serves: 6-10
Prep Time: 6-7 hours

3 **lbs. venison**	1 **tsp. meat tenderizer**
1 **lb. fresh mushrooms**	¼ **tsp. dill weed**
1-2 **fresh green bell peppers**	¼ **tsp. seasoned salt**
2-3 **large onions**	1 **garlic clove**
4 **carrots**	**Optional:**
3 **celery stalks**	1 **bottle white wine**
1 **lb. unsalted butter**	4 **shots Southern Comfort**
1 **tsp. salt, pepper**	2 **12-oz. cans beer**
1 **tsp. Accent seasoning**	

Cut meat, mushrooms, peppers and onions into small pieces. Cut
carrots and celery into thin pieces. Brown half of meat,
mushrooms, peppers and onions in butter. Layer in Dutch oven
after browning. Add seasonings and half the wine, beer and
Southern Comfort. Add carrots and celery. Repeat the above for
other half of meat. Cover and cook over low fire for 5-6 hours.
Serve over rice, mashed potatoes or egg noodles.

W.E. Wagner
Cupertino, California

Whitetail Snack Loaf

Serves: several
Prep Time: 25 hours

2 **lbs. ground venison**	1 **T. onion powder**
2 **T. fast-curing salt**	3 **T. whole mustard seeds**
2 **T. liquid smoke**	1 **T. coarse black pepper**
2 **T. garlic juice (not salt**	1 **tsp. cumin**
or powder)	1 **tsp. red pepper, crushed**

Mix all ingredients by hand in large pan. Separate mixture into 5
or 6 loaves. Wrap in waxed paper and refrigerate for 24 hours.
Remove from wrap and bake at 350 degrees for 45 minutes. If
freezing loaves for later use, bake only 35 minutes.

Shorty Goodyear
Lyndon, Kansas

Mountain Top Venison Stew

Serves: 2-4
Prep Time: 2 hours, 30 minutes

1 **8-oz. venison ham**	1 **tsp. catsup**
flour	1 **tsp. instant coffee**
crackers (optional)	1 **16-oz. can red kidney**
dash of meat tenderizer	**beans**
salt, pepper and garlic	1 **16-oz. can potatoes**
salt, to taste	1 **16-oz. can sliced carrots**
½ **onion, diced**	1 **8-oz. can peas**
1 **tsp. Worcestershire**	¼ **green pepper, diced**
sauce	

Cut venison into bite-size pieces and shake in mixture of crushed crackers, flour, meat tenderizer, salt, pepper and garlic salt. Brown meat in pot used to cook stew. Add water to cover. Add onion, Worcestershire, catsup and 1 tsp. instant coffee. Cover and cook on low heat for 2 hours. Add kidney beans, potatoes, carrots, peas and green pepper. Cover and cook on medium heat for 30 minutes. Add water as needed.

Russell Shoate
Glade Valley, North Carolina

Venison Mushroom Meat Loaf

Serves: 4-6
Prep Time: 1 hour, 30 minutes

3 **lbs. ground venison**	4 **bacon strips**
2 **cups stuffing**	**garlic salt or powder**
1 **can mushroom soup,**	**black pepper**
condensed	**mushrooms, sliced**

Mix meat, stuffing and ¾ cup soup in large bowl. Form into loaf and put mixture in loaf pan. Top with bacon strips and remaining soup. Add garlic salt/powder and pepper to taste. Garnish with mushroom slices and bake at 350-375 degrees for 1 hour or until done to your preference.

Mark Johnson
Brewster, New York

Backcountry Venison Stew

Serves: 8
Prep Time: 3 hours

2 lbs. venison, cubed	½ tsp. black pepper
4 T. bacon drippings	¾ cup onion, chopped
water	4 medium potatoes, cubed
1 tsp. garlic salt	6 medium carrots, sliced
1 tsp. Worcestershire sauce	1 green pepper, chopped
1½ tsp. salt	2 cups celery, sliced
	3 T. flour

Cut venison into 1-inch cubes. Brown in hot bacon drippings in heavy Dutch oven. Add water to cover, seasonings and onion. Cover and simmer about 2 hours. Add potatoes, carrots, pepper and celery. Cook about 20 minutes or until vegetables are tender. Add more seasonings to taste. Dissolve flour in ¼ cup cold water and stir into stew. Cook 5 minutes and serve hot.

J. Wayne Fears
Heflin, Alabama

Canned Smoke & Sour Venison Stew

Serves: 4-6
Prep Time: 1 hour, 30 minutes

1 cup venison stew meat	1 beef bouillon cube
⅓ cup lima beans	1 cup potatoes, diced
⅓ cup string beans	½ tsp. salt
⅓ cup carrots, sliced	½ tsp. Worcestershire sauce
⅓ cup celery, sliced	⅛ cup sour wine
2 T. onion, chopped	1 T. Drake's crispy fry mix
½ tsp. garlic, sliced	warm water
2 T. home-cured venison ham	

Pack raw ingredients in quart jar in above order to within one inch of top, seal and process for 90 minutes at 10 lbs. pressure.

Willard Foster
Midland, Michigan

Indian Venison Jerky

Serves: varies
Prep Time: 3 days

5 lbs. venison   **pepper**
salt

Cut venison into ¼-inch strips. This is a time when you'll appreciate having a good, sharp knife. Salt and pepper each piece. Put the strips of venison into a colander to drain. Let sit 5 hours in colander, draining. Hang in cool place for 3 days and your venison jerky is ready to eat.

Lewis Lytle
Las Vegas, Nevada

The Best Venison Jerky

Serves: varies
Prep Time: 24 hours

½ venison ham, well trimmed	**1 cup apple wine (red or white)**
⅓ cup sugar	**½ tsp. garlic salt**
⅓ cup non-iodized salt	**½ tsp. onion salt**
2 cups soy sauce	**1 T. coarse ground pepper**
1 cup water	**1 tsp. liquid smoke**

Slice meat with the grain into ¼- to ½-inch slices. Reserve pepper except for ½ tsp. which will be used immediately in combining ingredients. Except for meat, combine all ingredients, including the ½ tsp. pepper, in a large glass or plastic container. Mix well. Add meat to mixture and let stand for 8-10 hours. Now, you can feel free to go to work. After meat has marinated, remove from container to dry. Spread paper towels over newspapers and lay meat slices on them. Use remaining pepper to season to your taste. Allow to air dry for 8 hours. Next, being careful not to lose too much pepper, lay meat on oven grates. Allow meat to dry at 150 degrees for 4-8 hours, checking every 2 hours to determine if the drying process is done.

Ron Lawrence
Creswell, Oregon

Guido's Jerky

Serves: several
Prep Time: 10-12 hours

beef or venison, lean cut	**1 tsp. Accent brand**
¼ cup Worcestershire	**seasoning**
sauce	**1 tsp. garlic powder**
¼ cup soy sauce	**1½ tsp. onion powder**
1 T. liquid smoke	**salt and pepper**

Take beef or venison and cut into ⅜-inch strips, 6 inches long with the grain. Trim off fat. Combine Worcestershire sauce, soy sauce, liquid smoke, Accent, garlic powder and onion powder in container. Mix until dissolved. Dip meat into mixture. Lightly salt and pepper 1 side only. Place a toothpick through end of each strip. Place aluminum foil in oven to catch drippings. Suspend strips from top oven rack. Turn heat to 120 degrees or lowest setting. Allow oven door to stand slightly open so moisture will escape. Heat jerky strips 10-12 hours or until meat turns dark and there is no moisture left, dehydrating meat, not cooking it. Store in airtight container to seal in freshness.

Don "Guido" Villemez
Harvey, Louisiana

Camp Jerky

Serves: varies
Prep Time: 8 hours

leftover venison scraps	**pepper**
salt	**garlic powder**

Use leftover scraps from boning out deer or elk. Cut meat into strips 1-2 inches wide, 3-5 inches long and not more than ½-inch thick. Sprinkle meat with salt, pepper, and garlic powder on all sides. Arrange meat to hang from rack or tripod, at least 3 feet above fire in smoke, using wire or string hangers. Smoke at least 8 hours. Use portable tripod, if possible, so you can move meat in same direction as blowing smoke.

Paula Del Giudice
Reno, Nevada

Venison Or Beef Jerky

Serves: 6
Prep Time: overnight, plus 6-8 hours

3 lbs. venison or beef	**2 tsp. seasoned salt**
½ cup soy sauce	**2 tsp. onion powder**
½ cup Worcestershire sauce	**⅔ tsp. garlic powder**
2 tsp. Accent	**⅔ tsp. black pepper**

Cut meat into ⅜-inch strips. Combine all ingredients to make marinade sauce. Put meat strips in marinade sauce and marinate in refrigerator overnight. Next morning, take strips out and put in oven rack and bake at 150-200 degrees for 6-8 hours. The longer it bakes, the crispier it gets. When done, put into airtight containers. It should keep up to 2 years.

Jeff Fischer
Bonduel, Wisconsin

Deer Jerky

Serves: 4
Prep Time: 7 hours

2 lbs. flank or brisket	**½ tsp. onion powder**
¼ cup soy sauce	**dash of Tabasco sauce**
1 T. Worcestershire sauce	**1 T. taco sauce**
¼ tsp. pepper	**1 tsp. liquid smoke**
¼ tsp. garlic powder	

Trim off fat. Cut meat with the grain into long ⅛- to ¼-inch thick strips. Partially frozen meat is easier to cut. Combine all other ingredients in bowl and stir until dissolved. Pour over meat strips, cover tightly and marinate overnight. Remove from sauce and arrange strips close together on rack. Do not overlap. Set rack on cookie sheet and bake at 150 degrees for 7 hours, turning once. Keep in airtight container.

Ronald Orr
Ogallala, Nebraska

Ragged Mountain Buckskin Jerky

Serves: 4
Prep Time: 24 hours

venison roast
⅓ **cup sugar**
¼ **cup salt**
2 **cups soy sauce**
1 **cup red wine**
1 **tsp. Worcestershire sauce**

½ **tsp. Tabasco sauce**
½ **tsp. onion powder**
½ **tsp. pepper**
½ **tsp. garlic powder**
¼ **tsp. liquid smoke**

Trim all fat from meat. Slice with the grain into pieces about ¼ to ½ inch thick. (Meat slices better when semi-frozen.) Mix all ingredients together. Place meat in cool brine and leave overnight. Remove from brine and air dry. Place the prepared meat strips in smoker for 12-16 hours, making sure to check periodically for proper dryness. Use 3 panfuls of aspen (poplar) chips in early part of drying process if desired.

Dion Luke
Glenwood Springs, Colorado

Venison Jerky

Serves: varies
Prep Time: overnight, plus 8 hours

1 **lb. meat, cut into thin strips**
½ **cup soy sauce**
½ **cup Worcestershire sauce**
2 **tsp. seasoned salt**

2 **tsp. onion powder**
2 **tsp. Accent seasoning powder**
⅔ **tsp. garlic powder**
⅔ **tsp. pepper**

Mix all ingredients. Marinate meat overnight. Cook on rack, using foil to catch drippings, at 150 degrees for 6-8 hours until dry. Store in airtight containers. Will keep up to 2 years if you don't eat it all before then.

Randy Bonnet
Bussey, Iowa

Ground Deer Jerky

Serves: 12
Prep Time: 16-20 hours

2 **lbs. lean ground venison**	½ **tsp. onion powder**
½ **cup soy sauce**	1 **tsp. Tabasco sauce**
2 **T. Worcestershire sauce**	2 **T. taco sauce**
½ **tsp. garlic powder**	2 **tsp. liquid smoke**
½ **tsp. pepper**	

Place ground meat in large bowl. In a separate bowl, mix all ingredients together and then pour them over the ground meat. Mix well. Place in refrigerator for 12 hours. Roll out into thin strips or patties and place on cookie sheet. Bake at 150 degrees for 4-8 hours. Drying time will depend on thickness of strips or patties so check every 2 hours or so to determine when they're dry. When they are dry, store in container in refrigerator or freezer for use at a later time.

Ronald Orr
Ogallala, Nebraska

Jerky

Serves: several
Prep Time: 8 hours

3 **lbs. venison**	3 **T. black pepper**
2 **T. cayenne pepper**	3 **T. salt**
4 **T. marjoram**	2 **T. garlic salt**
4 **T. thyme**	

Slice venison into finger-size strips. Mix other ingredients. Add meat to mixture. Mix well until all pieces are coated. Place each piece on a toothpick and hang from oven rack (placed at top of oven). Turn oven temperature to 150-175 degrees and dry the meat for approximately 8 hours. Jerky will keep for several months in an airtight container. It will keep longer if put in sealed bags and placed in the refrigerator or freezer.

Anonymous

Northwoods Jerky

Serves: varies
Prep Time: 24 hours

2 **lbs. venison, cut in**	1 **T. Worcestershire sauce**
⅛-inch strips	¼ **tsp. garlic powder**
¼ **cup soy sauce**	½ **tsp. onion powder**
¼ **tsp. black pepper**	

Mix seasonings. Add meat. Let stand 1 hour. Cover and refrigerate overnight. Place meat on oven racks. Do not overlap. Place in oven, but not within 4 inches of heat source. Place foil on lower rack to catch drippings. Bake at 150-175 degrees for 6-10 hours until dry and almost crisp. Keep oven door open about 1 inch during first few hours of drying, allowing moisture to escape. Cool on absorbent paper. Pat off beads of accumulated fat. Store in an airtight plastic bag or jar for quick nourishment for backpacking trips or for nibbling when watching television.

Alfred's Oriental Venison Jerky

Serves: several
Prep Time: 24 hours

4 **lb. venison roast**	2 **oz. bourbon or brandy**
¼ **cup salt**	½ **tsp. onion powder**
¼ **cup brown sugar**	½ **tsp. garlic powder**
2 **cups water**	1 **tsp. ginger, grated**
1 **cup apple cider or cider**	1 **tsp. orange peel, grated**
vinegar	6 **white cloves (optional)**
½ **cup soy sauce**	

Trim fat from meat and cut into ¼- to ½-inch thick slices. Place meat into marinade made by combining above ingredients in glass or ceramic bowl. Marinate at least 8 hours in cool place. Remove to rack and allow to air-dry until glazed. Do not rinse. Smoke for 12-16 hours depending on degree of dryness that you prefer. Use 3 panfuls of hickory or cherry wood chips to add special flavor to the meat.

Alfred Sabino
Ringwood, New Jersey

Hanky Panky Game Balls

Serves: 4-6
Prep Time: 30 minutes

2 **lbs. ground venison**	**Sauce:**
1 **dozen crackers, crushed**	¾ **cup white vinegar**
2 **eggs**	1 **cup water**
2 **T. flour**	1 **cup brown sugar**
2 **T. bacon, diced**	¼ **cup soy sauce**
1 **T. garlic salt**	1 **pkg. chicken soup**
¼ **tsp. pepper**	2 **T. cornstarch mixed**
1 **T. butter**	**with 2 T. water**
½ **cup red wine**	2 **T. grated mozzarella**

Mix together first 7 ingredients and form into balls. In large fry pan melt butter and brown meatballs evenly. Add wine. Simmer until liquid evaporates and meat is cooked. In 2-qt. saucepan, bring first 5 sauce ingredients to a boil. Stir in cornstarch until thickened. Reduce heat and simmer 3 minutes. Place meatballs in warmed serving dish, cover with sauce and cheese.

Major E.M.S. Deneumoustier
Barrie, Ontario

Cocktail Meatballs

Serves: several
Prep Time: 1 hour, 45 minutes

2 **lbs. ground venison,**	2 **T. onion, grated**
1 **cup fine bread crumbs**	1-2 **T. shortening**
1 **egg, slightly beaten**	2½ **cups pineapple juice**
1 **tsp. salt**	1 **cup barbecue sauce**
½ **tsp. pepper**	¼ **cup flour**
½ **cup milk**	

Mix together first 7 ingredients and form small meatballs. Brown meatballs in hot shortening. Mix pineapple juice, barbecue sauce and flour. Add meatballs to sauce. Bake in a covered dish for 90 minutes at 350 degrees. Serve hot or cold on toothpicks.

James D. Roberts
Bremerton, Washington

Barbecued Venison Meatballs

Serves: 4-6
Prep Time: 1 hour

1½	lbs. ground venison		Sauce:
1	egg, beaten	½	cup catsup
⅓	cup milk	½	cup water
1	cup soft bread crumbs	¼	cup brown sugar
½	cup onion, chopped	2	T. vinegar
1	tsp. salt	½	tsp. salt
⅛	tsp. pepper	1	T. Worcestershire sauce
½	T. Worcestershire sauce	¼	tsp. pepper
1	T. shortening	½	tsp. celery seed (optional)

In a bowl, combine venison, egg, milk, bread crumbs, onion, salt, pepper and Worcestershire sauce. Shape mixture by rounding tablespoonfuls into balls. Melt shortening in large skillet, brown. For sauce: Place all ingredients in a pan and bring to a boil. Pour over meatballs and bake at 350 degrees for 25 minutes.

Donn L. Conrad
Bloomdale, Ohio

Fried Venison Meat Loaf

Serves: 6
Prep Time: 20 minutes

1	lb. ground venison	1	onion, finely chopped
	salt and pepper	¼	green pepper, chopped
1	egg	22	Ritz crackers, crushed
2	dashes Worcestershire sauce	½	cup milk

Mix all ingredients well. Form into hamburger patties. Brown in a skillet with hot oil. Excellent when topped with chili sauce, catsup or steak sauce.

John Zanon
Norway, Michigan

Venison Meat Loaf

Serves: 4-6
Prep Time: 1 hour

2½ **lbs. ground venison with beef suet**
¼ **cup canned milk**
1 **garlic clove, minced**
1 **large onion, grated**
1 **tsp. Worcestershire sauce**
salt and pepper

Blend all ingredients in large mixing bowl. Transfer ingredients to a well-oiled baking dish. Let sit in cool place for 30 minutes, allowing meat to absorb seasonings. Bake in preheated oven at 350 degrees for 1 hour. Place 2-3 bacon slices over loaf before baking if desired.

Lorene Heugel
Leavenworth, Kansas

Italian Venison Meat Loaf

Serves: 4-6
Prep Time: 1 hour

1½ **lbs. ground venison**
1 **cup Italian style bread crumbs**
¾ **cup onion, chopped**
1 **8-oz. can tomato sauce**
1 **egg, slightly beaten**
1¼ **tsp. salt**
½ **tsp. pepper**
4-6 **bacon slices**
3 **hardboiled eggs**
2 **T. olive oil**

Preheat oven to 350 degrees. In large bowl, combine venison, ¾ cup bread crumbs, onion, tomato sauce, egg, salt and pepper. Mix gently but thoroughly. If desired, place bacon strips on bottom of loaf pan. Place half of mixture into pan. Place hardboiled eggs lengthwise down center of meat. Pat remaining meat over eggs to form rounded loaf. Combine remaining bread crumbs with olive oil and press evenly over loaf. Bake 45-50 minutes.

Greg Kowalczyk
Blasdell, New York

Fluffy Meat Loaf

Serves: 6
Prep Time: 2 hours

1½ **lbs. lean ground venison**	¼ **tsp. pepper**
3 **medium soft bread slices, torn into pieces**	¼ **tsp. celery salt**
	¼ **tsp. garlic salt**
1 **cup milk**	2 **T. catsup**
1 **egg, beaten**	1 **T. Worcestershire sauce**
1¼ **tsp. salt**	¼ **cup onion, minced**

Heat oven to 350 degrees. Mix all ingredients thoroughly. For better browning, shape into loaf pan or shallow baking dish. Bake 90 minutes or until done and be prepared for lots of compliments.

Mrs. Michael Wagner
Rockport, Illinois

Don's Venison Meat Loaf

Serves: 8
Prep Time: 1 hour

1 **lb. ground venison**	⅓ **cup catsup**
1 **lb. pork sausage**	½ **tsp. garlic salt**
¾ **cup salted crackers, crushed**	¼ **tsp. pepper**
	1 **T. Worcestershire sauce**
½ **cup onion, minced**	1 **T. A-1 steak sauce**
2½ **oz. sliced mushrooms**	½ **tsp. curry powder**
1 **T. mustard**	⅓ **cup cheddar cheese, grated**
1 **egg, slightly beaten**	

Combine all ingredients and shape into loaf in 13x9x2 baking dish. Bake the venison meat loaf in preheated oven at 350 degrees for 1 hour. Let stand 5 minutes before slicing into individual servings and serve with mashed potatoes and salad or make a tasty meat loaf sandwich.

Donald Wyatt
Weyers Cave, Virginia

Gordon's Venison Stew

Serves: 8
Prep Time: 3 hours, 30 minutes

2½ **lbs. venison, 1½-in. cubes**	½ **cup Worcestershire sauce**
⅓ **cup flour**	¼ **tsp. pepper**
⅓ **cup salad oil**	4 **beef bouillon cubes**
1 **cup onion, chopped**	5 **medium potatoes**
1 **garlic clove, minced**	1 **16-oz. bag carrots, cut up**
3 **cups water**	1 **10-oz. pkg. peas**
1 **tsp. salt**	

About 3-4 hours before serving, coat meat with flour and brown in oil. Remove from pan. Add onions and garlic. Cook until tender. Gradually stir in water, salt, Worcestershire, pepper and bouillon. Return meat. Simmer 2 hours, 30 minutes. Add potatoes and carrots. Simmer 20 minutes. Stir in peas and cover. Simmer 5-10 minutes until vegetables are tender.

Gordon Zurn
Waubun, Minnesota

Venison Roast Stew

Serves: 4-6
Prep Time: 4 hours

3½ **lbs. venison roast**	2 **cups water**
salt and pepper	1 **celery stalk**
garlic powder	4 **carrots**
onion powder	4 **potatoes**
cooking oil	3 **garlic cloves, minced**
4 **onions, sliced**	2 **small cans Hot V-8 Juice**
1 **pkg. onion soup mix**	**mushrooms**

Sprinkle roast with salt, pepper, garlic and onion powder. Brown on both sides in hot oil. Place browned roast in oblong roasting pan. Put onions and soup on top of roast with juice. Add 1 cup water and celery. Cover with foil. Bake at 350 degrees 3-4 hours. During last hour, add remaining ingredients. Thicken gravy.

Leland Clyde Brown, Jr.
Boca Raton, Florida

Cedar Creek Lodge Meat Loaf

Serves: 8-10
Prep Time: 2 hours, 30 minutes

2 **lbs. ground venison**	1 **egg, beaten**
½ **lb. pork sausage**	¼ **cup celery, chopped**
1 **tsp. salt**	1 **cup soft bread crumbs**
dash of pepper	¼ **cup parsley, chopped**
1 **onion, minced**	1 **cup milk or tomatoes**

Combine all ingredients and mold into loaf. Line pan with foil and cook meat loaf uncovered at 350 degrees for 2 hours or until done.

J. Wayne Fears
Heflin, Alabama

Rolled Italian Venison Loaf

Serves: 4
Prep Time: 2 hours

1 **lb. ground venison**	1 **tsp. chili powder**
2 **white bread slices, crumbled**	½ **tsp. pepper**
1 **egg, beaten**	3 **oz. mozzarella or Monterey Jack cheese, grated**
1 **T. fresh parsley, chopped**	1 **cup mushrooms, chopped**
1 **tsp. oregano**	

Combine all ingredients except cheese and mushrooms. Mix well. Preheat oven to 350 degrees. On sheet of waxed paper, shape mixture into rectangle ¼-inch thick. Sprinkle with cheese, leaving ½-inch border on all sides. Top cheese with mushrooms. Starting from narrow end, lift waxed paper and roll meat (jelly roll style), removing waxed paper at same time. Seal open ends of roll by pinching together. Spray 9x5x3 loaf pan with non-stick cooking spray. Put loaf in pan and bake 45-55 minutes until done.

Bobbi Futterer
San Antonio, Texas

Crispy Venison Meat Loaves

Serves: 8
Prep Time: 30 minutes

1½ **lbs. ground venison**
¾ **cup whole wheat flakes, crushed**
2 **eggs, beaten**
½ **cup onion, minced**
2 **T. parsley, minced**
½ **tsp. thyme**
1½ **cups whole wheat flakes, uncrushed**

In mixing bowl, stir eggs, onion, parsley, thyme and crushed whole wheat flakes into venison. Reserve uncrushed flakes for later. Shape this mixture into 8 loaves 3½ inches long. Roll in uncrushed flakes. Place in greased, shallow pan. Bake at 350 degrees for 30 minutes. Garnish with parsley and onion rings, and relish with applause.

Wyatt Coughlan
Acton, Massachusetts

Kent's Venison Meat Loaf

Serves: 6
Prep Time: 1 hour

1 **lb. ground venison**
1 **lb. ground pork or beef**
4 **day-old bread slices**
½ **cup milk**
2 **eggs, slightly beaten**
1 **medium onion, chopped**
1 **garlic clove, minced**
2 **T. Worcestershire sauce**
1 **tsp. salt**
½ **tsp. pepper**

Heat oven to 350 degrees. Soak bread in milk until saturated. Place remaining ingredients in mixing bowl. Break bread into bits and combine with milk. Add to mixing bowl. Thoroughly blend the meat, bread, eggs and seasonings and place the mixture into a loaf pan that you have lightly but thoroughly greased. Put the pan in the oven and bake for 1 hour, pouring off fat as it accumulates. Let cool for 10 minutes before slicing.

Kent Carney
Urich, Missouri

Venison Burger Bake

Serves: 4-6
Prep Time: 45 minutes

1 **lb. ground venison**	¼ **cup milk**
salt and pepper	1½ **cups cabbage, shredded**
2 **cups Jiffy baking mix**	½ **medium onion, diced**
½ **cup milk**	1 **cup broccoli, diced**
1 **can cream of mushroom soup**	

Season venison with salt and pepper. Lightly fry venison and set aside. Make dough from baking mix and milk. Spread half of dough in greased pie plate. Mix cooked venison, soup and milk. Pour mixture into pie plate. Sprinkle with shredded cabbage, diced onion and diced broccoli. Top with the remaining dough. Bake in the oven at 400 degrees for approximately 20-30 minutes. Serve warm with green salad.

Rex Morgan
Kansas City, Missouri

Corned Venison Reuben Bake

Serves: 4
Prep Time: 30 minutes

2 **cups corned venison, diced or shredded**	2 **cups Swiss cheese, shredded**
1 **cup sauerkraut**	3 **cups rye bread, diced**
1 **cup Thousand Island dressing**	

Mix together venison, sauerkraut, Thousand Island dressing and cheese. Then, add the bread. Put in lightly greased baking dish, about 1½ inches deep. Bake at 350 degrees for 30 minutes or until brown. Serve warm.

Eugene Halliwill
Ashland, Ohio

Bowhunter Venison Pie

Serves: 6
Prep Time: 1 hour, 30 minutes

1½	**lbs. ground venison**	2	**T. Worcestershire sauce**
1	**10-oz. pkg. pastry mix**	¼	**tsp. thyme and**
½	**cup sharp cheddar**		**marjoram**
	cheese, grated	1½	**cups dry bread cubes**
½	**tsp. paprika**	1	**10-oz. can beef bouillon**
	dash of cayenne pepper		**or consomme**
1	**small onion, minced**	½	**tsp. salt**

Prepare pastry mix, adding cheese, paprika and cayenne before adding liquid. Roll half a pastry on lightly floured board, fit into 9-inch pie pan. Cook venison and onion in skillet until meat loses its red color and meat breaks up with fork. Drain excess grease. Add Worcestershire, thyme and marjoram, mix well. Mix bread cubes, bouillon and salt and let stand a few minutes. Add to beef-onion mixture, stir well and pour into pastry-lined pan. Roll remaining pastry and put over top, crimping edges. Bake at 375 degrees for about 45 minutes. Serve warm or cold.

Ed Botwright
Hyattsville, Missouri

Venison & Leek Pie

Serves: 4
Prep Time: 1 hour

1¼	**lbs. ground venison**	1	**T. garlic, chopped**
1	**pkg. pie dough**	1	**T. paprika**
4	**T. butter**	1¼	**lbs. leeks, thinly sliced**
	salt and pepper	3	**eggs**
¼	**tsp. cayenne pepper**	¾	**cup sour cream**

Line pie dish with dough. Brown venison in butter, seasoning with salt, pepper, cayenne, garlic and paprika. Then add leeks. Cook until they are translucent. Cool slightly and mix in eggs and sour cream. Pour into dish and bake at 450 degrees for 10 minutes. Reduce to 300 degrees; bake 30 minutes more.

Anonymous

Berky's Venison Muffins

Serves: 6
Prep Time: 1 hour

1 **lb. ground venison**	1 **tsp. Accent**
½ **lb. ground pork**	½ **tsp. thyme**
2 **cups soft bread crumbs**	1 **tsp. onion powder**
1 **cup milk**	½ **tsp. pepper**
1 **egg, beaten**	1 **tsp. garlic powder**
1 **tsp. Worcestershire**	⅓ **cup brown sugar**
sauce	⅓ **cup catsup**
2 **tsp. salt**	

Grease muffin pan. Mix above ingredients except brown sugar
and catsup. Divide mixture into 12 equal portions and pack
mixture lightly into wells. Bake at 350 degrees for 40 minutes.
Meanwhile, blend brown sugar and catsup and set aside. After
20 minutes of baking time, spoon 2 tsp. catsup mixture on each
venison muffin and continue baking. Serve hot.

Bill Berkant
Wilkes Barre, Pennsylvania

Venison Bleu Cheese Burgers

Serves: 8
Prep Time: 4 hours, 30 minutes

2 **lbs. ground venison**	1 **garlic clove, chopped**
½ **cup red wine**	½ **cup butter**
2 **tsp. salt**	½ **cup bleu cheese**
¼ **tsp. pepper**	½ **cup red wine**
1 **onion, grated**	2 **tsp. parsley, minced**

Mix venison, wine, salt, pepper, onion and garlic thoroughly.
Refrigerate for several hours. Form mixture into 8 patties. Cook
burgers in melted butter until done. Crumble bleu cheese on top
of patties and cover for 2-3 minutes before removing from skillet.
Stir the wine and parsley into the remaining juice. Heat and serve
over burgers.

Stewart Rolf
San Francisco, California

Venison Cheeseburger Pie

Serves: 4
Prep Time: 1 hour

1 **lb. ground venison**	1 **fresh tomato, diced**
1 **single pie crust**	¼ **cup green pepper,**
½ **lb. hot sausage**	**chopped**
1 **tsp. salt**	**Cheese Topping:**
½ **tsp. oregano**	1 **egg**
¼ **tsp. pepper**	¼ **cup milk**
½ **cup dry bread crumbs**	½ **tsp. salt**
1 **8-oz. can tomato sauce**	**Worcestershire sauce**
¼ **cup onion, chopped**	2 **cups cheese, shredded**

Heat oven to 425 degrees. Prepare pie crust for 9-inch pie. In skillet, brown meat, drain. Stir in salt, oregano, pepper, crumbs, tomato sauce, onion, tomato and green pepper. Pour in pie shell. Combine cheese topping ingredients, mixing the egg, milk, salt and Worcestershire sauce with 2 cups shredded cheese. Pour this mixture over the meat in the pie shell and bake for approximately 30 minutes.

Keith Dixon
Niehoopany, Pennsylvania

Special Burgers

Serves: 2-4
Prep Time: 15 minutes

1 **lb. ground venison**	1 **T. Worcestershire sauce**
¼ **cup catsup**	1 **tsp. sugar**
1 **T. mustard**	½ **cup milk**
1 **tsp. vinegar**	**dash of salt**

For this quick and easy lunchtime treat, mix all ingredients thoroughly in mixing bowl. Spread venison on hamburger bun halves. Place under broiler for 2-5 minutes until done.

Mike Gaddy
Nunda, New York

Buck And Bread

Serves: 8
Prep Time: 30 minutes

1 lb. ground venison	1 egg yolk
½ cup onion, chopped	1 T. water
½ cup ripe olives, chopped	
½ tsp. salt	**Mushroom Sauce:**
½ tsp. basil	½ lb. mushrooms
⅛ tsp. pepper	2 T. butter
2 T. parsley, chopped	1 beef bouillon cube
4 cups buttermilk mix	1 T. flour
¾ cup cold water	1 cup water

Brown venison with onions. Remove from heat and stir in olives, salt, basil and pepper. Set aside. Mix parsley into buttermilk mix. Quickly mix in ¾ cup cold water until mixture forms soft dough. Turn dough onto floured surface, knead 8-10 strokes. With rolling pin, roll dough into 12x10-inch rectangle. Evenly spread cooled meat mixture on dough, leaving ½-inch edges. Starting at narrow end, roll up dough (jelly roll style). Tuck ends under. Place roll, seam side down, on cookie sheet. Beat egg yolk with 1 T. water. Brush roll with mixture. Bake at 425 degrees 30 minutes. Meanwhile, cook mushrooms in butter and bouillon. Blend flour with water, and gradually stir into mushrooms. Cook, stirring constantly until sauce thickens. Slice roll and serve with sauce.

Dixie Luke
Glenwood Springs, Colorado

Pickled Venison

Serves: several
Prep Time: 1 hour

cooked venison, sliced	⅔ cup sugar
⅓ cup vinegar	2 T. mixed pickling spices
⅔ cup water	wide mouth gallon jug

Heat all ingredients until warm, adding salt to taste. Pour over cooked, sliced meat. Let stand 24 hours before serving.

Joseph Cooney
Nanticoke, Pennsylvania

Venison Bake

Serves: 4
Prep Time; 1 hour

2 **lbs. venison**	½ **cup flour**
¼ **cup vegetable oil**	1½ **cups hot water**
1 **cup carrots, sliced**	3 **beef bouillon cubes**
1 **large onion, sliced**	**rice or noodles, cooked**

In heavy skillet, pour in vegetable oil to heat. Add carrots and onions. Saute for 2 minutes. Remove carrots and onions from skillet. Cut up venison into bite-size pieces and dredge in flour until well-coated. Brown meat in hot oil. Return carrots and onions to skillet. Saute for an additional 2 minutes. Add hot water and beef bouillon cubes. Stir until bouillon has dissolved. Pour into casserole dish. Cover and bake at 350 degrees for 1 hour. To serve, pour over prepared rice or noodles.

Edward Dull
Ashland, Ohio

Venison Sausage And Noodles

Serves: 6
Prep Time: 1 hour

1 **lb. venison sausage**	1 **can cream of mushroom**
2 **cups fine noodles**	**soup**
2 **T. pimento, chopped**	½ **cup crumbly blue**
2 **T. green pepper,**	**cheese**
chopped	½ **cup soft bread crumbs**
¼ **cup milk**	1 **T. butter**

Brown sausage, stirring to crumble. Drain. Cook noodles until tender in unsalted boiling water. Combine sausage, noodles, pimento and green pepper. Add milk to soup. Heat, stirring constantly. Add blue cheese, stirring until cheese melts. Combine sauce and noodle mixture. Turn into greased 1½-qt. casserole. Mix crumbs and butter and sprinkle over top. Bake at 350 degrees for 30 minutes.

Dave Van Liere
Wolcott, New York

Venison Bundles To Go

Serves: 6-8
Prep Time: 45 minutes

1-2 lbs. ground venison	**1 tsp. ground cumin**
4 large eggs	**1 tsp. salt**
2 8-oz cans tomato sauce	**16 taco shells**
2 cups small bread cubes	**8 American cheese slices**
2 tsp. chili powder	

Mix together venison, eggs, tomato sauce, bread cubes, chili powder, cumin and salt. Divide this mixture into 16 portions. Lightly press portions into taco shells. Place on broiler pan rack. Bake at 350 degrees for 20 minutes. Turn the shells over and bake 20 minutes more. A few minutes before done, place half cheese slice on meat in each shell. Drain the shells on paper towels. Serve warm with guacamole and sour cream, or add lettuce, tomato and dollop of mayonnaise. It's a real South of the Border delight.

Walter Squier
Portland, Connecticut

Venison Spaghetti

Serves: 6-8
Prep Time: 1 hour, 30 minutes

2 lbs. ground venison	**2 celery stalks, chopped**
2 large onions, chopped	**olive oil**
½ green pepper, chopped	**salt and pepper**
2 garlic cloves, chopped	**32 oz. spaghetti sauce**

In a large pan, brown the onion, green pepper, garlic and celery in olive oil. When the mixture is adequately brown, add the ground venison and break it up and brown. Then, add salt and pepper. Now, pour the spaghetti sauce over the browned meat and spices. Bring the sauce to a boil. Simmer 15 minutes or until juices become thick. Then, pour the sauce over spaghetti which you have cooked and drained. Add garlic bread and enjoy.

Sue Volkmann
Pittsburgh, New Hampshire

Luau Venison

Serves: 8-10
Prep Time: 2 hours

5 **lbs. boneless venison, cubed**	1 **cup celery, chunked**
¾ **cup flour**	3 **green peppers, cubed**
¾ **cup cooking oil**	¼ **cup packed brown sugar**
1 **cup water**	2 **T. sliced fresh**
1 **can pineapple chunks, drained**	**gingerroot or ¾ tsp. ground ginger**
3 **large white onions, thickly sliced**	¼ **cup soy sauce**
	4-5 **cups hot cooked rice**

Dredge meat in flour. Heat oil in large skillet over medium-high heat. Brown meat in batches. Return all meat to pan and add water. Cover, reduce heat to medium or medium-low and simmer until meat is tender, about 45 minutes. (Time will vary depending upon age of deer.) Remove meat. (Thicken gravy by combining 1 T. flour and ¼ cup water. Stir into pan juices, increasing heat to medium.) Add pineapple, onions, celery and peppers to roasting pan. Mix brown sugar, ginger and soy sauce into gravy. Pour over vegetables in roaster. Add meat. Cover. Bake at 350 degrees for 30 minutes or until vegetables are tender but not soft. Lightly mix ingredients. Serve over cooked rice.

Anonymous

Venison Breakfast Hash

Serves: 4
Prep Time: 35 minutes

1¼ **lb. cooked venison steak, finely diced**	2 **potatoes, cooked and diced**
¼ **lb. bacon, diced**	**salt and white pepper**
½ **onion, diced**	⅛ **lb. butter**

Mix all ingredients except butter. Melt butter in pan. Add hash mixture to butter and fry until golden brown and crispy. Top with poached eggs. For brunch, serve with sliced tomato salad.

Anonymous

Venison Tidbits

Serves: 4-6
Prep Time: 1 hour, 15 minutes

2 lbs. venison
1 lb. bacon
1 cup Worcestershire sauce

2 cups water

Cut meat into 1-inch cubes. Wrap bacon around meat and secure with toothpicks. Place meat in skillet. Pour Worcestershire and water over meat. Cover and simmer 1 hour. Remove cover and cook 15 minutes.

Mark Bishop
Angleton, Texas

Pigs On A Bass Bed

Serves: 4-6
Prep Time: 2 hours

4-6 lbs. venison steaks
2-3 bass fillets
2 cups flour
1 cup cornmeal
3 eggs
1 T. Old Bay seasoning

salt and pepper, to taste
garlic and onion powder, to taste
1 can beer
longhorn cheese, grated

Boil steaks in water until tender. Save water. Cut steaks into ½-inch finger strips and set aside. Cut belly bones from bass fillets and set aside. Mix flour, cornmeal, eggs, Old Bay seasoning, salt, pepper, garlic and onion powder. Add beer and mix well. Add enough flour to make thick dough. Roll dough out to ¼-inch thickness and cut into 4x5-inch squares. Put salted water on to boil. Cut bass fillets into finger strips. Put 2 meat pieces and fish on each dough square. Roll up fairly tight, pinch and close. Add to boiling water. When rolls float on top, wait another 2 minutes and remove. Place in pan on tinfoil and cover with cheese. Bake at 325 degrees until cheese melts.

Howard Bailey
North Las Vegas, Nevada

Seaside Venison

Serves: 6-8
Prep Time: 3 hours, 30 minutes

6-8 lbs. venison brisket
1 lb. small cooked shrimp
1 lb. crab meat
1 medium onion, diced
1 cup mushrooms, diced

1 tsp. black pepper
1 tsp. thyme
1 tsp. mustard
1 tsp. flour
beef bouillon

Form pocket in brisket by splitting lengthwise, stopping a few inches from each end. Remove about 1 lb. venison. Put shrimp, crab and 1 lb. venison through meat grinder. Mix onion, mushrooms and spices into ground meat. Stuff brisket with ground meat and sew up pocket with poultry string. Place brisket in large roasting pan, add enough beef bouillon to cover one-third of brisket. Bake at 300 degrees for 2 hours, basting every 15-20 minutes with bouillon.

David Calhoun
Pekin, Illinois

Venison Chow Mein

Serves: 8-10
Prep Time: 2 hours

2 lbs. venison, cubed in
½-inch pieces
10 cups water
2 large onions, sliced
1 celery stalk, sliced
½ lb. bean sprouts

bamboo shoots
1 small can chopped
mushrooms
soy sauce
salt and pepper

Brown venison cubes in large skillet. Transfer to 4-qt. stew pot. Cover with water and boil 30 minutes. Add onions and celery. Boil until tender. Add bean sprouts, bamboo shoots and mushrooms. Boil 10 minutes. If soup is too thin, add cornstarch mixed with water to desired thickness. Serve with chow mein noodles and rice.

Dennis Sharp
Clifton, Arizona

Walter's Deer

Serves: varies
Prep Time: 3-4 hours

1 **venison hindquarter, boned**	2 **bottles Italian dressing**
4 **bacon strips**	1 **pt. dry white wine**
1 **tsp. red pepper**	1 **large onion, sliced**
salt, to taste	1 **large can mushrooms**
2 **garlic cloves**	4 **carrots, diced**
	4 **potatoes, diced**

Place bacon strips in open hindquarter. Sprinkle in red pepper and lightly salt. Add garlic, roll and tie. Place rolled hindquarter in deep pan. Add Italian dressing and wine. Place onion on top of meat, pour on mushrooms, carrots and potatoes. Place on covered charcoal grill with fire in one end and meat on the other for 4 hours. (Can be done in oven at 325-350 degrees for about 2 hours, 30 minutes or until done.) Baste occasionally. When cooked, slice thin and serve either as entree or as sandwiches.

Walter L. Allen
Montgomery, Alabama

Canadian Goulash

Serves: 8-12
Prep Time: several hours

4-6 **lbs. venison cubes**	1 **pinch caraway seeds**
cooking oil	½-**inch lemon peel strip**
½ **tsp. seasoned salt**	1 **tsp. coarse horseradish**
1 **tsp. marjoram**	¼ **cup catsup**
¼ **tsp. pepper**	**flour to thicken**
1 **T. onion, minced**	

In large hot frying pan, add oil and venison. Turn to keep from burning. After all meat is browned, add remaining ingredients and 2 T. flour. Add water gradually to cover venison. Simmer several hours until tender. If gravy is thin, add flour paste.

David Swalby
Fond du Lac, Wisconsin

Saskatchewan Venison

Serves: 4-6
Prep Time: 3 days plus 3 hours, 30 minutes

4 lbs. venison	**8 T. butter**
1½ cups red wine vinegar	**cooking oil**
½ cup dry red wine	**flour**
2 carrots, sliced	**1 T. sugar**
2 onions, sliced	**gingersnaps**
your favorite spices	

Mix vinegar, wine, carrots and onions. Pour over meat and marinate 3 days in refrigerator. Turn occasionally to absorb flavors. Take meat out of refrigerator and pat dry with paper towels. Save marinade. Brown meat in 4 T. butter and cooking oil in Dutch oven, sprinkling meat with flour as it is turned. Heat the marinade, pour over meat, cover and simmer for about 3 hours until tender. Strain off liquid and skim fat. Melt 4 T. butter, blend in same amount of flour, 1 T. sugar and cooking liquid. Stir until smooth and thickened. Add about 1 T. crushed gingersnaps and sprinkle over meat. Cook slowly for another 30 minutes.

Glen Hill
Saskatoon, Saskatchewan

Peppered Venison Rack

Serves: 4-6
Prep Time: 3 hours

1 venison loin or rack	**½ cup whole black**
1 cup brandy and red	**peppercorns**
wine combined	**salt**

Marinate trimmed venison rack in sealed container with brandy and red wine. Turn once or twice while marinating. Crush peppercorns with bottom of frying pan. Push peppercorns into roast. Bake at 375 degrees until internal roast temperature is 145 degrees. Let stand after roasting for 10 minutes. Slice with that knife you just sharpened. Serve with fried potatoes and a fresh green vegetable.

Anonymous

Venison Pizza

Serves: 6-8
Prep Time: 2 hours

1 **lb. ground venison**	3 **cups grated cheese**
6 **cups unbleached flour**	1 **small onion, chopped**
1½ **cups buttermilk**	**chives (optional)**
4 **T. butter or margarine**	2 **cans pizza sauce**
4 **T. honey**	**oregano**
½ **tsp. salt**	**garlic powder**
1 **pkg. yeast**	**pepper**
¼ **cup warm water**	**thyme**

Measure flour into large bowl. In separate container combine buttermilk, butter, honey and salt. Heat buttermilk mixture to lukewarm. Dissolve yeast in warm water. Add yeast and milk mixture to flour and combine to make firm dough. Turn dough out and knead for 5 minutes. Put dough in greased bowl, cover and let rise until double in bulk. Prepare toppings. Fry venison, crumbling it as you fry. After dough rises, punch it down, divide in half and roll out 2 parts to fit baking sheets. Spread pizza sauce on dough. Sprinkle with seasonings and top with grated cheese and crumbled venison. Bake 20-30 minutes at 350 degrees.

Mary Smith
Lewiston, Minnesota

Poontock

Serves: 3-4
Prep Time: 1 hour

2-3 **lbs. venison**	1 **large onion, chopped**
salt and pepper	1 **large lemon, peeled and**
flour	**sliced**

Salt, pepper and flour venison. Fry until lightly brown on both sides. Place meat in large pot. Add onion and lemon. Cover contents with water and cook on low heat. Allow to slow boil for 30 minutes to 1 hour. Makes its own gravy.

Bill Morrison
Camden, Arkansas

Homemade Egg Noodles And Venison

Serves: 6
Prep Time: 3 hours

1-2 qts. home-canned venison or 2 lbs. chunked venison
6 eggs, beaten
1 tsp. salt
¼ tsp. baking powder
5 cups flour
1 onion or ¼ cup dry onion
2 beef bouillon cubes
salt and pepper

Mix eggs, salt, baking powder and flour until mixture is stiff. Sprinkle flour on and under mixture on a board and roll as thin as possible. Sift flour over rolled mixture and roll up like cinnamon rolls. Slice in thin pieces and unroll to dry. Place in airtight container and store in cool place or freezer until ready to use. In large kettle, heat meat, onion and bouillon in 1½ qts. water until boiling. Don't be impatient. It only seems like it takes forever. Also, remember that if you're using fresh meat allow longer stewing time. Add salt and pepper to taste. Add noodles and simmer 30 minutes.

Mary Beth Kibler
Sand Springs, Montana

Spaghetti Squash With Venison

Serves: 6-8
Prep Time: 1 hour, 15 minutes

2 lbs. ground venison
1 large spaghetti squash
4 large onions, chopped
1 qt. spaghetti sauce
pepper, to taste
4 T. soy sauce

Cook squash 45 minutes at 375 degrees. Fork squash out of skin. Fry onions and venison in oil until brown. Now, mix the browned onions and venison with the squash and add the spaghetti sauce, soy sauce and pepper to taste. Cook for 15 minutes and serve.

Charles Riegel
Hudson, New York

Venison A La Calabrase

Serves: 2-3
Prep Time: 45 minutes

**2-3 lbs. venison, boned and
chopped into bite-size
pieces**
¾ cup cooking oil
1 lb. onions
½ cup water
1 lb. green peppers, sliced
**1 lb. hot green peppers
(optional)**

1 cup tomato sauce
salt and pepper
fresh parsley
garlic powder
oregano
fennel seeds

Heat ¼ cup oil in large skillet. Add meat and brown on all sides
at high heat. While browning, spice to taste. After meat is
thoroughly browned, remove from pan. Fry onions in same pan
and add to meat. Stir in ½ cup water to gather up all the gravy in
bottom of pan. Simmer 3 minutes, add to onions and meat. In
clean skillet, fry sliced peppers in oil at high heat. Add peppers
to meat and onion mixture. Put more oil, tomato sauce and rest of
spices into skillet. Fry at high heat (do not boil). Cook for 5-8
minutes. At this time, stir in cooked meat, onion and pepper.
Cook another 5 minutes, stirring constantly.

Thomas Varbero
Harrison, New York

Marinated Venison

Serves: varies
Prep Time: 12 hours

venison steaks
1 bottle beer
½ cup soy sauce

1 tsp. garlic salt
1 tsp. onion powder

Combine all ingredients. Pour over sliced venison. Marinate
overnight. Flour and fry venison steaks in hot fat or oil until
cooked.

Mary Beth Kibler
Sand Springs, Montana

Venison Navy Contact Mines

Serves: 6-8
Prep Time: 1 hour, 30 minutes

venison round	**cooking oil**
1 onion	**salt and pepper**
8 bacon slices	**3 T. flour**

Cut 4 slices (½-inch thick) from venison round. Divide each slice into 4 equal pieces. Peel onion and cut into 16 pieces. Cut bacon slices in halves. Slap each venison piece with broadside of cleaver. Wrap onion piece in bacon piece. Wrap bacon piece in venison piece. Secure resulting ball with toothpick (should look like a Navy contact mine). For those of you who weren't in the Navy, contact mines are round with spines or points on them which cause detonation when they come in contact with an object. Brown in hot oil in Dutch oven. Add salt and pepper to taste. When browned, cover with water and simmer 1 hour. Remove "mines" from oven. Mix flour with enough water to obtain milk consistency. Add this to boiling mixture, stirring constantly. When proper consistency, return "mines" to Dutch oven. Cover and simmer for 10-15 minutes. Serve on mashed potatoes with a green salad and bread, if you like.

Morton Anderson
Columbus, Ohio

Venison Carlos

Serves: varies
Prep Time: 5 days

venison backstrap	**buttermilk**

Slice backstrap into thick strips. Crosshatch each strip. Place a layer in flat baking pan. Cover with buttermilk and continue to layer until all meat is in pan. Place in refrigerator for 5 days. Remove and place strips on charcoal grill for 2-3 minutes. Serve as an appetizer.

Walter Allen
Montgomery, Alabama

Jimbeaux's Venison Bambino

Serves: 8-10
Prep Time: 30 minutes

2 **lbs. young venison backstrap**	2 **garlic cloves**
sherry cooking wine	2 **T. lemon juice**
¼ **cup butter**	**vermicelli**
1 **onion, thinly sliced**	**flour**
	milk

Slice venison into thin medallions and place in tall container. Add just enough sherry to cover meat. Work sherry into meat with wooden spoon. Melt butter in skillet. Chop garlic and onion coarsely. Simmer in butter 5 minutes. Add lemon juice, meat and sherry. Cover and simmer 10 minutes, turning meat occasionally. Boil pasta in water while removing meat and garlic from skillet. Put meat on warm plate in oven and make thin gravy in skillet using flour and milk. Stir until smooth. Add meat to gravy and simmer until pasta is done. Quickly drain and serve pasta topped with meat and gravy.

James Kelley
Denver, Colorado

Hungry Boy Casserole

Serves: 4-6
Prep Time: 45 minutes

1½ **lbs. ground venison**	¼ **cup water**
1 **cup celery, chopped**	1 **tsp. salt**
½ **cup onion, chopped**	1 **tsp. paprika**
½ **cup green pepper, chopped**	1 **can pork and beans**
1 **can tomato soup**	1 **container biscuits**

Fry venison with celery, onion and green pepper. Add soup, water, salt, paprika and pork and beans. Place in casserole and put biscuits on top of meat mixture. Bake at 425 degrees for 25-30 minutes or until biscuits are golden brown.

Wayne Umlor
Conklin, Michigan

Venison Roll-Ups La Barb

Serves: 8-10
Prep Time: 1 hour, 30 minutes

3-4 lbs. venison	**2 eggs, beaten**
1½ lbs. beef suet	**2 T. Romano cheese,**
2 cups seasoned Italian	**grated**
bread crumbs	**1 lemon**
1 cup onion, sliced	**1 tsp. oregano**
lengthwise	**¼ lb. butter**
1 T. parsley, chopped	

Cut meat across grain into ½-inch thick slices. Pound out until ¼ inch or less. Thinly slice beef suet. Mix bread crumbs, onion, parsley, eggs and cheese in bowl. Lay out meat pieces. On one end, place suet piece and 1 T. bread crumb mix. Roll up. Make another the same way. Stick both roll-ups together with toothpicks. Continue until all meat is gone. Barbecue over nice coal bed, turning frequently. Baste with melted butter, lemon and oregano mix.

Joe LaBarbera
West Allis, Wisconsin

Triple K's Venison

1 venison breast	**1 tsp. flour**
¼ lb. butter	**1 cup hot water or stock**
salt and pepper	**1 T. currant jelly**
cracker crumbs	

Cut venison breast into steaks. Heat butter in pan and rub steaks with salt and pepper mixture. Dip steaks in cracker crumbs and fry in hot butter until golden brown. When both sides are browned, place steaks in covered dish. Add flour to butter and stir until brown. Add cup of boiling water with currant jelly dissolved in it and stir for a few minutes. Strain this mixture over meat and serve.

Danny Kokaska
Tinley Park, Illinois

Field Tips

Preparation for a wild game feast you'll be proud to serve your friends and family begins long before the processed meat is pulled from the freezer to thaw. The highest quality wild game meat is the result of planning that should be started even before you go hunting.

For example, having the right tools on hand once game is brought to bag isn't something that should be left to the last minute. Nor is knowing the distance to the nearest available locker plant and the logistics of getting your animal to it on the weekend or in the middle of the night. The following pages address the proper procedures to ensure delicious wild game meals that you and your family are sure to enjoy. As hunters, you deserve the best after all the time and effort you've spent afield. It isn't easy bringing home the bacon, or the venison, duck or antelope, for that matter. Here's hoping your hunt is a success, and that you get your wild game home and in the freezer in the best possible condition.

Recovering Big Game
by Mark LaBarbera

The old adage, "You can't cook it if you don't shoot it," is missing one step. After you shoot it, you have to find it. As Uncle Ignazino LaBarbera would tell us younger hunters years ago, "Tracks make thin soup. You boys better get on that deer's trail if you want to eat tonight."

Iggy and his brother Giuseppe shared some trailing tips back then that have proven effective over the years. For some of you, the tips in this big game recovery guide may be new. For others, some of them will be old hat. Consider it, then, a refresher course.

Whether you connect on your target and it doesn't drop in sight, the animal should be trailed until it is found or until you are sure that it was not mortally hit. After a hit, follow these steps:

1. Sit tight. Watch where the game goes until it's out of sight, but also make sure you pin-point the spot where the animal was standing when you shot. Also, try to picture how the animal reacted when you shot.

2. Note your position since many hunters forget where they were when they shot. And pick out a specific landmark to help you remember where the game was last seen. Note the time before leaving your stand.

3. But don't let anxiety overcome you. Over-anxious hunters push game that may have otherwise stayed nearby to die. Veteran hunters recommend waiting one hour, and at least twice that long for a gut shot, but you'll have to judge what's appropriate for your situation. Hunting on public land, near major roadways and in an area with heavy hunting pressure or hungry predators may force you to pursue your animal sooner.

4. When it's time to move, go first to where you shot. Check for blood, hair or other signs. Bowhunters can look for their arrow.

5. Follow any blood sign or obvious trails the game left. If none, follow the path you recall the animal taking toward where you last saw it.

6. Mark the beginning of the trail with flagging or toilet paper, but remember to come back later and remove this from the woods.

Field Dress Tasty Venison Correctly

Once you've recovered your deer and your composure, dress the animal immediately following these guidelines from information supplied by the Nebraska Game and Parks Commission.

1. Roll the carcass on its back with the rump lower than the shoulders and spread the hind legs. Cut along the centerline of the belly from breastbone to base of tail. Cut through the hide, then through the belly muscle. Avoid cutting into the paunch and intestines by holding them away from the knife with your free hand while guiding the knife with your other hand.

2. With a small, sharp knife, cut around the anus and draw it into the body cavity, so it comes free with the complete intestines. Avoid cutting or breaking the bladder.

3. Reach into the cavity and pull down on the liver to expose the diaphragm. To access the upper chest cavity, cut the diaphragm away from the rib cage. Reach up into the neck as far as possible and grasp the gullet, large blood vessel and windpipe and sever them with the same small, sharp knife.

4. Roll the deer on its side and pull on the gullet and windpipe. This will pull away the entrails from the body easily, spilling them onto the ground. Save the heart and liver and place them in a plastic bag to keep them clean.

5. Turn the deer belly-down to drain remaining blood from the body cavity. If you hang the deer to drain, hang with the head down to allow quicker cooling of meat. Use a clean cloth to wipe the inside of the body cavity, removing any fluids from the entrails that may have escaped when the animal was shot. It is not necessary to flush the body cavity with water.

Dragging Out Your Trophy & Your Meat

To make dragging go as smoothly as possible when trying to get your deer out of the woods, bring the forelegs up and tie them inside the antlers to streamline the animal. A light rope or nylon cord tied around the neck just below the head works well, especially if the other end is tied to a strong stick to distribute the weight among available hands. This works ideally for two hunters dragging a single deer.

Meat Handling Tips

While warm weather on tap for deer season makes hunting comfortable for the hunter, it also makes caring for the venison you collect a potential problem.

University of Nebraska Extension Meat Specialist Dwight Loveday advises field dressing the animal as quickly and carefully as possible to avoid meat contamination. Also, it should be stored at temperatures below 40 degrees.

But in warm temperatures it may be difficult to find an area where the temperature stays that cool. "The hunter should still field dress the deer quickly and carefully. Then he should hang the deer in as cool an area as possible to let the meat go through the state of rigor mortis—contraction of the muscles that stiffens the animal—before freezing or butchering the deer," he said.

Loveday said it takes 10-12 hours for the meat to go through rigor mortis. If the flesh is not allowed to go through that stage prior to being frozen or butchered, the result will be tough meat, because it contracts during thawing or cutting.

"It is important to keep the meat as cool as possible, out of the sun. Usually hanging the carcass overnight will allow the rigor to occur. It should also be taken to a processor or processed by the hunter and iced-down as quickly as possible following the rigor mortis state," he said.

To help keep the meat cool, many hunters purchase inexpensive styrofoam coolers to carry the iced-down, boned meat on the trip home, according to Game and Parks Commission Outdoor Education Instructor Dick Turpin.

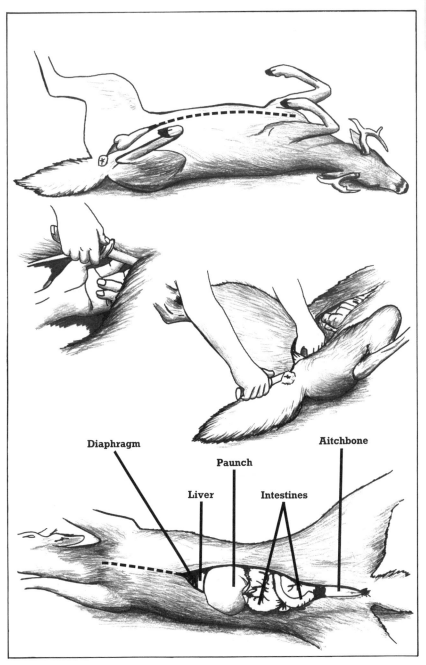

By carefully following these steps, even a first-timer can field dress a deer with little waste or mess.

Another great way to keep meat cool in a remote camp is to put the animal in a breathable cloth bag—a number of companies make such products. This will keep flies and dirt off the meat. Then hang the animal in a shady area. Allow the cool night air to flow in and around the bagged carcass. Then before daylight in the morning, hang two or three layers of sleeping bags over the animal. This insulates the cooled carcass from the effects of the warming daytime temperatures.

"It is the responsibility of the hunter to properly care for the meat he takes in the field so it will be enjoyable later on the table. Too many hunters work very hard to find and take their game and then don't properly care for it. How the animal is treated after the shot determines the quality of the meat from that time on," Turpin said.

Meat Cutting Tips That Help Save Money

Merle Ellis has a few money saving tips to share. Ellis, who has a syndicated television series on 76 stations and writes a meat-cutting column for 126 newspapers, offered the following tips during a visit to Minneapolis, where NAHC headquarters is located.

First of all, he suggested to "spend some time learning the basic cuts of meat—which are tender and which not—and how each should be cooked."

Ellis says meat cutting can be confusing to people because a lot of the cuts of meat are disguised by misleading names. Surprisingly, he said, "There are only nine basic cuts to learn and at least four of those end up going into hamburger anyway." He said a real way to save money is learning how to cut, bone and trim meat.

That's something us hunters have known for a long time. But we take it one step further and actually harvest the meat. One example Ellis used: "A chuck roast can be cut apart for two nice steaks, some stew meat and scraps perfectly suitable for stir-frying."

Ellis said meat quality is about the same in all parts of the country. He also said whether you put tender meat on your table depends on what you begin with and how you prepare it.

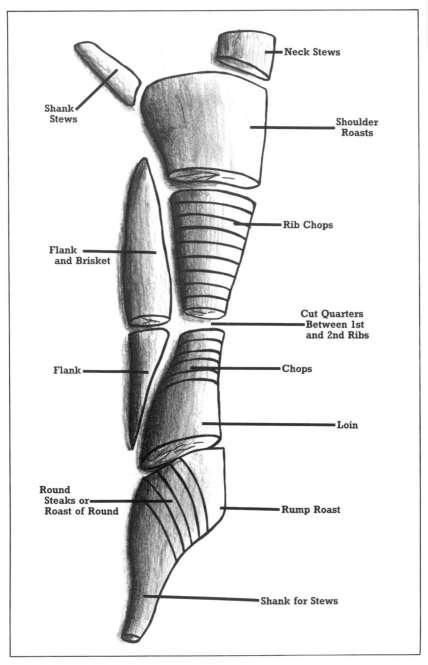

These are the basic cuts from a side of venison. With experience you'll be able to efficiently custom butcher your own game.

"Obviously," he said, "cuts of meat from parts of the animal that get the most exercise are going to be tougher than cuts like a tenderloin that just sort of rides along as the animal moves."

Although he likes to marinade and use commercial tenderizers, he says the best way to tenderize is by proper cooking.

"Marinades add flavor and tenderize the area of the meat that they touch, but they do not penetrate very deeply," he said. Commercial meat tenderizers, which are composed of three fruit enzymes, work in the same way.

"The thing to remember," he said, "is that dry heat toughens, and moist heat breaks down connective tissues. You can stew a 35-year-old buffalo to tenderness if you want to. It's all in the cooking."

When the cooking expert uses a marinade, he usually leaves it on the meat for less than an hour, because he says it draws out the moisture and makes the surface of the meat mushy.

One other tip Ellis offers concerns seasoning meat before cooking.

"When meat is seasoned before cooking, the flavor becomes part of the surface and you can taste it in the finished product," he said.

Your Easy Guide To Proper Caping
by Mark LaBarbera

Hunting the deep woods of my new state of residence last year was more difficult than deer hunting the agricultural areas of central Wisconsin, my home state. So, when I finally connected on a nice white-tailed buck, naturally I wanted it mounted to remember the achievement. A hunting buddy advised me where to cut the hide and it all seemed simple enough.

I brought the cape to Marv Gaston's Taxidermy Unlimited in Burnsville, Minnesota, and presented it and the antlers to Marv with a proud smile on my face.

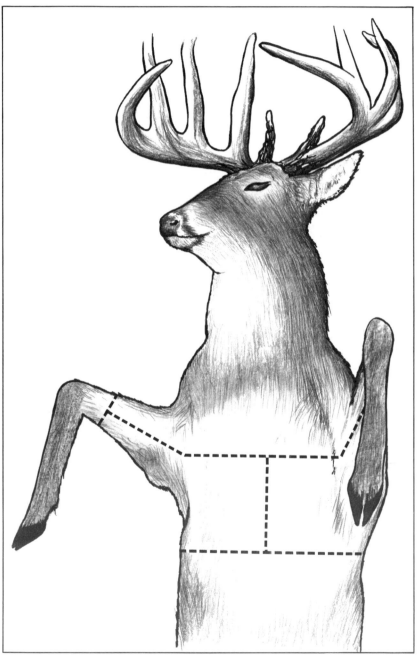

When making cuts for a cape, be sure to leave plenty of hide for the taxidermist to work with. Too much is far better than too little.

Marv picked up the cape like an inquisitive husband picks up his wife's new bikini. "Where's the rest of it?" he asked.

"That's it right there," I said stunned, and pointed to what he held.

"All of it?" he asked.

"Yep!" I said.

"Well," he shrugged, "we'll see what we can do."

Marv explained one simple rule pertaining to big game field care for those of us who want our trophy mounted: "Too much cape is better than not enough cape, so always cut a little farther back than you think is proper."

I talked to a number of taxidermists and hunters with different opinions on how to skin deer for mounting and came up with a simple step-by-step process that works for elk, moose, antelope and similar big game, in addition to deer.

Start out by field dressing your deer, but don't cut forward of the breastbone. Some hunters prefer to reach into the chest cavity to clean it out. If you prefer to split open the breast completely, wait until after this caping process is complete. Follow your state check-in regulations for registering game and then follow these steps.

Step 1

Some taxidermists work better if you can provide two easy measurements taken before you cape the game animal. Measure from the tip of the nose to the corner of the eye and measure completely around the neck right behind the ears. (If you don't have a tape measure, use your drag rope or belt and count off the distance with a dollar bill, which is always six inches long.)

Step 2

Cut the hide from between the ears (a) to a point (b) on top of the back and directly above any spot just behind the front shoulder. Always cut with the grain of the hair and in a straight line down the neck's middle.

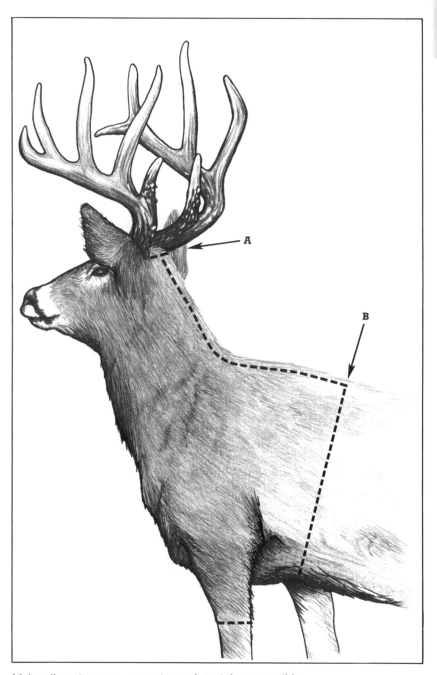

Make all caping cuts as precise and straight as possible.

Step 3

From the top of the back (b), cut straight down to the center of the brisket. Do this on both sides.

Step 4

Cut from there inward under the brisket to a point almost directly between the front legs, then down the insides of the legs to a point about eight inches down.

Step 5

Now cut around the front legs to complete the knife work.

Step 6

Peel the hide forward off the legs, shoulders and neck, right up to the base of the antlers.

Step 7

With a knife or saw, cut the muscles and vertebrae that attaches the head to the rest of the neck. Twist the head and cape to separate them from the neck.

Take the head and cape to the taxidermist right away in something protective and breathable, like a burlap bag, so he can skin out the head completely. If you can't get to a taxidermist immediately, roll up the hide, hair inward, and place it in a plastic bag inside your freezer for not more than two weeks.

On elk, moose and other types of hunts, you may not be able to haul around the cape and head, and may have to completely skin out the head yourself. If so, follow these steps:

Step 8

Use a blunt instrument (even a screwdriver will do) to free the hide around the antlers by prying it carefully.

Step 9

Continue to free the skin toward the eyes in a circular motion, being careful not to cut the eyelids or tear ducts. Put your finger under the skin around the eyes and feel where the eye membrane is connected. Cut it and continue toward the tear duct, which you then cut as close to the bone as possible. The eyelashes and eyelids must stay attached to the cape, not the skull.

Step 10

Work in a circular motion toward the corner of the mouth. Then put your finger on the underside, cut as close to the gums without cutting the lips and work to the middle of the lower jaw. At this point the skin will fall free. You will have to cut the lips free from the upper jaw without slicing them.

Step 11

Next, work on the nose. To know where to make the final cuts, turn the head so the top of the skull is facing you. Feel the end of the skull where the cartilage joins it. From here make a diagonal cut toward the lip. This should completely free the cape from the skull.

Step 12

Remove the antlers by cutting from the back of the skull, completely through it just at the top of the eye socket. This same step is used if you only want to mount the antlers on a plaque for yourself. If you can't get your cape to a freezer, treat it like you would the rest of the hide. Carefully scrape away any red meat still on it without cutting holes in the skin. Use non-iodized salt to cover the skin. Remove the salt after 24 hours and salt again. The required amount of salt for a deer head is three pounds, and five pounds for a complete hide. This should keep the hair from slipping, or falling out, until you reach your favorite or nearest taxidermist. Roger Tourville at A-1 Taxidermy, Saint Paul, Minnesota, says you don't have to abandon hopes of having a good mount just because you cut a hole in your hide. Likewise, he says, taxidermists have ways to cover up bullet or arrow holes, as long as you haven't shaved away too much hair.

Now it's up to you to memorize these informative steps so you can follow them when you down your big game trophy this hunting season. Good luck and good hunting.

Getting Meat Ready For The Freezer
by Annette and Louis Bignami

Freezing food has to be the safest and easiest way to preserve game. Since we eat game and game birds in place of domestic meats we take special care to ensure that the food we eat comes out of the freezer in the same good shape that it went in.

The mechanics of freezing are simple. What's most important is a careful consideration of portion size and future recipes so you don't face a whole frozen turkey when you just want breast meat to smoke. We also use the freezer to store extra servings of our favorite game and birds to tenderize them. We age birds in their feathers in the refrigerator for one to three days. We hang deer for a night or two; then bone. Since we live in California it's not possible to hang game and birds outdoors for longer periods. The weather is much too hot. At 40 to 50 degrees, hang it for a longer period.

We bone big game. This eliminates bone chips and ensures compact packages that wrap and freeze in minimum space. Cutting game along muscle groups also makes the final result more uniform than is the case with steaks that might have tender and tough sections.

We freeze small birds like quail four at a time in quart plastic milk containers. Some pheasants freeze whole in half-gallon containers. However, we portion most of our pheasants, sage grouse and turkeys. Breasts are individually wrapped and used for supremes. Legs and thighs go six or eight at a time, with shot up bird parts, into plastic milk cartons for later use in enchiladas, pasties and other dishes. We save backs and necks for stock. This is more flexible than freezing birds whole. Note: if you butcher-wrap birds, tuck the legs inside the body cavity for a compact package less likely to freezer-burn.

Other Big Game

Webster's definition of "venison" is a broad one. Historically, it includes the flesh of any wild animal taken by hunting. And that definition works pretty well for most of the recipes in the "Venison" chapter of this book, particularly if you limit the discussion to "antlered" game. Moose, elk or caribou meat can usually be substituted for deer meat in any of those recipes with quite satisfactory results.

On the other hand, the delicious meat of these and other animals like pronghorn antelope, wild sheep, goats and buffalo are certainly unique. All can benefit from special handling, and there are some recipes that bring out the uniquely delicious flavor of these wild meats better than any other. These, then, are the recipes which comprise this chapter.

Though the game animals themselves and the delicious wild game feasts they can produce are each different, there are some common field care and cooking tips that can benefit them all:

* Fresh meat will keep for several days if sealed in a jar and sunk underwater in a spring or creek.

* Salt moose steaks down in a crock. Sprinkle each layer with a few vinegar drops, put in a cool place. They will keep for several weeks.

* Edible organs of game are highly perishable. Prepare and cook as soon as possible.

* When roasting a lean piece of meat, drying out can be prevented by fastening strips of fat around the meat with a string.

* Less tender meat is made tender and flavorful by long slow cooking in moist heat.

* A little ground beef fat added to lean ground wild game is delicious.

*The best pemmican is made from dried, powdered meat. It can be used with lard, bear fat, goose fat or moose fat. Smoke the dried meat. Pound it and make a nice powder. Mix with water to form a batter. Some people like to add berries and sugar. In winter, put it outside to freeze and keep it frozen. In summer, make it more like a dough and cover it. It keeps well for a long time. Pemmican is used especially in the winter by trappers when they walk all day and want to travel light. A piece the size of a date square is enough for a meal.

*Whether you are preparing venison, moose, elk, buffalo or beef, the following chart and a good meat thermometer will help you to cook meat to its preferred doneness.

Doneness	Meat Temperature
Still Kicking	0 - 20 degrees
Raw	40 - 100 degrees
Rare	120 degrees
Medium Rare	130 degrees
Medium	140 degrees
Medium Well	150 degrees
Well	160 degrees
Burnt Crisp	200 - 250 degrees

*When all else fails remember to keep your sense of humor and follow these axioms of Wild Game Cookery:

No recipe is ever a total failure; it can always serve as a bad example.

You can't prepare a wild game meal if you didn't bag any wild game.

Culinary expertise is inversely proportional to kitchens ruined and meals burned.

If anything can go wrong, check the oven because it may have already.

When you return from the store and begin to prepare a wild game recipe, there will always be one ingredient you forgot to buy.

According to your hunting buddies, there is always an ingredient which, when added to or subtracted from your recipe, will provide a better tasting meal.

The one who complains about the camp cook's meals becomes the new cook.

Having the butcher drop meat into the bag you are holding does not justify telling your dinner guests that you "bagged" this meal.

Sparta Hunt Steak

Serves: 8-10
Prep Time: 1 hour

3 lbs. elk round steak, cubed	**4 T. bacon drippings**
2 tsp. salt	**2 cups tomato juice**
¼ tsp. pepper	**1 cup carrots, diced**
7 T. flour	**1 cup celery, diced**
	1 cup onion, chopped

Dredge meat in seasoned flour. Brown in drippings; remove. Add remaining flour and tomato juice. Stir until thick. Boil 4 minutes. Add meat, other ingredients. Cover. Simmer 50 minutes.

Rick Sinchak
Warren, Ohio

Elk Roulade

Serves: 6-8
Prep Time: 1 hour, 30 minutes

2 lbs. elk round steak	**2 T. shortening**
4-6 bacon slices, finely chopped	**½ cup white wine or sherry**
1 onion, finely chopped	**1 cup water**
¾ cup flour	**½ lb. mushrooms, sliced**
1 T. salt	**cornstarch**
½ T. pepper	**salt and pepper, to taste**

Cut meat into 2-inch squares. Pound meat until it doubles in width and size and is ⅛-inch thick. Spread bacon slices and onion on flattened meat. Roll meat up and tie with meat string or hold with toothpicks. Secure so roll will not open while cooking. Roll each piece in mixture of flour, salt and pepper. In large skillet, add shortening and brown all pieces evenly. When done, add wine and water. Simmer 30 minutes. Add mushrooms and more water if necessary. Simmer until meat is tender. Thicken with cornstarch and water. Add salt and pepper. Serve with rice, mashed or baked potatoes.

Walter Weichold
Stockton, California

Barbecued Elk Teriyaki Steak

Serves: 6
Prep Time: 30 minutes

2 24-oz elk sirloin steaks	**salt and pepper**
teriyaki sauce	**garlic salt**

Brush steaks generously with teriyaki sauce. Lightly add salt, pepper and garlic salt. Marinate in sauce at least 1 hour. After marination, place steaks on barbecue grill over hot coals. Cook on both sides and remove from grill when steaks are about medium-rare. Slice steaks diagonally into thin strips. Do not over-cook steaks as they will cook some while slicing. This may be used as a French Dip.

Kay Trogdon
Victor, Montana

Creamed Elk Or Moose

Serves: 6
Prep Time: 1 hour

4-5 lbs. round steak (elk or moose)	**4 medium onions, chopped**
½ T. salt	**¼ lb. butter**
¼ T. pepper	**½ cup beef broth**
½ tsp. marjoram, dried	**1 cup sour cream**
1 cup flour	**4-5 T. Parmesan cheese, grated**

Sprinkle both sides of steak with salt, pepper, marjoram and flour. Pound meat with wooden mallet until flour disappears. Chop onions into thick slices. Saute onions with butter in large, heavy skillet: When onions are transparent, remove from skillet. Place steak in skillet and brown over high heat. Mix together beef broth, sour cream, cooked onions and cheese in a separate bowl, and pour over meat. Simmer slowly until tender, which should be about 1 hour.

Avis Roe
Golden Valley, Minnesota

Chinese Fajita

Serves: 4
Prep Time: 30 minutes

1 **lb. elk steak**	1 **T. cooking sherry**
1 **T. oil**	1 **T. Worcestershire sauce**
1 **onion, thinly sliced**	6 **flour tortillas**
1 **bell pepper, thinly sliced**	**sour cream, guacamole**
seasoned salt, pepper	**or salsa**

Slice steak diagonally across the grain into ¼-inch strips and set aside. Prepare vegetables. Coat wok with oil and heat to medium high for 1-2 minutes. Add meat and stir-fry until meat loses pinkness. Add all seasonings. Stir-fry until vegetables are crisp-tender, about 5 minutes. Scoop cooked mixture into tortillas. Top with sour cream, guacamole or salsa. Roll and serve.

Frank Dunkle
Washington D.C.

Shogun Elk

Serves: 6
Prep Time: 30 minutes

1 **lb. boneless elk steak**	2 **T. cornstarch**
1 **small cauliflower head**	½ **tsp. sugar**
2 **T. butter**	1½ **cups beef broth or water**
1 **green pepper**	1 **cup green onion, sliced**
¼ **cup soy sauce**	3 **cups cooked rice**
1 **garlic clove, minced**	

Cut ½-inch steak into cubes. Prepare 4 cups of cauliflower flowerettes. Brown meat in butter about 5 minutes. Add cauliflower, ¾-inch green pepper pieces, soy sauce and garlic. Stir so soy sauce coats vegetables. Cover pan and simmer until vegetables are barely tender. Blend cornstarch, sugar and beef broth. Add to meat mixture with green onions. Stir constantly, cook until well heated and sauce thickens.

Dixie Luke
Glenwood Springs, Colorado

Six Lakes Elk Shish Kabab

Serves: 6
Prep Time: 4 hours

2 lbs. elk steak or   **small potatoes,**
tenderloins, cut in strips   **precooked**
green peppers,   **mushrooms, whole**
quartered   **tomatoes, quartered**
onion, thickly sliced   **bacon slices**

Marinade:

½ **cup salad oil**   1 **tsp. thyme**
¼ **cup lemon juice**   ½ **cup onion, chopped**
1 **tsp. salt**   ½ **tsp. pepper**
1 **tsp. marjoram**   1 **garlic clove, minced**
¼ **cup parsley, snipped**

Mix marinade ingredients. Add meat strips or cubes and stir to coat. Refrigerate overnight or let stand at room temperature for 2-3 hours, turning occasionally. Roll up steak strips and wrap in bacon slices. Skewer meat with vegetables. Broil over hot coals, brushing on melted butter or margarine. Turn often.

Peg Puche
Jackson Hole, Wyoming

Elk Stir-Fry

Serves: 4
Prep Time: 30 minutes

2-4 lbs. steak or stew meat   1 **8-oz. can bamboo shoots**
olive oil   1 **16-oz. can bean sprouts**
6-8 celery pieces, diced   1 **bunch onions, diced**
1 **8-oz. can water**   **2-4 cups rice**
chestnuts, diced   **soy sauce**

Heat wok to 375 degrees. Add olive oil. Cut steak or stew meat into cubes. Brown meat and drain. Put all ingredients, except rice, into wok and cook until tender (10-20 minutes). While cooking, shake soy sauce over. Serve on rice.

John Dougherty
Torrington, Wyoming

Pocket Stew

Serves: 4
Prep Time: 20 minutes

1 **lb. elk steak**	2 **bell peppers, chopped**
2 **medium carrots, thinly sliced**	1 **medium onion**
2 **celery stalks, thinly sliced**	4 **mushrooms, thinly sliced**
1 **large potato, cut into small chunks**	**pinch of sage**
	salt and pepper
	1 **T. butter**

Cube steak into 1-inch squares. Divide each ingredient into 4 equal parts. Lay out four 18-inch pieces of foil. Place a pile of each ingredient in middle of each piece of foil. Add pinch of sage, salt and pepper and ¼ T. butter. Fold foil tightly around ingredients. Place a pocket stew in each hunter's pack. To cook, place on bed of coals. After 10-15 minutes, turn over once. Cook or bake at 350 degrees for 20 minutes.

Kenneth Binam
Fruita, Colorado

Hunter's Chili

Serves: several
Prep Time: 2 hours

1½-2½ **lbs. elk burger**	1 **beef bouillon cube**
1 **large onion**	1 **can kidney beans**
2 **hot peppers**	½ **tsp. garlic**
1 **bell pepper**	2 **tsp. salt**
1 **T. butter**	2 **tsp. Italian seasoning**
1 **28-oz can whole tomatoes**	2 **tsp. chili powder**
1 **6-oz. can tomato paste**	1 **bay leaf**
1 **cup water**	

Brown meat. Chop onion and peppers and fry in butter until limp. Add all ingredients and simmer for 2 hours.

Richard Atkins
Green River, Wyoming

Honeyed Elk Roast

Serves: 8
Prep Time: 5 hours

3-4	**lbs. elk roast**	**6**	**thin lemon slices**
	water	**6**	**bacon slices**
½	**cup vinegar**		**Sauce:**
½	**cup burgundy wine**	**¼**	**cup butter**
1	**tsp. MSG**	**¼**	**cup honey**
2	**tsp. salt**	**½**	**cup frozen orange juice**
2	**tsp. pepper**		**concentrate**
1	**tsp. garlic powder**	**½**	**tsp. rosemary**

Soak roast overnight in water with ½ cup vinegar. Remove from refrigerator, wash and dry. Splash on wine. Sprinkle on MSG, salt, pepper and garlic powder. Place lemon slices on top of roast. Place bacon on top of lemon slices and secure with toothpicks. Cook at 275 degrees for 5 hours. Melt butter in pan and add honey, orange juice and remainder of wine. Add rosemary. Baste roast often with honey sauce while baking.

Dion Luke
Glenwood Springs, Colorado

German Meat Salad

Serves: 4
Prep Time: 30 minutes

3	**cups venison, elk, venison sausage or a mixture of any kind, diced**	**¼**	**cup brown sugar**
		2	**cups mayonnaise**
		8	**bacon strips, diced**
½	**jar Grey Poupon mustard**	**8**	**green onions, diced**
		2	**celery ribs, diced**
¼	**cup white distilled vinegar**	**2**	**potatoes, diced**

Whip together mustard, vinegar and brown sugar. Mix in mayonnaise. Fold in bacon, onions, celery, potatoes and meat. Serve in cucumber boats, peeled and seeded.

Anonymous

Mahony's Moose Casserole

Serves: 4-5
Prep Time: 2 hours, 30 minutes

2 **lbs. moose meat, cubed**
1 **can cream of mushroom soup**
1 **pkg. dry onion soup mix**
1 **cup canned tomatoes or 2 fresh tomatoes**

Preheat oven to 325 degrees. Place meat in casserole and add mushroom soup, dry soup mix and tomatoes. Cover and bake for 2 hours.

Bill Mahony
Platteville, Wisconsin

Roast Moose (Six Day Marinade)

Serves: 8
Prep Time: 6 days plus 8 hours

6 **lb. moose roast**
  red wine or sherry
  salad oil
8 **peppercorns**
¼ **tsp. marjoram**
¼ **tsp. thyme**
1 **bay leaf**
1 **onion, sliced**
1 **carrot, cut into strips**
  pork-fat slices
½ **cup red wine**
½ **cup sour cream**
½ **cup red currant jelly**

Remove all fat from roast. Make marinade by combining 2 parts wine to 1 part salad oil. Put roast into bowl and sprinkle with peppercorns, marjoram, thyme and bay leaf. Cover with onion and carrot. Pour marinade over roast to completely cover. Cover bowl loosely with foil and marinate in refrigerator for 6 days. After 6 days, drain meat and discard marinade. Place meat on rack in roasting pan and cover with pork-fat slices. Roast uncovered at 275 degrees, allowing 1 hour per pound. Make gravy from drippings by adding ½ cup red wine. Bring to a boil over medium heat. Slowly add sour cream and red currant jelly. Serve with mashed potatoes and hot biscuits.

H. O. Stubblefield
Sidney, Montana

Spiced Pot Roast

Serves: 6
Prep Time: 4 hours

4 **lbs. moose rump roast**	1 **bay leaf, crushed**
2 **medium onions, chopped**	1 **T. pickling spice**
¼ **cup fat**	¼ **cup vinegar**
¼ **cup flour**	2 **T. brown sugar**
1 **tsp. salt**	4 **carrots, pared**
¼ **tsp. pepper**	1 **celery stalk, diced**
2 **cups canned tomatoes**	4 **potatoes, diced**

Fry onions in fat until golden brown. Dredge roast in flour, salt
and pepper. Brown roast on all sides in heavy pan with onions for
15 minutes. Combine remaining ingredients, pour over moose.
Cover pan and cook slowly in moderate oven or on top of stove
for 2-3 hours. Let liquid simmer. Add water if necessary. Pared
carrots, peeled onions, celery and potatoes may be added 45
minutes before meat is finished cooking. Remove meat, strain
liquid and thicken.

Daniel Hotten
Calvin, North Dakota

Moose Meatloaf

Serves: 6
Prep Time: 1 hour

2 **lbs. ground moose**	1 **T. Worcestershire sauce**
1 **pkg. onion soup mix**	¼ **tsp. pepper**
1½ **cups evaporated milk**	½ **tsp. garlic salt**

Sauce:

1 **10-oz. can tomato soup**	1 **T. lemon juice**
1 **T. Worcestershire sauce**	1 **T. brown sugar**

Combine meat ingredients and shape into loaf. Bake at 375
degrees for 30 minutes. Combine sauce ingredients and pour
over meatloaf. Bake an additional 30 minutes.

Toddy Watson
Ft. St. John, British Columbia

Polynesian Moose Bites

Serves: 6
Prep Time: 1 hour

2 lbs. ground moose	**¾ cup brown sugar**
⅓ cup uncooked oats	**2 T. cornstarch**
1 can water chestnuts, chopped	**1 8-oz. can crushed pineapple, drained (sav juice)**
2 T. soy sauce	
1 small onion, chopped	**1 cup beef bouillon**
½ tsp. garlic salt	**½ cup vinegar**
1 egg	**2 T. soy sauce**
½ cup milk	**⅓ cup green pepper, chopped**
shortening	

Combine first 8 ingredients and form into small meatballs. Brown in shortening and drain well. Mix firmly-packed brown sugar and cornstarch. Add pineapple juice, bouillon, vinegar and soy sauce. Bring to a boil, stirring occasionally until clear and thick. Boil for 1 minute. Stir in pineapple and green pepper. Add sauce to meatballs and simmer 5-10 minutes. Serve hot.

John Fisher
Logansport, Indiana

Moose Muffle

Serves: 6
Prep Time: 4-5 hours

moose muzzle	**salt**
water	**pepper**
onions	

Drop moose muzzle into kettle of boiling water. Parboil for 1 hour. Cool in cold water. Pluck loosened hairs and wash in cold water. Simmer in fresh water along with onions, salt and pepper until tender. Let cool in its juice. After cooling, extract bone and cartilage. Pack the rest in handy container and cover with juice This will jell when chilled. Slice for eating cold.

Robert Zabloudil
Waukesha, Wisconsin

Caribou Stew With Dumplings

Serves: 5-6
Prep Time: 2 hours

2 **lbs. caribou meat**	¼ **turnip, chopped**
¼ **cup flour**	¼ **cup carrots, chopped**
salt and pepper	2 **potatoes, quartered**
½ **onion, chopped**	2 **T. drippings**
water to cover	

Dumplings:

1 **egg**	½ **cup water or milk**
1 **tsp. salt**	1½ **cups flour**

Cut meat into pieces and dredge with flour, salt and pepper.
Brown with onions in oil. Cover with water. Simmer about 2 hours
or until tender. Add vegetables. When done, thicken gravy
drippings with 1 T. flour mixed with a little cold water. Season
with salt and pepper. One-half cup strained tomatoes may be
added. Serve with dumplings. To make dumplings: Beat egg
well, add salt and water and stir with flour until smooth batter is
formed. Drop by spoonfuls into stew. Cover until dumplings are
done. Serve warm.

Laurentian Ungava Outfitters
Lachute, Quebec

Foil Lunch For The Fire

Serves: 2
Prep Time: 1 hour

1 **lb. ground caribou**	1 **large onion, chopped**
10 **bacon slices**	1 **tsp. salt**
3 **carrots, chopped**	1 **tsp. pepper**
3 **potatoes, chopped**	1 **tsp. garlic powder**

Spread 5 bacon strips on foil, (dull side out). Put half the carrots,
potatoes and onions on top. Add spices to meat and put on top.
Add rest of vegetables and bacon and wrap. Lay on hot coals for
30 minutes on each side.

Kevin Mattice
George River, New Quebec

Curried Caribou "A La Biere"

Serves: 4
Prep Time: 30 minutes

4 large caribou fillets	**1 tsp. curry powder**
2 T. butter	**salt and pepper**
1 onion, sliced	**¼ tsp. parsley**
1 green pepper, sliced	**¼ tsp thyme**
1 can sliced mushrooms, drained	**1 can beer**

Fry fillets in butter in large frying pan. Add all vegetables, season with spices and add the beer. Let the mixture of fillets, vegetables, spices and beer cook until the vegetables are soft. Serve with rice that you prepared while the fillets cooked.

Lise Vanasse
Fort Chimo, New Quebec

Caribou Steak

Serves: 2-4
Prep Time: 1 hour, 30 minutes

1 caribou round steak flour	**1 onion, chopped**
½ tsp. salt	**½ cup sour cream**
¼ tsp. pepper	**1 cup canned tomatoes**
3 T. drippings	**½ tsp. sweet basil**

Mix flour, salt and pepper for dredging. Dredge steaks, rubbing flour well into both sides of meat. Sear steaks over hot fire in heavy skillet, using beef drippings. When steaks are well browned on both sides, remove from pan. Saute onions until soft in drippings. Replace steak in skillet with onions. Simmer slowly about 50 minutes, covered. Mix 2 T. flour into sour cream. Add tomatoes and basil and stir well. Pour over steaks. Cover and pour yourself a cup of coffee while you let the whole thing simmer for about 25 minutes or until done to your taste.

Laurentian Ungava Outfitters
Lachute, Quebec

Teriyaki Caribou

Serves: 4-6
Prep Time: 1 hour, 30 minutes

1-2 lbs. caribou	**1 tsp. ground ginger**
¼ cup soy sauce	**1 tsp. garlic powder**
3 T. brown sugar	**¼ tsp. pepper**
½ cup water	

Slice caribou into ¼- to ½-inch strips. Mix all ingredients together. Marinate caribou strips in sauce for 1 hour in a cool place. Remove from marinade, broil or pan-fry.

Arctic Rivers Guide Service—Kathy
Kotzebue, Alaska

Mountain Goat & Cabbage

Serves: 10
Prep Time: 3 hours

3 lbs. ground goat	**2 cups onions**
4½ tsp. salt	**2 cans tomato soup**
½ tsp. pepper	**2½ cups water**
2 eggs, beaten	**1 cup celery, chopped**
⅔ cup uncooked rice	**2 tsp. parsley, minced**
12 large cabbage leaves	**6 T. lemon juice**
4 T. butter	**2 tsp. sugar**

Mix together goat, 2½ tsp. salt, ¼ tsp. pepper and eggs. Mix in rice. Cook cabbage leaves in boiling salted water until tender. Drain. For sauce, melt butter in skillet. Add onions and cook until tender. Blend in tomato soup and water. Add celery, parsley, lemon juice, sugar and rest of salt and pepper. Simmer 10 minutes. Place about ¼ cup meat mixture on center of each cabbage leaf. Roll up, tucking ends in toward center. Use toothpicks to fasten leaves securely. Place rolls in large, heavy skillet. Pour sauce over rolls, cover tightly and cook 2 hours.

Rick Sinchak
Warren, Ohio

Texas Antelope Stew

Serves: 4
Prep Time: 2 hours

2 **lbs. antelope meat, cubed**	1 **can solid packed tomatoes**
salt and pepper	¼ **tsp. dried basil leaf**
flour	½ **tsp. celery seed**
2 **T. bacon fat**	¼ **tsp. cumin seed**
1 **onion, chopped**	5 **medium potatoes**
1 **small can mushrooms**	5 **carrots**
1 **T. Worcestershire sauce**	

Salt, pepper and flour meat and brown in bacon fat. Add onion, mushrooms and Worcestershire. Stir until onion is light brown. Add water to cover meat. Add tomatoes and simmer for 1 hour. Add basil leaves, celery seed and cumin seed. Simmer 30 minutes. Add potatoes and carrots. Cook until meat is tender. Note: If mushroom sauce is used in place of mushrooms, add when potatoes and carrots are added.

James Bresee
Pampa, Texas

Antelope Cabbage Casserole

Serves: 1-2
Prep Time: 1 hour

1 **lb. antelope burger**	¼ **tsp. pepper**
1 **onion, chopped**	½ **tsp. basil**
3 **T. butter**	1 **medium cabbage head**
2 **T. parsley, chopped**	1 **can tomato soup**

Preheat oven to 350 degrees. Saute onion in butter. Add meat, parsley and spices. Shred cabbage and place half in casserole. Add meat mixture. Place remaining cabbage in casserole. Pour soup on top. Cover and bake 1 hour.

Turk Tangert
Lancaster, Pennsylvania

Roast Antelope

Serves: 8
Prep Time: 5 hours

antelope roast
flour
salt and pepper
butter
3 onions, sliced
4 lbs. canned tomatoes
½ cup celery, diced

parsley
bay leaf
rosemary
thyme
2 cups dry red wine
12 oz. mushrooms

Flour, salt and pepper antelope and brown in Dutch oven.
Remove roast and fry in butter with onions. Put roast in pot and
add canned tomatoes, celery, parsley, bay leaf, pinch of
rosemary and thyme and wine. Cover and cook 4 hours at 350
degrees or until tender. Baste continuously. Remove roast and
add mushrooms to gravy and serve over hot rice.

Dan Sommer
West Allis, Wisconsin

Antelope Steaks Supreme

Serves: 3
Prep Time: 5 hours

3 round steaks
2 tsp. salt
¼ cup vinegar
1 bay leaf
1 garlic clove
salt and pepper
garlic salt

onion salt
flour
oil
**1 can cream of mushroom
soup**
1 can water

Put steaks in shallow pan with water to cover. Add salt, vinegar,
bay leaf and garlic. Soak 3-4 hours. Remove steaks, drain,
sprinkle with seasonings. Dredge in flour. Heat oil in skillet,
brown meat, cover. Simmer 40 minutes. Add soup and water and
simmer 20 minutes longer.

Karen Wood
Elko, Nevada

Granny Butler's Antelope Steak

Serves: 4
Prep Time: 30 minutes

1½ **lbs. antelope steak, each**	1 **tsp. salt**
about ½-inch thick	1 **tsp. pepper**
1 **cup milk**	1 **tsp. garlic powder**
1 **egg**	½ **cup cooking oil**
¾ **cup flour**	

With meat tenderizer, pound steak on both sides. Combine milk and egg in bowl. On plate, mix flour, salt, pepper and garlic powder. Dip antelope steaks in milk and dredge in flour mixture. In large cast iron skillet on medium-high heat, add oil and cook on both sides. Add more oil for remainder of steaks. Serve with mashed potatoes and carrots. Gravy can be made from skillet drippings if desired.

Kay Butler
Glenwood Springs, Colorado

Antelope Stroganoff

Serves: 6-8
Prep Time: 30 minutes

2 **lbs. antelope, boned**	1 **can mushroom soup**
½ **tsp. salt**	1 **cup water**
½ **tsp. pepper**	½ **lb. mushrooms**
3 **T. flour**	1 **T. horseradish**
4 **T. butter**	½ **cup white Chablis**
1 **cup onions, minced**	1½ **cups sour cream**

Cut antelope into 1½-inch wide and 2-inch long strips. Salt, pepper and flour meat pieces. In electric skillet, melt margarine. Brown onions and meat. Mix soup and water together. Pour over meat, stir. Add mushrooms, horseradish and wine. Cook over low to medium heat until tender. Test before serving. Stir in sour cream. Serve over rice or noodles. Serve with wine-glazed carrots, tossed salad and rolls.

Marvin Epling
Fairport, New York

Miner's Springtime Bighorn

Serves: 6
Prep Time: 1 hour, 30 minutes

1 **lb. sheep meat, trimmed and cut into 1-inch cubes**	1 **tsp. salt**
	¼ **tsp. black pepper**
	½ **tsp. cinnamon**
2½ **cups fresh rhubarb, sliced**	¼ **tsp. nutmeg**
¾ **cup sugar**	1 **cup parsley**
¾ **cup water**	1 **T. cornstarch**
¼ **cup butter**	1 **T. water**
	2 **cups cooked rice**

Mix sugar, water and rhubarb; set aside for 30 minutes. Drain, reserving syrup. In skillet, melt butter. Saute meat, onion and seasoning until meat is browned on all sides. Stir in parsley and saute a few more minutes. Stir in rhubarb syrup. Simmer 40 minutes, covered. Stir in drained rhubarb. Continue simmering, covered, for 20-30 minutes or until meat is tender. Combine cornstarch and 1 T. water. Stir into meat mixture. Cook gently 2-3 minutes longer until mixture thickens. Serve on hot cooked rice.

Dixie Luke
Glenwood Springs, Colorado

Junjik River Dall Roast

Serves: 4-6
Prep Time: 2 hours

1 **thick ram slab**	1 **T. parsley, chopped**
½ **cup flour**	1 **tsp. salt**
½ **cup cornmeal**	2 **T. onion, chopped**
5 **tsp. bacon fat**	3 **cups boiling water**
½ **tsp. pepper**	

Put slab on board and pound flour and cornmeal into it. Melt fat in large frying pan and brown roast. Add all seasonings and half the boiling water. Simmer 1 hour, covered. Add rest of water and simmer until tender.

"Alaska" Rick Sinchak
Warren, Ohio

Sheep Camp Steak

Serves: 6
Prep Time: 30 minutes

6 **1-inch thick sheep steaks**	3 **T. oil**
3 **T. Worcestershire sauce**	3 **T. vinegar**
2 **garlic cloves, minced**	½ **tsp. thyme**
¼ **tsp. pepper**	½ **cup pecans, coarsely chopped**
4 **T. parsley, chopped**	

In bowl, combine all ingredients except steaks and pecans. In deep platter, score meat evenly. Cover steaks with sauce. Let stand 1-2 hours. Remove meat and pour sauce into a cup. Grease grill lightly. Cook steak 7 minutes per side for a medium steak. Brush with sauce before turning. Turn steak and brush with remaining sauce. Sprinkle with pecans. Grill until cooked as desired. Carefully remove to platter. Let stand 5 minutes before serving. Serve with potato and green vegetable.

Dixie Luke
Glenwood Springs, Colorado

Roast Leg Of Dall Sheep

Serves: 6
Prep Time: 5 hours

1 **Dall sheep leg**	1 **cup cold water**
vegetable oil	4 **onions**
salt	1 **T. butter**

Clean meat with cold damp cloth. Rub roast generously with vegetable oil and salt. Place in roasting pan, adding cold water. Roast at 325 degrees for 3 hours, 30 minutes. During last hour, add whole onions and baste repeatedly. Add butter to water. Add more water if necessary. Roast until well done. Serve steaming hot.

Dan Sommer
West Allis, Wisconsin

Excellent Wild Sheep Chops

Serves: 4
Prep Time: 45 minutes

4 sheep chops, ⅝-inch thick	**1 celery stalk, chopped**
salt and pepper	**1 small onion, chopped**
	¾ cup water

After trimming fat from chops, salt and pepper them to taste. Fry in hot skillet until the chops are brown and crusty. Add vegetables and stir carefully to avoid burning. You may have to add a little oil if too dry. When vegetables are browned, add water and cover. Simmer until liquid is gone. Serve with mashed potatoes, if you like, and a salad.

Barbara Strong
Kingwood, Texas

Sheepherder's Chili

Serves: 6-8
Prep Time: 1 hour

2 lbs. ground lamb	**1 T. salt**
1 cup onions, chopped	**1 bay leaf**
¾ cup green peppers, chopped	**1 T. chili powder**
2 medium garlic cloves, minced	**2 4-oz. cans Ortega green chilies, diced**
1 28-oz. can tomatoes, chopped	**1 16-oz. can pinto beans, drained**

Brown lamb in large skillet until crumbled. Drain. Add onion, green pepper and garlic. Cook until vegetables are tender. Stir in remaining ingredients except beans. Simmer, covered, for 35 minutes. Don't leave for long because you need to stir it occasionally. Remove cover and add beans. Simmer, uncovered, 10 minutes or until the mixture is the desired consistency. Garnish with sour cream or Monterey Jack cheese, if desired.

Anonymous

Plumb's Sheep Or Goat Supreme

Serves: several
Prep Time: 1 hour, 30 minutes

1 shoulder or leg roast	**1 cup medium white sauce**
2 qts. water	**2 T. vinegar**
1 T. salt	**2 T. sugar**
6 fresh dill sprigs	**3 T. dill, finely snipped**

Put meat in large kettle, add water to cover, measuring as you do so. Add proportionate amount of salt and dill. Bring to boil uncovered, skim foam. Cover and simmer slowly until tender. Remove to warm serving platter and keep warm until meat has a chance to firm up (about 20 minutes). Prepare white sauce, add vinegar or lemon juice, sugar and snipped dill. Carve meat in thin slices and arrange on platter. Pour some sauce on top and serve rest in sauce boat.

Corey Plumb
Dryden, Michigan

Stewed Mountain Goat

Serves: 4-6
Prep Time: overnight plus 2 hours

4 lbs. goat meat, cubed	**3 large onions, thinly sliced**
juice of 2 limes	
2 garlic cloves, chopped	**2 bay leaves, crumbled**
1 T. oregano	**1 cup chicken bouillon**
½ tsp. pepper	**1 can beer**
1 tsp. salt	**sugar**
1 T. vinegar	

Place meat in glass bowl and sprinkle with lime juice. Refrigerate overnight (covered). Place meat in Dutch oven and add all ingredients except beer and sugar. Bring to a boil over high heat, and boil 10 minutes. Cover and reduce heat to medium and cook for 1 hour. Add beer and sugar, cover and continue to cook for 1 more hour or until tender. Serve with steamed potatoes, vegetable and baking powder biscuits.

Anonymous

Chili Caliente California

Serves: 4-6
Prep Time: 3 hours

2 **lbs. cabrito (goat), cut into ¼-inch cubes**
2 **T. beef fat**
2 **cups onions, chopped**
1 **8-oz. can hot chile peppers, minced**
1 **garlic clove, minced**
4 **cups tomatoes, chopped**
1 **T. sugar**
2 **tsp. salt**
¼ **cup water**
3 **T. chili powder**
2 **T. A-1 sauce**
1 **16-oz. can kidney beans, with juice**
2 **celery stalks, minced**
  water

Heat fat in large skillet. Add onions, hot chile peppers, garlic and goat cubes. Brown until onions are tender. Add remaining ingredients, cover and simmer for 2-3 hours, stirring occasionally. Add water if mixture is thicker than you desire.

Anonymous

Caribou Liver Skillet Cakes

Serves: 8
Prep Time: 1 hour

2 **lbs. caribou liver**
3 **cups hot water**
6 **T. onion, chopped**
2 **eggs, beaten**
2 **T. flour**
  salt and pepper, to taste
  bacon slices

Simmer liver in hot water for 10 minutes. Drain liver and put in food chopper and grind. Mix ground liver, onion, eggs, flour, salt and pepper. Shape into round cakes and wrap with bacon slices. Fasten with toothpicks. Fry until well done or to your liking. Serve as an appetizer or as a main course with your favorite vegetable and potato.

Rick Sinchak
Warren, Ohio

Wild Boar In Mustard Sauce

Serves: 6
Prep Time: 30 minutes

2 lbs. wild boar tenderloin
4 T. Dijon mustard
1 T. coarsely ground black pepper
salt, to taste
1 T. butter

2 T. olive oil
2 T. green peppercorns
3 T. dry white wine
3 T. cream or condensed milk

Slice boar tenderloin ¼ inch thick. Spread half the mustard and half the black pepper on 1 side. Saute slices in frying pan in butter and olive oil until done. Remove and place on serving platter. Crush peppercorns in frying pan. Add remaining mustard and pepper. Add wine and cream. Bring to a boil and reduce to creamy consistency. Pour hot sauce over boar slices and serve.

Keith Baker
Falls Church, Virginia

Santa Catalina Boar

Serves: 4
Prep Time: 2-3 hours

2 lbs. boar meat, cubed
¼ cup flour
1 tsp. salt
pepper, to taste
3 T. bacon fat
1 medium onion, chopped
1 garlic clove, diced

4 cups water
½ tsp. rosemary
1 T. parsley flakes
4 potatoes, peeled
4 carrots, peeled
4 small onions, peeled and sliced

Coat boar in flour mixed with salt and pepper. Heat bacon fat in deep pan and brown meat on all sides. Add onion and garlic clove and cook 5 minutes longer. Add water and seasonings and cook covered until meat is tender. Add potatoes, carrots and small onions and cook another 30 minutes.

Alan Conzelmann
Arcadia, California

Doug's Wild Hog Stew

Serves: 8
Prep Time: 2 hours, 30 minutes

4 lbs. wild boar, cut in large chunks
½ lb. Anaheim sweet peppers
1 lb. bell peppers
1 lb. mushrooms
1 lb. tomatillos
1 T. olive oil
1 8-oz. can tomato sauce
1 6-oz. can tomato paste
1 48-oz. can stewed tomatoes, drained
6 T. corn flour
1 tsp. cayenne pepper
1½ tsp. salt
¼ cup chili powder
1 T. cumin
1 T. paprika
1 tsp. oregano
1 tsp. onion powder
1 tsp. garlic powder
1 T. fruit brandy
¼ cup lemon juice
2 tsp. Worcestershire sauce

In large skillet, saute peppers, mushrooms and tomatillos in olive oil until tender. Add meat and stir until brown. Add remaining ingredients. Mix thoroughly. Cook on low heat for 2 hours, stirring frequently.

Douglas Cuciz
San Jose, California

Wild Boar Nabe

Serves: 4-6
Prep Time: 2 hours

1 lb. wild boar meat, cubed
1 cup fresh or dried mushrooms
1 cup carrots, sliced
2 cups potatoes, diced
½ cup cooking Sake or other cooking wine
2 T. soy sauce
2 T. vinegar
¼ cup misco paste

Cover meat with water and boil. After partially cooked, add other ingredients. Serve when vegetables are soft.

Norman Lund
Kofu Shi, Japan

Braised Wild Boar With Beer And Cumin

Serves: 6
Prep Time: 3 hours

3 lbs. wild boar leg, trimmed and cubed	**6 T. oil**
	1 pt. beer
1 T. powdered cumin	**1 garlic head, separated**
salt and pepper	**1 bay leaf**
4 T. flour	**1 pt. game stock**

Mix cumin, salt and pepper with flour. Dredge wild boar pieces
in flour and saute in hot oil until lightly browned. Drain meat.
Loosen any caramelized juices in pan with beer. Place garlic,
bay leaf, stock and beer in casserole with boar pieces and cover.
Braise at 350 degrees for about 2 hours or until tender. Skim off
any excess fat. If juices seem too light, strain meat pieces off.
Reduce to desired consistency. Return meat pieces to sauce and
correct seasonings. Serve on a bed of buttered noodles or rice.
Beer is a good accompaniment to this dish. Or serve The
Christian Brothers 1986 Napa Valley Zinfandel. The fruitiness and
body of the wine balances the spiciness of the dish.

Paul Rankin
Calistoga, California

Dick's Barbecued Wild Boar

Serves: 8
Prep Time: 4-5 hours

16 wild boar chops, about ¾-inch thick	**½ tsp. seasoned salt**
	1 cup wine vinegar
2 cups honey	**2 cups white wine**
1 small can dry mustard	

Combine all ingredients, except chops. Mix. Pour over chops in
large container. Marinate several hours. Remove chops and
barbecue over slow fire, 15-20 minutes each side, baste often.

Dick Jacobson
Minneapolis, Minnesota

Boar Adobo

Serves: 5-6
Prep Time: 1 hour, 30 minutes

2-3 lbs. boar meat, cut into 1½-inch chunks
vegetable oil
5 garlic cloves, finely chopped
ginger root, 2-inch piece
1½ tsp. salt

15-20 peppercorns, whole
2-3 bay leaves
¼ to ⅓ cup desired wine
⅓ cup vinegar
3-4 T. soy sauce
⅓ cup water

Brown meat in small amount of vegetable oil. Set aside. Drain off excess oil. Saute garlic and grated ginger root in remaining oil. Mix together remaining ingredients. Add meat and other ingredients to garlic and ginger in pot. Simmer slowly, stirring occasionally, until desired doneness.

Ray Fabrao
Lanai City, Hawaii

Javy Wrap-Ups

Serves: 2
Prep Time: 1 hour

½ lb. ground javelina
1 shot tequila
1 tsp. lime juice
1 garlic clove, minced
salt and pepper

1 egg
2 tsp. bread crumbs
1 onion, sliced
1 potato, sliced

Mix together ground javelina, tequila, lime juice, garlic clove, salt and pepper, egg and bread crumbs. Form into patties and freeze (for added flavor, refrigerate for 2 days before freezing). When in camp, lay potato slices and onion rings between patties and wrap in tinfoil. Place in hot coals for about 2-3 hunting stories or until onions and potatoes are cooked. Serve hot as a tasty treat.

Andrew Wyly
Tucson, Arizona

Buffalo Medallions

Serves: 2
Prep Time: 30 minutes

4 2-oz. buffalo medallions, cut from tenderloin	**¼ cup reduced veal stock**
1 T. butter	**2 tsp. heavy cream**
1 jigger Jack Daniels whiskey	**salt and pepper**

In small skillet, melt butter until light brown. Reduce heat and saute medallions on both sides for 3-4 minutes or until done to your taste. Place medallions on preheated plate. Discard butter. Place skillet back on heat and deglaze with Jack Daniels. Immediately add veal stock and reduce to half over medium heat. Add cream, stir well and season to taste. Spoon sauce on plate and top with medallions.

Mark Schultz
Bronson, Texas

Buffalo Jerky

Serves: 8
Prep Time: 8 hours

1½-2lbs. buffalo meat	**¼ tsp. garlic powder**
1 pkg. instant meat marinade	**¼ tsp. onion powder**
1¾ cups cold water	**¼ tsp. black pepper**
½ tsp. liquid smoke	**½ tsp. Tabasco sauce**

Cut meat with the grain in 6-inch strips about 1½ inches wide and ½-inch thick. Set aside. Mix together other ingredients. Place meat in container and cover with marinade while piercing meat slices deeply with fork. Marinate overnight in covered container in refrigerator. Remove meat strips. Drain slightly and place on rack, making sure strips do not overlap. Place cookie sheet under rack in a 150- to 175-degree oven for 5 hours. Cool and store in covered container in refrigerator. These larger pieces are not dried long and will be soft.

Anonymous

Microwave Cooking

*f*ast and good . . . Good and fast. Those seem to be key elements in all types of American cooking today. And they explain the popularity of the microwave oven.

At first that seems to be in conflict with the traditions of fine wild game cookery. But with some innovation and determination, Paula Del Giudice (pronounced ga-deece), the NAHC Charter Member who contributed this entire Microwave Game Cooking section, came up with marvelous meals—fast and good . . . good and fast.

If you don't own a microwave, these recipes can easily be converted for your regular oven. Simply cook at 350 degrees for three times as long as listed for the microwave.

Venison Peppers

Serves: 4
Prep Time: 30 minutes

1 **lb. ground venison**	1 **T. soy sauce**
4 **medium green peppers**	1½ **cups cooked rice**
1 **onion, chopped**	1 **cup tomato sauce**
1 **tsp. sage**	2 **T. water**
1 **garlic clove, minced**	

Cut tops off peppers. Remove seeds and rinse thoroughly. Place peppers in shallow microproof dish. Add water to cover bottom of dish. Cover and micro on high 2 minutes. Allow peppers to sit, covered, while preparing filling. In medium microproof dish, combine onion and crumbled ground meat. Micro on high 4 minutes, stirring 1-2 times to break up meat. Add sage, garlic, soy sauce, rice and tomato sauce. Fill peppers, packing well. Place in casserole dish. Add 2 T. water and cover well. Micro on high 8-10 minutes until peppers are tender. Let sit 2-3 minutes, covered, before serving.

Microwave Venison Stew

Serves: 4-6
Prep Time: 4 hours, 45 minutes

2 **lbs. venison stew meat, cut in small cubes**	3 **small zucchini, chopped**
flour	2 **potatoes, cut in chunks**
bacon fat	4 **medium tomatoes, quartered**
3 **carrots, sliced**	

Marinade:

1-1½ **cups burgundy wine**	12 **peppercorns**
1 **cup beef bouillon**	2 **garlic cloves, minced**
2 **T. oil**	**freshly ground pepper**

Mix venison with marinade ingredients. Cover and refrigerate at least 4 hours. Drain venison, reserving marinade. Dust venison with flour and brown in bacon fat in either skillet or microwave browning dish. Place cubes in 3-qt. casserole dish with remaining ingredients and marinade. Cover. Micro on high 3-5 minutes or until boiling. Simmer 30 minutes.

Easy Venison Ragout

Serves: 4
Prep Time: 50 minutes

1 **lb. venison stew meat, cut in 1-inch cubes**	¼ **cup burgundy wine**
1 **pkg. brown gravy mix**	2 **carrots, sliced**
2 **T. flour**	2 **potatoes, peeled and cubed**
freshly ground pepper	1 **cup frozen peas, thawed and drained**
1 **garlic clove, minced**	
1 **tsp. Worcestershire sauce**	1 **cup beef broth**

Lightly brown venison in browning dish or skillet. Remove meat to 3-qt. casserole. Add gravy mix and stir well. Add remaining ingredients. Stir well. Cook on 50 percent for 35 minutes or until meat and vegetables are tender. Stir occasionally during cooking time. Let stand 3-4 minutes before serving.

Moose Sauerbraten

Serves: 6
Prep Time: 3 days plus 30 minutes

1 **3-3½ lb. moose chuck roast**	**Marinade:**
2 **T. oil**	1 **onion, sliced**
¾ **cup gingersnaps, crushed**	2 **bay leaves**
	15 **peppercorns**
2 **tsp. sugar**	6 **cloves**
	1 **cup cider vinegar**
	½ **cup boiling water**

Place roast in bowl with marinade ingredients. Cover tightly and refrigerate for at least 3 days. Turn roast twice a day. Be careful not to pierce meat when turning. Drain meat, reserving marinade. Heat oil in skillet and brown roast on all sides. Put meat in glass baking dish. Add marinade micro on 60 percent until temperature probe reads 130-140 degrees. Remove meat and onions and cover with foil. Strain and measure liquid in casserole. Add water to bring 2 cups total liquid. Return to casserole and micro on high 3-4 minutes. Stir gingersnaps and sugar into liquid. Micro on high 2-3 minutes.

Three Bean Elk Chili

Serves: 6-8
Prep Time: 1 hour

1 **lb. ground elk**	1 **15-oz. can black-eyed**
1 **green pepper, diced**	**peas**
1 **onion, diced**	1 **tsp. salt**
2 **garlic cloves, minced**	1 **tsp. pepper**
1 **28-oz. can whole**	3 **T. chili powder**
tomatoes	¼ **tsp. cayenne pepper**
1 **15-oz. can pinto beans**	1 **tsp. cumin**
1 **15-oz. can kidney beans**	

Combine meat, green pepper, onion and garlic in medium microproof saucepan. Micro on high 4 minutes. Stir to break up meat. Micro on high 2 minutes more. Stir. In 4-qt. casserole, combine meat mixture and remaining ingredients. Adjust seasonings to taste. Cover well. Micro on high 5 minutes or until boiling. Micro on simmer for 25-30 minutes. Let sit 4-5 minutes.

Elk Sirloin Steaks

Serves: 4
Prep Time: 40 minutes

4 **sirloin-cut elk steaks,**	¼ **onion, coarsely chopped**
about 8 oz. each	¼ **tsp. ground pepper**
3 **T. soy sauce**	2 **celery stalks, sliced**
2 **T. steak sauce**	

In a small bowl, mix soy sauce, steak sauce, onions and pepper. In 2-qt. casserole, layer one steak with sauce. Continue layering steaks and sauce until steaks are stacked one on top of the other. Add celery around steaks. Place temperature probe into middle of steaks. Cover with waxed paper and micro on 80 percent until the temperature reaches 140 degrees, about 15-20 minutes. About halfway through, rearrange steaks so they cook evenly. Cover with foil 5 minutes before serving. Meat will be a little pink when cooked in this manner. Cook to a higher temperature if you wish to have meat well-done. My advice is to serve meat a little pink inside so it doesn't toughen.

German Style Caribou Pot Roast

Serves: 6 ·
Prep Time: 30 minutes

4 lb. caribou roast	**2 garlic cloves**
2 T. oil	**salt and pepper**
½ tsp. pepper	**¼ tsp. ginger**
1 cup water	**¼ cup catsup**
¼ cup flour	**2 T. vinegar**

In large skillet, heat oil and brown outside of roast. Season with pepper. Remove to larger casserole. Stir water into skillet and scrape to remove sediment. Pour water into casserole. Insert temperature probe into center of meat and micro on 70 percent or roast until temperature reaches 130 degrees. Put roast on platter and cover with foil, shiny side down, to finish cooking. Blend flour with juices in casserole. Micro on 50 percent 5 minutes. Stir in remaining ingredients. Micro on 50 percent 4-5 minutes. Pour gravy over roast.

Garden Fresh Gumbo

Serves: 8-10
Prep Time: 45 minutes

2 lbs. antelope round steak or stew meat, cut into bite-sized pieces	**1 cup corn**
	2 cups water
	salt and pepper
3 T. oil	**3 carrots, chopped**
1 onion, chopped	**1 zucchini, chopped**
2 celery stalks, chopped	**1 cup string beans, cut**
3 parsley sprigs, chopped	**Roux:**
1 garlic clove, chopped	**1 cup butter**
1 48-oz. can tomato juice	**1 cup flour**

Make roux by melting 1 cup butter in saucepan. Stir in flour and heat until boiling. Reduce heat. Stir constantly until dark brown. Don't overbrown or overcook. Set aside. Cook meat and onion in oil 5 minutes on high. Drain. Combine with remaining ingredients. Stir the roux into ingredients until completely blended. Cook on high 5 minutes. Stir. Simmer 25-30 minutes.

Doves Ole!

Serves: 3-4
Prep Time: 30 minutes

6 doves
4 T. olive oil
salt and pepper
½ onion, finely chopped
½ green pepper, thinly sliced
1 garlic clove, minced

1 cup carrots, finely chopped
1 cup celery, chopped
¾ cup tomato juice
1 bay leaf
¼ cup black olives, sliced

In skillet, brown doves in olive oil. Arrange doves in 8-inch square baking dish. Sprinkle with salt and pepper. In medium saucepan add a little fat (from skillet), onion, green pepper and garlic and micro on high 4 minutes. Add carrots, celery, tomato juice and bay leaf. Stir well and pour over doves. Cover tightly and micro on 80 percent for 13 minutes. Remove from microwave and add black olives. Cover with foil, shiny side down, for 5 minutes before serving.

Roast Pheasant

Serves: 2
Prep Time: varies

1 pheasant
salt and pepper
1 bay leaf

1 garlic clove
a few celery leaves
2 T. butter, melted

Sauce:
½ cup consomme
2 T. flour

2 T. butter, melted
3 T. Madeira wine

Sprinkle pheasant with pepper. Add salt. Place bay leaf, garlic and celery leaves inside pheasant. Tie legs together. Insert meat thermometer. Cover bird loosely. Micro on 70 percent or roast, until meat reaches 170-180 degrees and the bird juices run clear. Remove from microwave and brush with butter. Brown in oven/broiler. For sauce: Add consomme to pan drippings. Micro on high for 2 minutes. Blend flour with butter and stir into gravy a little at a time. Micro on 90 percent or reheat for 2-3 minutes until thickened. Stir well and add wine.

Brandied Woodcock

Serves: 2-3
Prep Time: 30 minutes

4 **woodcocks**	¼ **cup beef bouillon**
4 **T. butter**	**freshly ground pepper**
½ **medium onion, finely**	2 **cups baby carrots**
chopped	2 **T. flour**
2 **T. brandy**	**fresh parsley, chopped**

In large skillet, melt butter. Add onions and cook for 2-3 minutes.
Brown woodcocks on all sides. Pour in brandy and flame. Pour
woodcock mixture into a 2-qt. casserole. Stir in bouillon, pepper
and baby carrots. Cover and micro on 80 percent for 8-10
minutes. Place woodcocks and carrots on warm platter and cover
with foil. Add 2 T. flour to liquid and stir well. Microwave sauce
for 3 minutes at 80 percent. Pour sauce over woodcocks. Garnish
carrots with parsley.

Wild Rice And Sausage Stuffed Goose

Serves: 2-4
Prep Time: 1 hour

1 **goose, rinsed and dried**	3 **cups cooked wild rice**
2 **T. butter, melted**	2 **T. butter, melted**
2 **tsp. sage**	3 **celery stalks, sliced**
Stuffing:	½ **medium onion, chopped**
½ **lb. pork or game**	
sausage, cooked	

Mix all stuffing ingredients together in large bowl. Stir well to
combine. Loosely stuff and truss goose and tie legs together.
Shield tips of legs with small pieces of foil in newer microwave
ovens to prevent overcooking. Follow safety rules for foil use, and
don't use in older units. Mix melted butter and sage and brush on
goose. Insert temperature probe in thickest part of goose
between leg and breast. Micro on 70 percent or roast until meat
reaches 180-185 degrees, normally about 30-40 minutes. Turn
goose over halfway through cooking time to ensure the goose
will be completely cooked.

Squash And Squirrels

Serves: 4
Prep Time: 40 minutes

2 squirrels, cut in pieces	**Roux:**
3 T. butter	**½ cup butter**
½ medium onion, sliced	**½ cup flour**
2 cups chicken bouillon	
4 small crookneck squash (about 2½ cups), sliced	

Melt butter in frying pan. Add onions and saute until transparent. Add squirrels, cook 3-4 minutes each side. Put squirrels and onions in 3-qt. casserole. Add bouillon and squash. Cover. Micro on 70 percent 10 minutes. Meanwhile, make roux. Melt butter in saucepan on stove. When hot, add flour. Reduce heat and cook until caramel colored, stirring constantly. Remove squirrels from bouillon if too thick. Return squirrels to mixture. Micro on 70 percent or roast setting for 10-12 minutes until juices of squirrel run clear.

Rabbit In White Wine

Serves: 2
Prep Time: 30 minutes

1 large rabbit, cut in serving pieces	**¼ tsp. thyme**
3 T. butter	**¼ tsp. marjoram**
1 onion, sliced	**1 cup chicken bouillon**
1 carrot, sliced	**2 T. vinegar**
2 celery stalks, diced salt and pepper	**½ cup dry white wine**
	¼ cup sour cream

In 2-qt. casserole, micro butter 1 minute on high to melt. Stir in onion, carrot and celery to coat. Micro on high 2 minutes. In separate bowl, thoroughly mix salt, pepper, thyme, marjoram, bouillon, vinegar and wine. Mix thoroughly. Place rabbit pieces on top of vegetable mixture. Pour wine/seasoning mixture over both. Cover and micro on high 5 minutes. Micro on bake or 60 percent for 7 minutes. Stir. Micro on bake 5 minutes more. Stir in sour cream. Micro on bake 5 minutes to complete. Serve over buttered noodles.

Waterfowl

When it comes to the pursuit of waterfowl, hunting is the enjoyable part; cleaning is the chore. Of all game, waterfowl is probably the most time consuming and, in some ways, the most difficult to prepare.

Regardless, no game should ever be wasted! Even the less revered species of waterfowl can provide good eating if some special care is taken with their dressing and table preparation.

There are several methods of cleaning ducks and geese. The proper choice depends on the species, the cooking method you intend to use, how much time you have and the equipment and facilities you have available. Some methods, like skinning, may take only a few minutes. Others may take almost an hour for a large bird.

One common method is to dry pluck the birds. This can be done by hand or with any number of special duck-plucking machines. The motorized duck pickers can speed up the chore a great deal, but regardless, it is a messy and time consuming affair. You might as well sit down and make yourself comfortable.

Use a large grocery bag or paper sack to pluck over to help contain the feathers and down. If you intend to save the down, keep it separate from the main feathers.

There are several tricks to make dry plucking easier. The first is to pick the birds as soon as possible after they are killed. The feathers and down will release more easily then, and the skin isn't as prone to tear as it is after the bird has hung for some time. Always pull feathers out downward or toward the tail; they'll release more easily that way.

Though the preparation can be a hassle if you only have a few birds to dress, another good plucking method is to use paraffin. Float melted paraffin on top of a bucket of hot water and quickly dip the ducks a couple of times. Wrap the dipped birds in newspaper and allow the paraffin to cool and harden. Then peel off the newspaper, paraffin, feathers and down all in large chunks.

Before dipping the ducks, it is best to remove the wings so the paraffin can readily flow around and coat the entire bird. Leave the wings on while dry picking for convenience in handling the bird.

Once the majority of feathers and down are removed, it's time to take off the pin feathers. These are the small dark shafts starting new feathers. They can be removed by pinching them with your fingers or between the index finger and the blade of a knife.

You can further clean the bird after removing the pin feathers by using a torch to singe off the small "hair" feathers and tiny bits of down that may still be clinging to the skin.

Next cut off the head. Cut around the wing sockets with a sharp knife, bend the wing bone out of its socket and twist it off. You will probably have to cut some additional muscles to release the wing. Cut off the feet as well.

How the bird will be cooked determines how it will be gutted and cut up. If a bird is to be prepared whole they should be gutted by making a slice across the belly just below the rib cage. Slice down around the tail and remove the entrails and tail section at one time. Make sure the windpipe is pulled from the neck opening of the bird.

A method that is simpler, less messy and allows the bird to cook more thoroughly if they are not to be stuffed is to stand the bird on the base of its tail, and cut down through the ribs, along the backbone and each side of the neck. Do this on both sides of the backbone, then pull it out along with the neck and entrails all at once.

Once the birds are eviscerated, wash out the cavity. Soak the birds overnight in a pan of cold water with a bit of salt, vinegar, lemon juice or wine. Be sure you cut away any bloodshot areas or damaged flesh. Remove any shot pellets from under the skin and in the muscle. Steel shot can be devastating on expensive dental work!

Waterfowl were important to early hunters not only for the nutritious meat, but also to provide down for pillows, mattresses and clothing. If you wish to save the down from your waterfowl harvest, it can be used to make clothing or bedding.

Down used for these purposes must be cleaned to remove the dirt and debris it collects as well as lice and other "creepy crawlies". The simplest way to doing this is to place the down in cloth bags and hang it outside through the winter months. The sun, wind and rain will cleanse it.

Roast Wild Duck With Sausage Stuffing

Serves: 4
Prep Time: 3 hours (plus)

2 ducks	**bulk pork sausage**
salt and pepper	**2 cabbage leaves**

Wash and dry ducks. Salt and pepper outsides lightly. Take 1 small handful of bulk pork sausage and wrap sausage inside cabbage leaf. Stuff into each duck cavity. Cover and bake at 250 degrees for 3 hours or longer (the longer the better). The sausage stuffing can be eaten, too.

Paul S. Burke, Jr.
Edina, Minnesota

Helen's Sunday Ducks

Serves: 3-4
Prep Time: overnight plus 3 hours

2	**ducks**		**Stuffing mix (optional):**
	water	**2**	**duck gizzards**
2-3	**T. baking soda**	**4-5**	**dried bread slices**
2	**T. butter**	**1**	**onion, chopped**
1	**medium apple, sliced**	**1**	**T. butter**
1	**medium onion, sliced**	**2**	**eggs**
		2-3	**T. milk**
			salt and pepper

Rinse ducks thoroughly. Place in pot, covered with water. Add baking soda. Soak overnight. Drain and rinse again. Stuffing Mix: Boil gizzards 30 minutes until tender. Cool. Grind in meat grinder. Add dried bread slices, broken into small pieces. Saute onion in butter. Add to mix. Beat and add eggs and milk to mixture. Salt and pepper to taste. Place half of the mixture into each duck cavity and put in roaster. Rub skins with butter. Salt and pepper to taste. Place 2 apple slices on each duck. Add enough water to cover bottom of pan. After 30 minutes, place onion slices on duck. Roast at 350 degrees for 2-3 hours.

Bob Fratzke
Winona, Minnesota

Old Fashioned Duck & Dressing

Serves: 6
Prep Time: 2 hours

- **2 ducks**
- **12 cold biscuits**
- **1 pone (8-inch) of cold cornbread**
- **2 medium onions**
- **3 celery pieces, chopped**
- **3 T. margarine**
- **3 eggs**
- **2 tsp. black pepper**
- **2 tsp. sage (or enough to suit your taste)**

Soak ducks overnight in salt water. Be sure the down and pin feathers have been removed. Boil ducks in heavy pot with half an onion or potato until done. The vegetables will remove the wild taste. Remove ducks when done, and save broth. Set both aside. Cornbread Dressing: Crumble biscuits and cornbread together. Saute 1 onion and celery in margarine. Add to cornbread mixture, along with duck broth. The dressing should be of medium consistency—preferably on the thin side. Add eggs, black pepper and sage. Mix thoroughly. Place ducks in low pan for baking (a 13x9-inch sheet-cake pan is perfect) fill duck cavity and surround with dressing. Bake at 325 degrees for approximately 20 minutes or until dressing is done.

Turner Kirkland
Union City, Tennessee

Wild Duck Browning

Serves: 2
Prep Time: 3 hours, 30 minutes

- **1 duck**
- **salt and pepper**
- **1 medium onion**
- **½ cup red wine**
- **½ tsp. thyme**
- **pat of butter**

Rub inside of duck with salt and pepper. Place onion inside. Place on heavy foil and add wine, thyme and butter. Wrap tight. Bake at 325 degrees.

Don Gobel
Morgan, Utah

Roast Wild Duck

Serves: 2
Prep Time: 4 hours

1 duck	**marjoram**
salt and pepper, to taste	**rosemary**
1 orange, quartered	**1 orange rind, grated**
1 small onion, quartered	**2 bacon strips**
butter	**½ cup chicken broth**

Thaw duck thoroughly, and soak in salted water, covered, at least 1 hour. Rinse and dry duck. Season cavity with salt and pepper. Fill cavity with orange and onion. Tie cavity shut. Grease outside of duck with butter and place in Dutch oven. Season with salt, pepper, marjoram, rosemary and grated orange rind. Place bacon strips over duck. Add chicken broth and cover pan. Roast at 300 degrees for 3 hours, basting every 30 minutes and uncovering for the last hour.

Annette Glotzbach
Lutherville, Maryland

Wild Duck And Rice

Serves: 6-8
Prep Time: 5 hours

2-3 large ducks (frozen)	**2 large onions, diced**
salt and pepper	**2 celery stalks, diced**
water	**1 lb. rice**

Do not thaw ducks. Salt and pepper ducks and brown in open roasting pan at 450 degrees until browned on all sides. Cover with water. Add onions and celery and bake another 2-3 hours in covered roasting pan at 350 degrees. When breast meat falls away from bone, add rice to duck and broth and bake covered another 30-45 minutes, checking to see if rice is done. Serve with appropriate salad.

Harry Carle
Monette, Arkansas

Gourmet Wild Duck

Serves: 4
Prep Time: 45 minutes

1 **duck breast, thinly sliced**	1 **cup butter**
salt and pepper	½ **lb. fresh mushrooms, sliced**
garlic salt	**cooking oil**
flour	**dash of cinnamon**
1 **small can pearl onions or 1 medium onion, chopped**	1 **T. sugar**
	1 **T. Lea & Perrins sauce**
	1 **cup red wine**

Pat duck breasts dry and sprinkle with salt, pepper and garlic salt; dust with flour. Sear onions in melted butter and add mushrooms, cooking until tender. Brown duck in oil at high heat, 5 minutes on each side. Add duck slices to onion and mushrooms. Add dash of cinnamon, sugar, Lea & Perrins sauce and wine. Cover and simmer 15 minutes.

Cheryl Buster
Fort Collins, Colorado

Fool-Proof Duck In Orange Sauce

Serves: 2-4
Prep Time: 2 hours

1 **wild duck**	2 **T. orange marmalade**
1 **pkg. brown gravy mix**	1 **6-oz. can frozen orange juice, thawed**
¼ **cup flour**	1 **cup hot water**
1 **tsp. salt**	1 **oven cooking bag**
2 **T. sugar**	

Wash duck and wipe dry, inside and out. Combine next six ingredients and mix well. Add to hot water in cooking bag and mix well. Place duck in bag and close according to directions. Place in roasting pan and cut slits in top of bag. Bake at 350 degrees for 2 hours. Serve with pan gravy. More than one duck may be cooked in each bag.

Bobby Wright
Highland, Indiana

Fried Duck Steak

Serves: 2
Prep Time: 45 minutes

2 duck breast halves, boned	**cooking oil**
	flour
1 stick butter	

Heat 1 stick butter in oiled pan (do not scorch). Fry breasts coated with flour at high heat, turning frequently and adding butter until crispy brown on outside and pink in center.

Jay Strangis
Minnetonka, Minnesota

German Duck

Serves: 2-4
Prep Time: 1 hour, 30 minutes

1 duck, cut into pieces	**2 bacon slices**
1 small red cabbage	**1 medium onion, chopped**
2 T. red wine vinegar	**2 tart apples, sliced**
¼ cup flour	**1 T. sugar**
¼ tsp. salt, pepper	**¼ tsp. tarragon**
1 T. vegetable oil	**1 bay leaf**
2 T. butter	**½ cup white wine**
2 Polish sausages	

Preheat oven to 400 degrees. Shred cabbage and sprinkle with vinegar. In plastic bag, shake flour with salt and pepper. Add duck pieces; shake to coat. In Dutch oven, heat oil and butter over medium heat. Add duck and brown. Remove and set aside. Add sausage, brown lightly, set aside. Add bacon and cook until crisp; set aside and crumble. Remove all but 2 T. pan drippings. Saute onion. Add cabbage, sausage, apples, sugar, tarragon, bay leaf and wine. Cook until soft, about 20 minutes. Add duck and top with bacon. Cover and bake 35 minutes. Serve with wild rice or fluggy white rice, if desired.

Annette and Louis Bignami
Moscow, Idaho

Dave's Sweet And Sour Wild Duck

Serves: 4
Prep Time: 1 hour, 30 minutes

4 ducks
2 tsp. salt
½ tsp. lemon pepper
½ cup flour

1 T. mixed herbs (thyme,
oregano, basil)
¼ cup olive oil

Sweet and Sour Sauce:
1 cup tomato puree
2 cups red wine
2 T. capers

3 T. brown sugar
½ cup olives, chopped
1 T. dry mustard

Stir all ingredients for Sweet and Sour Sauce thoroughly until mixed. Let stand. Wash ducks thoroughly, pat dry, split down back and flatten. Sprinkle with salt and lemon pepper and roll in flour herb mixture. Brown in hot oil. Drain off fat and add Sweet and Sour Sauce which combines tomato puree, red wine, brown sugar and seasonings. Cover and simmer slowly until tender, about 1 hour.

Dave Johnson
Milwaukee, Wisconsin

Puddle Jumpers Fricassee

Serves: several
Prep Time: 1 hour, 30 minutes

2 ducks
salt and pepper
½ cup flour
1 onion, minced
¼ cup butter

1 cup mushroom caps
2 bay leaves
1 green pepper, sliced
1 cup water
¼ cup burgundy wine

Cut ducks into bite-size pieces. Sprinkle salt and pepper into flour and roll duck pieces in combination. Put duck, onion, butter, mushrooms, bay leaves and green pepper in big frying pan. Brown duck and add water and wine. Cover and simmer 1 hour.

John Sindberg
Greenfield, Wisconsin

Teal In Wine Sauce

Serves: 4
Prep Time: 2 hours

4 small ducks or duck breasts	**2 onions, thinly sliced**
4 T. butter	**1 bay leaf**
2 T. flour	**2 cloves**
1 cup red wine	**½ tsp. Tabasco**
2 cups beef broth	**salt and pepper**
	½ tsp. parsley

Brown ducks in butter. Transfer to deep pot or casserole. Add flour to butter and thicken. Stir in other ingredients except parsley. Bring to a boil, then simmer 5 minutes, stirring often. Pour sauce over ducks and add parsley. Simmer 90 minutes.

Bobby Wright
Highland, Indiana

Wild Duck (Crockpot Method)

Serves: 4
Prep Time: 5 hours

4 medium-sized duck breasts	**¼ cup wine vinegar**
1 tsp. salt	**½ cup catsup**
1 tsp. pepper	**1 T. steak sauce**
1 cup bread crumbs	**1 tsp. Kitchen Bouquet**
3 eggs, beaten	**2 bay leaves**
butter/bacon drippings	**2 garlic cloves, minced**
¼ tsp. paprika	**2 T. Worcestershire sauce**
4 whole cloves	**½ cup burgundy wine**
	6-8 oz. currant jelly

Cut each breast into 3-4 pieces. Combine salt, pepper and bread crumbs. Dip pieces into beaten eggs and roll in seasoned bread crumbs. Brown on all sides in butter or bacon drippings. Mix all other ingredients except wine and jelly in small bowl with a little water and pour over meat in Crockpot. Simmer 3-4 hours. During last 10 minutes, add wine and jelly.

Reprinted with permission from the
Minneapolis Tribune

Red Wine Duck Breasts

Serves: 4
Prep Time: 1 hour, 30 minutes

4-8 duck breasts	**1 shallot or small onion,**
1 cup flour	**finely chopped**
¼ lb. butter	**¼ T. thyme**
½ cup brandy	**1 T. parsley, chopped**
2 cups red wine	**¼ lb. butter**

Dredge duck breasts in seasoned flour. Fry duck in hot butter
until brown. Pour off butter. Add brandy. Burn off alcohol. Add
red wine, shallots, and thyme. Cover and slow cook 20 minutes.
Set aside duck breasts. Reduce sauce until syrup-like. Add
parsley and swirl butter. Pour sauce over duck and serve.

Anonymous

Hawaiian Honeyed Duck

Serves: 2
Prep Time: 2 hours, 30 minutes

2½ lb. duck	**3 T. orange juice**
salt and pepper	**2 tsp. lemon juice**
1 tsp. ground ginger	**1 tsp. orange peel**
1 tsp. ground basil	**¼ tsp. dry mustard**
½ tsp. pepper	**1 unpeeled orange**
¾ cup honey	**½ tsp. cornstarch**
¼ cup butter	

Combine 2 tsp. salt, ginger, basil and ½ tsp. pepper. Rub half
mixture inside duck. Heat honey, butter, orange juice, lemon
juice, orange peel and mustard, stirring until butter melts. Rub
2-3 T. of this mixture inside duck. Stuff with orange slices. Put 4 T.
of honey mixture inside duck. Turn duck and rub on remaining
seasoning mixture. Place bird on aluminum foil. Cover with
remaining honey mixture. Wrap duck, roast 2 hours at 325
degrees. Unwrap and baste with drippings—then bake
unwrapped 20-30 minutes. Add cornstarch to drippings.

Bob Allen
Des Moines, Iowa

Duck Scallopini

Serves: 2-4
Prep Time: 3-4 hours

**3-4 duck breasts, cut in
bite-size pieces**
**2 large cans tomatoes,
crushed**
2 large cans tomato sauce
1 small can tomato paste
**2-3 tsp. oregano
olive oil**

**¼ lb. fresh mushrooms,
sliced**
5 green peppers, sliced
**1 large onion, finely
chopped**
8 garlic cloves, crushed
1 1-lb. pkg. frozen peas

In large pan mix tomatoes, tomato sauce, tomato paste and
oregano. Saute mushrooms, green peppers, onion and garlic in
olive oil until tender, add to tomato sauce. Add duck to sauce,
simmer 3-4 hours in covered pot. Add peas 15 minutes before
serving with garlic bread and Parmesan cheese.

Suzanne Smith
Conway, Washington

Marinated Duck Jerky

Serves: several
Prep Time: 48 hours

6-8 duck breast fillets
¼ cup soy sauce
**½ cup white distilled
vinegar**
¼ cup teriyaki sauce

**⅓ cup Worcestershire
sauce**
1 T. onion salt
1 T. garlic powder
1 T. seasoned pepper

Slice duck fillets into ⅛-inch thick strips. Mix all ingredients
together and marinate meat in mixture for 24 hours. Stir. Then
marinate for another 24 hours. Put strips on foil-covered cookie
sheet for easy clean up. Crack oven door open with pencil—not
in broil position. Bake in oven at 180-225 degrees. Store in paper
bag, not plastic.

T. G. Fasold
Sunbury, Pennsylvania

Wild Goose A L'Orange

Serves: 4-6
Prep Time: 4 hours

1 **6-8 lb. goose**	⅛ **tsp. salt**
¼ **tsp. tarragon leaves**	¼ **cup currant jelly**
1 **T. onion, minced**	2 **T. port**
2 **T. butter or margarine**	1 **orange, pared**
½ **cup orange juice**	1½ **tsp. cornstarch**
⅛ **tsp. dry mustard**	**orange slices**

Skewer goose neck skin to back, cross wing tips over back. Place breast-side up on rack in roasting pan. Cook tarragon and onion in butter until onion is tender. Add orange juice and 2 T. shredded peel, mustard, salt and jelly. Stir over medium heat until jelly melts. Reduce heat, stir in wine and orange sections. Reserve half of sauce for glaze; baste with remainder during 3½-hour cooking time at 325 degrees. Stir reserved sauce slowly into cornstarch, cook over medium heat, stirring constantly, until mixture thickens and boils 1 minute; serve with goose. Serve goose on a bed of brown rice. Garnish with orange slices.

Arlen Chaney
Lewiston, Idaho

Wild Goose With Raspberries

Serves: 4
Prep Time: 2 hours, 30 minutes

1 **large goose**	1 **medium onion, sliced**
salt and white pepper	1 **12-oz. jar raspberry**
1 **carrot, sliced**	**preserves**
2 **celery ribs, sliced**	½ **cup brandy**

Season goose and place on bed of sliced carrots, celery and onions in roasting pan. Roast at 325 degrees for 2 hours, basting every 10 minutes with preserves and brandy mixture. Pierce goose between breast and thigh. When liquid runs clear, goose is done.

Anonymous

Goose Steak In Mushroom Gravy

Serves: 6
Prep Time: 1 hour

2 **goose breasts**	2 **onions, cut in rings**
salt and white pepper	12 **large mushrooms, whole**
1 **cup flour**	½ **T. thyme**
½ **cup oil**	3 **cups cream**

Slice goose breasts into ¼-inch steaks. Season slices with salt and pepper, dredge in flour. Fry slices in oil and arrange on platter. Fry onion rings and lay on goose slices. Fry mushroom caps and lay on slices. Form a paste with remaining flour. Add thyme and cream. Bring to a boil and strain over platter. Serve with rice.

Anonymous

Wild Goose Supreme

Serves: 6-10
Prep Time: 3 hours, 15 minutes

1 **10-lb. wild goose**	4 **T. parsley flakes**
2 **tsp. salt**	1½ **cups celery, chopped**
½ **tsp. pepper**	½ **cup onions, chopped**
6 **cups cooked chestnuts**	1 **pt. raw oysters, drained**
1½ **cups melted butter**	**and cut in halves**
salt and pepper, to taste	**bacon strips**
1 **tsp. sage**	½ **cup gin**
¾ **cup evaporated milk**	1 **T. juniper berries**
3 **cups bread crumbs**	**flour**

Rub salt on inside and outside of goose. Sprinkle with pepper, set aside. Prepare dressing: Put chestnuts through a blender and chop fine. Combine with butter, salt, pepper, sage, canned milk, bread crumbs, parsley, celery, onion and oysters. Mix well and spoon dressing into cavity of goose. Close with skewers and tie up. Place goose in large roasting pan breast side up. Cover with bacon strips and add gin and juniper berries. Roast at 350 degrees 3 hours. Remove goose and keep warm. Skim off fat and heat drippings. Add flour to thicken.

Anonymous

Booger Woods Goose

Serves: 2-4
Prep Time: 4 hours

1 **goose**	½ **cup milk**
cold water	**salt and pepper**
3 **T. salt**	**paprika**
½ **cup celery, chopped**	**garlic**
½ **cup onion, chopped**	**Glaze:**
1 **lb. scrapple**	½ **cup honey**
6 **bread slices**	3 **T. barbecue sauce**
1 **egg**	4 **T. orange marmalade**
1 **tsp. poultry seasoning**	1 **tsp. black pepper**

Soak goose for 1 hour in cold water and salt. Combine celery, onion, scrapple, bread, egg, poultry seasoning and milk in large bowl. Salt and pepper to taste. Remove goose from water and pat dry. Stuff goose with above ingredients. Place in roasting pan with ¼ cup water. Combine glaze ingredients and brush on goose. Sprinkle paprika and garlic over goose to taste. Cover and place in oven at 350 degrees for 2 hours. Every 30 minutes remove goose and brush on glaze until a thick coating covers.

John Alex Paxson
Philadelphia, Pennsylvania

Bachelor's Snow Goose

Serves: several
Prep Time: overnight plus 1 hour

1 **goose**	**butter**
white wine	**salt and pepper**
2 **onions**	

The night before serving, baste goose in white wine and place onions inside. Let sit overnight. Place goose in shallow pan and cook at 400 degrees. Baste with butter and white wine for 45 minutes. Season with salt and pepper.

Mark LaBarbera
Minneapolis, Minnesota

Stuffed Canada Geese

Serves: 4-6
Prep Time: 24 hours

1-2 Canada geese
salt and pepper
garlic powder
onion powder
3-4 cups water

1 large can mushrooms
(do not drain)
1-2 pkgs. Lipton Onion Soup
Mix (dry)

Season geese with salt, pepper, garlic and onion powder inside and out. Pour water in roasting pan. Your favorite sage and onion stuffing recipe will work well here for stuffing the birds. Put birds in pan, breast side up. Add mushrooms and juice. Sprinkle soup mix over birds. Roast 2-3 hours at 325 degrees the day before serving. Make gravy from juice. Slice meat from bones when cold, put in gravy in roasting pan. Save some gravy for reheating the stuffing. When ready to serve, reheat geese in gravy for 1-2 hours at 250 degrees along with stuffing and enjoy.

Bill Minta
East Troy, Wisconsin

Goose In A Crockpot

Serves: 4-6
Prep Time: 4-5 hours (high)
8-10 hours (low)

2-3 goose breasts, cut into
1-inch strips
1 onion, sliced
dash garlic salt
½ cup catsup
2 T. Worcestershire sauce
2 T. brown sugar

2 tsp. salt
2 tsp. paprika
½ tsp. dry mustard
½ cup applesauce
¼ tsp. cinnamon
1 cup water
1 T. flour

Place goose strips in Crockpot and cover with onion. Combine other ingredients, except flour, and pour over meat. Cook on low 8-10 hours or high 4-5 hours. Thicken with flour. Serve over rice.

Cheryl Buster
Fort Collins, Colorado

Fajitas De Ganza And Tacos Al Carbon

Serves: 2-3
Prep Time: 1 hour, 30 minutes

- 1 **goose breast, sliced in ½-inch wide strips**
- 1 **lime or lemon seasoned salt pepper**
- 1 **large yellow onion, sliced soy sauce**
- 2-3 **large tomatoes, finely chopped**
- 1 **large yellow onion, finely chopped**
- 2 **jalapeno peppers, finely chopped**
- 1 **pkg. tortillas**

Squeeze lemon or lime on meat and salt and pepper. Slice onion to cover breast strips and cover with soy sauce. Marinate for 1 hour. While meat is marinating, chop tomatoes, onion and jalapenos. Fire should be hot (coals, not flames), about 6-10 inches from meat. While grilling meat, cook marinade. Serve as you would any steak. To make tacos, dice fajita and, on a hot tortilla, put a handful of diced meat, some onion, tomato and jalapeno pepper garnish. Roll up taco and enjoy.

Charles Barry
Houston, Texas

Jalapeno Pepper Goose

Serves: 2
Prep Time: 4 hours, 30 minutes

- 1 **whole goose**
- 1 **whole jalapeno pepper**

several bacon slices

Make a clean slice on each side of the breast bone where the bone curves. Slice pepper and stuff into each cut. Add bacon strip to each cut. Lay more bacon over goose and pin with toothpicks. Place in smoker or on slow fire for 4 hours, or until done and serve.

Chuck Barry
Houston, Texas

Sweet And Sour Snow Goose

Serves: 2
Prep Time: 3 hours

1 **goose, skinned**	3 **apples, diced**
1 **jar sweet & sour sauce**	2 **apples, halved**
1 **can crushed pineapple**	1 **orange, diced**
1 **can ring pineapples**	

Heat oven to 275 degrees. Place sweet and sour sauce, crushed pineapple, diced apples and diced orange into bowl. Add all juices from pineapple ingredients and mix thoroughly. Stuff cavity with apple halves. Place goose into covered roaster, baste generously every half hour. During last half hour, place pineapple rings on top of goose.

Tommy Everman
Iowa Falls, Iowa

Goose Stroganoff

Serves: 2-4
Prep Time: 30 minutes

2 **cups leftover goose meat, cut into small pieces**	1 **cup mushrooms, sliced**
water	1½ **T. butter**
salt, to taste	1½ **T. flour**
½ **onion, sliced**	1 **cup beef bouillon**
½ **celery stick, sliced**	1½ **tsp. prepared mustard**
1 **beef bouillon cube**	1 **cup sour cream**
	paprika
	parsley sprigs

Put meat in sauce pan with enough water to cover. Add salt, onion, celery and beef bouillon cube. Simmer until heated through. Saute mushrooms in deep skillet with butter until tender. Add flour and broth slowly, stirring constantly until broth thickens. Add meat, mustard and sour cream. Bring to boiling point, but do not let boil. Serve on hot buttered rice with a dash of paprika and parsley sprig.

Anonymous

Chicken-Fried Goose

Serves: 2
Prep Time: 1 hour

1 goose	**flour**
1 lime	**salt**
2 eggs	**pepper**
1 cup milk	**garlic powder**

Fillet thigh and breast meat and cut halfway through at ¾-inch intervals across grain. Use meat hammer to tenderize fillets. Squeeze juice of lime over meat. Mix eggs and milk in bowl. Combine flour, salt, pepper and a pinch of garlic powder in separate bowl. Dip meat in liquid, then flour, then liquid, then flour. Chickenfry in hot skillet. Pour off grease and mix cream gravy in same pan. Serve with mashed potatoes and green beans and enjoy.

Chuck Barry
Houston, Texas

Goose Roast

Serves: 6
Prep Time: 4 hours

2 wild geese	**salt and pepper**
wild rice	**6 bacon slices**
bread dressing	

Clean geese thoroughly and season with salt and pepper inside and out. Cut 4 bacon slices into small chips and add to bread dressing. (This will add a slight smoke flavor to dressing and geese.) Stuff geese with wild rice and bread dressing. Spoon stuffing into cavity, skewer and sew. Place geese in large roaster and lay 2 bacon strips on each breast. If birds are real fat, put rack under them to keep them out of grease. Bake at 350 degrees for 3 hours, depending on size of birds. It usually takes 15-20 minutes per pound.

Pete Jackson
Bloomington, Minnesota

Cleo's Roast Goose With Apple Stuffing

Serves: 6
Prep Time: 5-6 hours

1	**goose, remove all fat**	1	**tsp. salt**
	salt and pepper	1	**tsp. pepper**
3	**cups apples, diced**	¾	**cup apple cider**
½	**cup water**	6	**cups toasted bread**
1½	**onions, chopped**		**crumbs**
1	**tsp. celery seed**	4	**bacon slices**
¾	**cup butter, melted**		

Soak goose in salt water for 30 minutes. Drain. Rub inside and outside with salt and pepper. Prick breast, legs and wings with fork. Cook apples in ½ cup water. Cook onions and celery seed in butter for 3 minutes. Mix apples, onions, apple cider, celery seed, salt and pepper with bread crumbs and stuff body and neck cavity. Place in shallow roasting pan, breast side up. Lay bacon slices on top of goose. Roast uncovered at 325 degrees for 4-5 hours.

Kenneth Crummett
Sugar Grove, West Virginia

Roasted Goose

Serves: 4
Prep Time: 3-4 hours

1	**goose**		**salt, pepper and parsley,**
1	**large oven roaster bag**		**to taste**
¼	**cup celery, diced**	¾	**cup hot water**
¼	**cup onions, sliced**	4-5	**smoked-dried-beef**
1	**pkg. dry chicken broth**		**slices**

Place goose in roaster bag. Combine celery, onions, chicken broth, seasonings and water. Pour mixture over goose and inside cavity. Lay dried-beef slices on top of goose. Seal bag. Bake at 250 degrees for 3-4 hours. Remove from bag. Gently peel outer, darkened skin. Meat should pull away from bone.

B. Lewandowski
Greenlane, Pennsylvania

Bristol Bay Goose

Serves: 2-4
Prep Time: 2 hours

1 **good-sized goose**	1 **tsp. garlic powder**
½ **cup flour**	5 **T. cooking oil**
½ **cup bread crumbs**	2 **onions, diced**
1 **tsp. salt**	2 **T. lemon juice**
½ **tsp. pepper**	1 **tsp. paprika**

Cut up goose and soak in cold water for 1 hour. Roll pieces in mixture of flour, bread crumbs, salt, pepper and garlic powder. Brown goose in cooking oil and add onions and lemon juice. Sprinkle on paprika. Cover and cook until tender.

"Alaska" Rick Sinchak
Warren, Ohio

Waterfowl Delight

Serves: 4-6
Prep Time: 1 hour, 30 minutes

1 **goose breast or 4 large duck breasts flour, sage, salt and pepper**	1 **cup onion, chopped**
	3 **bacon slices, fried crisp and crumbled**
1½ **butter or margarine sticks**	½ **tsp. thyme**
1 **cup fresh mushrooms, chopped**	¼ **tsp. garlic salt**

Cut meat into finger-sized strips, cutting with the grain. Roll each piece in 2 mixtures of 10 parts flour and 1 part each of sage, salt and pepper. Brown meat in iron skillet with 1 stick of margarine, keeping heat low and turning often to avoid burning. When brown, remove from skillet and set aside. Add mushrooms, onions and celery to skillet and cook until soft. Add meat, bacon, thyme, garlic salt and ½ stick of margarine. Simmer 30 minutes, stirring frequently. Serve with wild rice.

Kenneth Martin
Philpot, Kentucky

Canada Goose Sandwich Spread

Serves: several
Prep Time: 1 hour, 30 minutes

- 1 **Canada goose**
- 2 **chicken bouillon cubes**
- 1 **tsp. parsley**
- ½ **tsp. pepper**
- 1 **small onion, chopped**
- 1 **cup mayonnaise**
- 2 **T. barbecue sauce**
- 1 **celery stalk, chopped**
- 1 **medium dill pickle**
- 2 **hard boiled eggs**
- ¼ **cup dill pickle juice**
- ¼ **cup prepared mustard**

Place goose in large pan. Cover with cold water. Add bouillon cubes, parsley, pepper and onion. Cover with tight-fitting lid and boil slowly until tender. Remove from heat and let cool in broth while still covered. Remove meat from bone and chop or grind into large bowl. Mix thoroughly with mayonnaise, barbecue sauce, chopped celery, pickles, eggs, juice and mustard. Store in covered plastic or glass container. Serve as needed. Will keep for a few days in refrigerator or frozen for 2 weeks.

Bruce Hodgdon
Shawnee Mission, Kansas

Sizzling Goose Hash

Serves: 2-4
Prep Time: 30 minutes

- 2 **cups leftover goose meat, diced**
- 3 **T. butter**
- 1 **large onion, diced**
- 2 **large potatoes, steamed, peeled and diced**
- 1 **tsp. salt**
- ¼ **tsp. freshly ground pepper**
- 1 **tsp. marjoram**
- 1 **tsp. caraway parsley sprigs**

In heavy skillet, heat butter. Saute onion until tender. Add meat, potatoes, salt, pepper, marjoram and caraway. Cook over moderate heat, turning occasionally, until mixture is heated thoroughly and starts to brown. When sizzling, sprinkle with parsley sprigs and serve immediately.

Anonymous

Coot 'N' Gravy

Serves: 4
Prep Time: overnight plus 1 hour, 30 minutes

3-4	**coot**	**1**	**T. salt**
	salt water	**¼**	**tsp. peppercorns**
	olive oil or butter	**1**	**bay leaf, whole**
6-8	**gingersnaps**	**1**	**medium onion, sliced**
	Marinade:	**1**	**carrot, sliced**
2	**cups burgundy or claret**	**2**	**T. sugar**
¼	**cup cider vinegar**	**3**	**whole cloves**

Skin coot, removing all fat. Soak in salt water for 1 hour; then in marinade overnight in glass bowl. Drain birds and put marinade on low heat. Brown birds in oil. Pour marinade over birds a little at a time. Cook until tender. Remove meat and add 6-8 gingersnaps to liquid. Stir until dissolved.

Joe LaBarbera
Milwaukee, Wisconsin

Steve's Coot Stew

Serves: 2
Prep Time: 2 hours

2	**coots**	**6**	**egg-sized onions**
1	**T. salt**	**5**	**carrots, cut into 1-inch**
1	**tsp. pepper**		**sections**
	flour	**5**	**peeled tomatoes, diced**
⅛	**lb. butter**		**pinch of marjoram**
1	**qt. water**	**2**	**T. parsley, chopped**
3	**T. wine/cider vinegar**	**2**	**bay leaves**

Salt and pepper coots, dredge sections thoroughly with flour and brown in large skillet with butter. Fill thick, iron pot with water and wine. Put browned coot sections, along with butter gravy (thinned out with a little water), into pot with vegetables, marjoram, parsley and bay leaves. Simmer (with cover on pot) for 2 hours or until coot is tender.

Steve Czerniak
Milwaukee, Wisconsin

Coot & Eggs

Serves: 2
Prep Time: 30 minutes

4 coot	**4 eggs**
8 bacon slices	**salt and pepper**
½ onion, finely chopped	**cheddar cheese, thinly**
1 garlic clove	**sliced**

The idea for this recipe was actually created by fellow NAHC Member Mike Boeselager who was bound and determined to convince me that coot are as good to eat as any of the "gourmet ducks." By golly, if he didn't. Skin and fillet breasts. If you prefer to eliminate the "gamey" flavor, soak overnight in marinade of 50 percent vinegar, 50 percent water. Fry bacon. Remove and place on paper-towel lined plate in warm oven until ready to serve. Saute onion and garlic in bacon grease. Add coot breasts and fry until done to the equivalent of a medium-rare steak. As breasts finish, fry eggs to your liking. Salt and pepper to taste. Serve with a tall stack of butter-soaked toast, sharp cheddar cheese and lots of coffee. You won't find a hardier breakfast to keep you warm in a cold duck blind.

Bill Miller
Chaska, Minnesota

Fried Marsh Hen

Serves: 4
Prep Time: 2 hours

12 marsh hens	**3 cups Bisquick**
salt and pepper	**1 lb. shortening**

Cut marsh hens into thirds, leaving breasts whole. Salt and pepper to taste. Place Bisquick and birds in large brown paper bag. Shake well. Be sure all birds are well covered with Bisquick. Fry in iron skillet, half filled with shortening, until brown. Make gravy with drippings and serve over rice.

George J. Osborne
Jacksonville, Florida

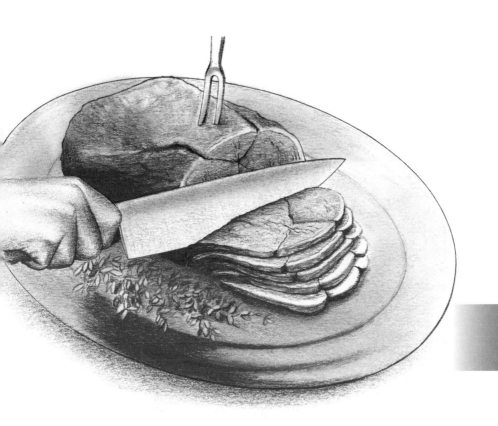

Kitchen Cutlery

Reprinted by permission of Chicago Cutlery

The single most important utensil in the kitchen is a good knife! A few quality, properly selected kitchen knives will do the work of dozens of space-consuming gadgets.

Knives are made from one of three types of steel—carbon, stainless or high-carbon stainless. Carbon steel was the most commonly used knife steel for many years. It is a soft metal that is easy to resharpen, but will stain and rust easily, even if cleaned and dried after each use. When highly polished, it is nearly impossible to tell the difference between carbon and stainless steel until put into use.

Stainless steel is widely used in the manufacturing of low-end household cutlery because of the ease of caring for this type of blade and its general durability and good looks. Stainless steel is the hardest and strongest of the three, making it the most difficult to sharpen. However, stainless steel is virtually stain and rust-resistant. Resharpening stainless steel must generally be done at the factory.

The present manufacturing trend is to make high quality knives of high-carbon stainless steel. This high quality stainless steel has the properties of ordinary stainless steel because it resists rusting and staining, but has enough carbon content so it readily takes a sharp edge and can be kept sharp at home with a butcher steel, hone or stone.

Quality knives generally have a hardwood or simulated wood handle. In addition to being made of a durable material, the handle should be properly balanced and mated to the blade and constructed to give the maximum amount of safety. Many knife handles are contoured to allow the user to grip the knife naturally. A shoulder or "guard" near the blade is a safety feature to help prevent slipping when the blade meets sudden resistance. As you hold different knives, think about how your hand will feel after a long chopping or slicing session. Comfort is of extreme importance.

Knife blades are generally ground one of three ways: hollow ground, flat ground, or taper ground. On a hollow ground knife, the blade is thinned out in an attempt to reduce "drag." This process tends to thin out the knife just behind the final edge of the blade, often causing a weak spot in the knife blade. On flat grinding, the knife is thinned uniformly, from the back of the blade to the point. On taper ground knives an additional grind is made on the knife which eliminates a shoulder, giving the edge an even, more uniform and smooth taper. This minimizes the blade's resistance as it cuts, making it seem sharper and drastically reducing the amount of time and effort needed to restore the edge. It also gives a hollow-ground appearance without undermining the strength or resilience of the blade.

No one knife can do every job in the kitchen. An assortment of good knives will assure you of having the right tool to meet every cutting need. Knives should never be used for purposes other than those for which they are intended. Unless specifically designed for cutting through bones, knives should never be used for this purpose. The following knives and sharpening implements are suggested items, and their common uses are detailed:

2¼- to 3-inch Parer Used for cleaning and paring foods. Generally use only the first inch or so of the knife. Not for dicing or chopping.

4-inch Steak Knife For individual table use.

5- to 6-inch Utility A good all-around knife for slicing cold cuts, cheese, tender vegetables. Also good for trimming meat and fat from bones.

8-inch Butcher For heavy cutting. Splitting up large roasts and dividing other cuts of meat.

8- or 10-inch Slicer For slicing meat and poultry.

4-, 6-, 8- or 10-inch Chef or Cook's Knife Most versatile of all knives. Used for most vegetables and fruits for cutting into chunks, julienne strips, bias cut, dicing or slicing.

7½-inch Narrow Slicer Ideal for slicing bread or tender vegetables, such as tomatoes.

6¾- or 7½-inch Fillet Flexible blade for filleting all types of fish.

10- or 12-inch Meat Slicer For slicing beef from beef rounds. An excellent carver. Ideal ham slicer or for cutting any large cut of meat.

6-inch Boner—Curved or Straight For boning meat and poultry. Good for small vegetables and cutting up chickens.

8- or 10-inch Bread Knife Used for slicing bread and delicate fruits and vegetables.

Chinese Pattern Chef Knife A good all-around knife, especially for Oriental food preparation. Excellent for dicing and chopping meats, fish or shrimp, and various cuts for vegetables, including bias or diagonal. The wide blade is also useful for transferring food from the cutting board to container.

Professional Cleaver For heavy cutting and chopping jobs, such as cutting through bones and separating frozen foods.

8- or 10-inch Butcher Steel For realigning the edge of a knife. Used each time knife is used. (Also referred to as a sharpening steel.)

Crock Stick Sharpener Used to put a new edge on knives or scissors. White alumina ceramic rods placed in a "V" provide the sharpening angle. Use when a dull blade needs a new edge. A good knife goes a long way toward accomplishing professional cutting results. And combined with the knowledge of specialty cutting operations, and some practice . . . *VOILA!* A pro is born!

How To Use A Chef Knife The Chef Knife is the most versatile of all knives for food preparation, designed for slicing and cutting of fruits and vegetables. Place your thumb and forefinger on the sides of the blade near the handle. The 2- to 3-inch section of blade closest to the handle is used more than the point, and placing the hand in this area gives greater control.

Hold the food firmly with your other hand, curling your fingers down and under. If your fingers are curled under properly, the knuckles can be used against the blade of the knife as a cutting guide. Do not lift the knife higher than necessary to get the food under it. If you guide the knife along by lightly touching the blade to your knuckles, and don't lift the knife very high, there is far less danger of cutting yourself. Use a rocking motion with the knife and push forward and down as you cut.

Dicing First cut the food into pieces about 2 inches long using the above method. Cut each of these pieces into thin strips lengthwise. Then cut crosswise to dice.

Bias Cut The knife remains perpendicular to the table, and the food is turned diagonally to the blade. Cut across the food at an angle to produce a long, slender cut. Celery cut in this fashion is more tender since the strings are cut short.

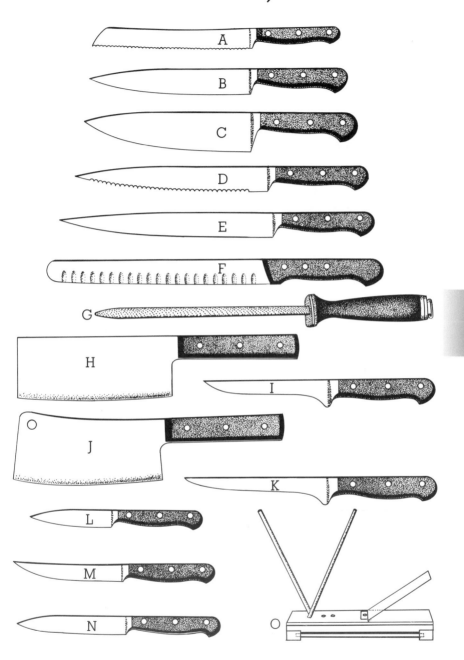

Suggested kitchen cutting tools include: bread knife (A); butcher knife (B); chef's knife (C); narrow slicer (D); slicer (E); meat slicer (F); butcher steel (G); pattern chef knife (H); 5-inch boning knife (I); standard cleaver (J); fillet (K); parer (L); steak knife (M); utility knife (N); crock stick sharpener (O).

How To Use A Chinese Pattern Chef Knife In Oriental cooking, all vegetables are cut to bite-size pieces. The cooking time is usually quite short; therefore uniform cutting is important for even cooking. Your Chinese Pattern Chef Knife is versatile enough for almost all of your Chinese food preparation ... from bias cutting celery to chopping meat for meatballs to scooping vegetables into your wok.

Hold the Chinese Pattern Chef Knife as instructed for the Chef Knife and follow the same methods of cutting. To chop meat or fish, first dice the food. Then, chop by holding the handle firmly and swinging the knife up and down in the center of the pile of food. As the food scatters, use the blade to again form a pile and chop through it. Continue this until the meat or fish has a fine texture.

Bear

Trying to convince some people that bear meat is just as delicious and better for you than domestic beef or pork is nearly impossible. To some extent the prejudice against bruin steaks is understandable. If one believes the adage "you are what you eat", seeing bear raid resort town dumps can result in a formidable mental barrier.

But those who have hunted bear know that bear in the wild share little resemblance to those dumpster-raiding clowns in habits or in diet! And maybe we should quit trying to convince our dinner guests that bear is great table fare, anyway—that way there'll be more for us!

Bear meat certainly is different from other wild meats like venison, and as such it needs different handling in the field and for the dinner plate.

Bear fat should be removed immediately when the animal is skinned. It turns rancid very quickly.

If a gamey piece of meat is tough, try a vinegar and salt combination. By mixing one tablespoon of salt and two tablespoons of vinegar in one quart of water, you can neutralize and tenderize a gamey piece of meat. Some people prefer to use wine or lemon juice, but in each instance it is best to soak the meat for 24 hours.

There are some things that just can't be rushed. And cooking bear meat is one of them. Randell L. Zarnke, disease and parasite biologist with Alaska's Fish and Game Department of Agriculture, revealed that preparing pork in microwave ovens does not always bring the meat to a sufficiently high temperature to destroy Trichinella larvae, the cause of the disease trichinosis.

"A similar situation could occur with bear meat," Zarnke said, "since bears are notorious sources of trichinosis for humans." Zarnke said several Alaskans per year suffer from trichinosis as a result of eating improperly prepared bear meat.

The problem with microwave cooking, according to the study, is microwave ovens do not always produce uniform temperatures throughout the product. "Cold spots" resulting from uneven heating may permit survival of micro-organisms including Trichinella.

The study cautions that even methods such as thawing in the microwave then charbroiling or precooking in the microwave then deep-fat frying did not kill the trichinae in infected pork. The best protection the bear consumer has against this parasite is to make sure all meat parts are heated to at least 137 degrees.

Black Bear Roast

Serves: 4-6
Prep Time: 4 hours, 15 minutes

1 bear roast	**1 can sliced mushrooms**
1 pkg. onion soup mix	

Remove all fat from roast and wash well. Place on a piece of heavy foil. Sprinkle package of onion soup mix and can of mushrooms over roast. Seal tightly and bake at 350 degrees for 4 hours or until well done.

Vera Schmidt
Patten, Maine

Bear Roast Marinade

Serves: 14
Prep Time: overnight plus 6 hours

10 lbs. bear roast	**3 cups water**
1½ cups vinegar	**2 cups red wine**
½ cup olive oil	**3 bay leaves**
½ tsp. nutmeg	**½ tsp. allspice**
1 tsp. dill seed	**½ tsp. red pepper**
1 tsp. garlic salt	**1 tsp. paprika**
1 cup celery, chopped	**1 cup onion, finely**
⅛ lb. butter	**chopped**
1 T. pepper	**2 T. salt**
½ tsp. sage	**8 cloves**

Combine all ingredients except meat and cloves and simmer 30 minutes. Before marinade cools, add meat and allow to marinate overnight. Place meat and marinade in roaster and bake 30 minutes per pound at 325 degrees. Bear has the consistency of pork and should be served well done. About 3 minutes before roast is done, pour off marinade and use for gravy. Rub butter over roast and stick in cloves. Serve with sweet potatoes, sauerkraut and well spiced cole slaw. Marinade too spicy? Omit onions, garlic salt, allspice, nutmeg, dill seed and paprika.

Anonymous

Violet's Roasted Black Bear In Red Wine

Serves: 4-6
Prep Time: 3-4 days plus 2 hours, 30 minutes

4 lbs. bear roast	**1 garlic clove, pressed**
2 cups dry red wine	**(juice only)**
1 cup canned consomme,	**¼ tsp. oregano**
undiluted	**¼ tsp. celery seed**
2 medium onions, chopped	**1 tsp. salt**
2 bay leaves	**1 tsp. freshly ground**
2 cloves	**pepper**

Mix all ingredients except meat. Pour marinade over meat and let stand 3-4 days in cold place, turning meat every day. Remove meat from marinade and drain. Sear in hot shortening until brown. Pour marinade over meat. Bake for 2 hours at 250 degrees. Remove meat. Strain all liquid into bowl, skim off fat and use to make gravy.

Joe Corrao
West Allis, Wisconsin

Bear Pot Roast

Serves: 6
Prep Time: 4 hours

2 lbs. bear roast	**2 bay leaves, whole**
1 10½-oz. can beef broth,	**¼ cup celery, sliced or**
consomme, or beef	**diced**
bouillon with 2 cups	**½ cup carrots, sliced**
water	**4-6 medium potatoes, diced**
1 small onion, sliced or	
diced	

Place meat on rack in Dutch oven or heavy roasting pan. Add liquid, onion and bay leaves. Cover. Roast slowly for 3 hours at 300 degrees. Add celery, carrots and potatoes. Cook another 30-45 minutes, covered, at 350 degrees until done. Remove bay leaves and serve.

Glenn Helgeland
Mequon, Wisconsin

Bear Roast

Serves: 6
Prep Time: 27 hours

6-8 lb. bear roast	**3 cups burgundy wine**
salt	**4 T. margarine, melted**
pepper	

Salt and pepper bear roast to taste and marinate in burgundy wine for 24 hours. Keep in refrigerator and turn at least once. After marinating roast, place in baking dish. Use 1 cup burgundy wine and melted margarine to baste roast. Cover dish with aluminum foil and roast at 340 degrees for approximately 2 hours, 30 minutes or until well done. For a complete meal, potatoes and carrots can be added to baking dish before placing roast in oven.

Kenneth W. Crummett
Moyers, West Virginia

Marinated Bear Roast

Serves: 6-8
Prep Time: 2 days plus 2 hours, 30 minutes

6-8 lb. bear roast	**½ tsp. pepper**
1 cup cooking oil	**1 bay leaf**
½ cup red wine	**1 tsp. salt**
2 onions, chopped	**½ tsp. thyme**
1 garlic clove, pressed	**3 T. margarine**
1 T. juniper berries, crushed	

Mix ingredients, except margarine, and pour over bear roast in a stainless steel or glass baking dish. Refrigerate 2 days but don't leave town on another hunting trip—turn roast twice daily. Now you're ready to cook. After marinating roast, melt 3 T. margarine in a heavy skillet and brown roast on all sides. Strain marinade and pour over roast. Cover and bake at 325 degrees for 2 hours, 30 minutes or until tender. Use drippings for gravy. Serve over mashed potatoes with green vegetable on the side.

Anonymous

Pepper Bear Steaks

Serves: 4-6
Prep Time: 1 hour

2 lbs. bear round, cut into ¾-inch strips
1 T. shortening
1 can consomme
1 can water
1 large green pepper, sliced
½ lb. mushrooms, thinly sliced
1 large onion, thinly sliced
cornstarch
soy sauce
coarse black pepper, freshly ground
salt

Brown meat in shortening. Add consomme and water, simmer 30 minutes or until tender. Add sliced vegetables and steam until limp. Thicken broth with cornstarch and water. Sprinkle with soy sauce and coarse black pepper. Serve over rice. This makes a great meal for a busy weeknight because it is quick to prepare.

Anonymous

Un-Bear-Able Steaks

Serves: 4
Prep Time: 1 hour

1½ lbs. bear meat
2 green peppers
12 oz. consomme
12 oz. water
¾ lbs. mushrooms
1 T. shortening
1 onion
soy sauce
black pepper
cornstarch

Brown bear meat in shortening. Add consomme and water and cook at low heat until tender. Throw in mushrooms, onion and green pepper and cook until soft. Add cornstarch mixed with water to thicken broth and sprinkle with soy sauce. Add plenty of black pepper and cook until tender, which should be less than a half hour. Serve with a salad, baked potato and the green vegetable of your choice.

John Sinberg
Greenfield, Wisconsin

Lambrusco Bear Steak Tips

Serves: 6
Prep Time: 1 hour, 30 minutes

1½ lbs. bear steak, cut in bite-size pieces
2 T. oil
½ pkg. instant onion soup mix (1.5 oz.)
1 cup water

½ cup Lambrusco (or burgundy if you prefer sweeter wine)
1 can mushroom stems, pieces and juice
salt and pepper, to taste

Brown meat in hot oil. Add remaining ingredients and simmer approximately 1 hour. Serve with cooked buttered noodles or fluffy rice. Note: We prefer to marinate bear meat. Some people find bear meat a bit strong for their tastes; others don't. To be safe, especially with guests, we put bear meat in the refrigerator for 24 hours in a marinade of 2 T. white vinegar to 2 cups water (use same ratio with quantity sufficient to cover meat) in a non-metal container.

Glenn Helgeland
Mequon, Wisconsin

Northwoods Braised Bear Delight

Serves: 4
Prep Time: 4 hours

1 bear roast
3 T. Kitchen Bouquet
2-3 T. cooking oil
4 garlic cloves, sliced
⅓ cup onions, chopped
⅓ cup celery, chopped

2 T. cornstarch dissolved in ⅛ cup water
1 18-oz. can tomato sauce
½ cup brown sugar
½ tsp. salt
½ tsp. black pepper

Soak meat in saltwater for 1 hour and drain. Precook meat over open coals and baste with Kitchen Bouquet until brown. In Dutch oven, add oil and saute garlic, onions and celery until brown. Mix in cornstarch paste until smooth. Add remaining ingredients. Cook for 1 hour or until meat is tender.

Mark Dorfman
Nanuet, New York

Gourmet Bear Steaks

Serves: 2 Prep Time: 1 hour

**2 bear steaks, about
¾-inch thick
salt and pepper
1 12-oz bottle Catalina
dressing**

**1 small can mushrooms
1 small can tomato sauce
1 small can ripe olives
1 small onion, chopped**

Salt and pepper steaks. Pour ½ bottle Catalina dressing in skillet. Brown steaks. Mix rest of dressing with remaining ingredients and pour over steaks. Bake 45 minutes at 350 degrees.

Bear Steaks With Pennaz

Serves: 2
Prep Time: 1 hour

**2 thick bear steaks
salt and pepper
1 12-oz. bottle French
dressing**

**1 8-oz. can tomato sauce
1 8-oz. jar green olives
1 8-oz. can mushrooms**

Season meat. Brown with French dressing in frying pan. Smother steaks with remaining ingredients in baking dish. Bake at 325 degrees 45 minutes.

Steve Pennaz
Minneapolis, Minnesota

Bear Sausage

Serves: 50
Prep Time: 1 hour

**12 lbs. bear meat, cubed
¼ cup sausage seasoning**

**¼ cup ground sage
1 T. black pepper**

Trim meat and mix with sausage seasoning, sage and pepper. Grind in meat grinder. Roll into logs or patties to freeze.

John Williams
Cashmere, Washington

Frank's Bear Stew

Serves: 2-4
Prep Time: 1-2 hours

2 lbs. bear meat, cubed	10 juniper berries
2 T. olive oil	1½ pts. water
2 T. flour	8 medium potatoes, diced
¼ tsp. black pepper	1 small can mushrooms
⅛ tsp. cayenne pepper	(optional)
1 tsp. salt	

Cook bear meat with olive oil in small Dutch oven until done. Stir in flour, black pepper, cayenne pepper and salt. When all water and oil is absorbed in flour, add juniper berries, water and potatoes. Simmer 30 minutes in closed Dutch oven. Add mushrooms if desired.

Frank Whitley
Orick, California

Baked Bear Stew

Serves: 6
Prep Time: 2 hours, 30 minutes

3 lbs. bear stew meat	¼ tsp. pepper
2 cups onions, minced	½ cup unsifted flour
2 garlic cloves, minced	⅓ cup salad oil
2 bay leaves	¾ cup red cooking wine
1½ tsp. salt	2 cups water
1½ tsp. monosodium glutamate (MSG)	1 6-oz. can tomato paste
	cooked noodles

Place bear meat, onion, garlic and bay leaves in shallow baking pan. Sprinkle with mixture of salt, monosodium glutamate and pepper. Bake uncovered 10 minutes at 425 degrees. Reduce heat to 300 degrees and bake 30 minutes longer. In pan, combine flour, salad oil, red cooking wine, water and tomato paste. Cook until smooth. Pour over meat, cover and bake at 300 degrees for 1 hour to 90 minutes.

Dion Luke
Glenwood Springs, Colorado

Black Bear Spaghetti Sauce

Serves: 24
Prep Time: 3 hours, 30 minutes

2 lbs. ground bear	**1 garlic clove, crushed**
2 28-oz. cans tomatoes	**salt and pepper**
2 5½-oz. cans tomato	**oregano**
paste	**bay leaves**
2 large onions, diced	**½ tsp. chili powder**
1 green pepper. diced	**2 T. Worcestershire sauce**
1 10-oz. can mushrooms,	**1 tsp. cornstarch**
drained	

Brown meat in frying pan. Drain excess fat. In large pot, combine tomatoes (mashed up), tomato paste, onions, green pepper, mushrooms and garlic. Stir. Add bear meat. Stir. Add remaining spices and stir. Let simmer 3 hours uncovered. Halfway through, add cornstarch to thicken. Stir occasionally. Serve with your favorite pasta, and a nice green salad with Italian dressing for a special taste treat.

Kris & Karen Fielding
Sudbury, Ontario

Mild Bear Chili

Serves: 4-6
Prep Time: 1 hour

1 lb. ground bear	**1 19-oz. can kidney beans**
⅓ cup onion, chopped	**1 can brown beans**
½ green pepper, chopped	**1 tsp. salt**
1 10-oz. can tomato soup	**1 dash pepper**
¼ cup milk	**2 dashes chili powder**

Brown meat with onion and green pepper. Add remaining ingredients and simmer on low heat for 30 minutes. Serve with crackers or bread.

Glen Hill
Saskatchewan, Canada

Bear Chili

Serves: 2-3
Prep Time: 1 hour

1 lb. ground bear meat	1 celery stalk, diced
1 qt. cold water	6 T. mild chili powder
1 garlic clove, crushed	1 6-oz. can tomato paste
1 onion, diced	salt and pepper, to taste

Add bear meat to cold water, making sure meat is completely separated. Bring to a boil and add garlic, onion and celery. Simmer until vegetables are done. Stir in chili powder and simmer 10 minutes. Add tomato paste and simmer another 10 minutes. This basic recipe can be multiplied to make any quantity desired. It can also be used as chili-mac, by serving over spaghetti or macaroni, or chili and beans, by adding a large can of your favorite beans and serving with crackers.

Ruth Ann Robinson
Montrose, Colorado

Char-Broiled Barbecue Bear Ribs

Serves: 4-6
Prep Time: varies

1 side of bear ribs
favorite seasonings
butter
favorite barbecue sauce
honey

Cut ribs into desired sizes. Season well on both sides, cover and refrigerate 1-12 hours. When grill is ready, put ribs on, adding slices of butter to each chunk of ribs. Turn often, adding butter with each turn. When ribs are almost ready, prepare barbecue sauce using ¾ of your favorite sauce and ¼ honey. Brush on sauce, let sit a while, then brush on other side.

John Zanon
Norway, Michigan

Bear Meatballs

Serves: 8-10
Prep Time: 1 hour, 30 minutes

1½ lbs. bear burger	1 tsp. garlic powder
¾ cup bread crumbs	1 pkg. onion soup mix
½ cup beer	2 cans cream of
2 eggs	mushroom soup
1 tsp. salt	¾ can water

Mix ingredients, except soup and water, in bowl. Form into meatballs and brown in skillet. Drain grease. Put browned meatballs in casserole with soup and water. Bake 1 hour at 375 degrees and serve with grated Parmesan or Romano cheese sprinkled on top of meatballs.

Bill Berkant
Wilkes Barre, Pennsylvania

Bear Stroganoff

Serves: 4-6
Prep Time: 30-45 minutes

2 cups bear meat, cubed	¼ tsp. pepper
½ cup onion	1 can sliced mushrooms
¼ cup butter, unsalted	1 can cream of celery
2 T. flour	soup
1 tsp. salt	1 cup sour cream
1 garlic clove	4 cups egg noodles

Saute onions in butter. Add bear meat and brown. Make sure onions are tender and bear is well done. Stir in flour, salt, garlic, pepper and mushrooms. Cook 5 minutes, stirring constantly over medium-low heat. Stir in soup, heat to boiling, stirring constantly. Add a little water if necessary. Reduce heat and simmer uncovered 10 minutes. Prepare egg noodles. Stir in sour cream and heat. Serve over bed of noodles.

Frank Whitley
Eureka, California

Bear Tenders

Serves: varies
Prep Time: 1 hour, 30 minutes

1 lb. bear meat, cubed	**¼ cup pineapple juice**
2 T. margarine	**¼ cup smoked barbecue**
pepper	**sauce**

Brown bear cubes in margarine. Add pepper to taste. Pour pineapple juice over meat, simmer 20 minutes. Drain. Coat with barbecue sauce. Add water and simmer, covered, 30-45 minutes.

B. Lewandowski
Greenlane, Pennsylvania

Guide's Bear Oriental

Serves: 4-6 people
Prep Time: 24 hours

1-2 lbs. bear meat	**1 can oriental baby corn,**
¼ cup soy sauce	**halved**
¼ cup cornstarch	**1 can sliced water**
1 T. sesame seed oil	**chestnuts**
2 T. vermouth	**¼ pound snow pea pods**
½ tsp. sesame seeds	**1 medium onion, sliced**
¼ cup peanut oil	**½ cup water**
¼ cup sesame seed oil	**1 beef bouillon cube**
1 bunch fresh broccoli,	
bite size	

Trim fat and cut meat into 2-inch strips. Marinate meat in soy sauce, cornstarch, sesame seed oil, vermouth and sesame seeds overnight. Heat peanut oil and small amount of sesame seed oil in wok on high heat. Stir-fry meat until browned, remove and set aside. Add more oil, then stir-fry all vegetables, approximately 5 minutes. Add water and bouillon cube. Stir. Cover for 3 minutes. Stir after 1 minute, 30 seconds. Add meat and continue cooking for a few minutes.

Anthony Guide
Middlesex, New Jersey

Pickled Grizzly Paws

Serves: 3-4
Prep Time: 3 hours

4	grizzly paws, split	1	bay leaf
3	cups cider vinegar	1	T. salt
2	onions, sliced	2	cups celery, diced
1	dozen peppercorns	2	tsp. parsley, minced
6	whole cloves		

Put paws in pot, cover with water. Add vinegar and bring to a boil. Skim the top. Add remaining ingredients. Simmer 2 hours. Serve cold.

Rick Sinchak
Warren, Ohio

Tomatoed Bear Roast

Serves: 4
Prep Time: 2 hours, 30 minutes

2	lbs. bear meat	chili pepper
2	T. shortening	2 cans tomato soup
	black pepper, ground	1 small can tomato sauce
	garlic salt	1 onion, sliced

Brown meat in shortening. Sprinkle with seasonings. Add tomato soup, sauce and onion. Simmer 2 hours, covered.

Tore's Bear Kabob

Serves: 6-8
Prep Time: overnight plus 1 hour

2	lbs. bear meat, cubed	2-3	large onions
¾	cup Italian dressing	2-3	green peppers

Marinate meat overnight in salad dressing. On skewers, alternate meat, onion and peppers. Grill over coals. Season to taste.

Ronald Torgersen
Windgap, Pennsylvania

Celebrity Chefs

Through the first 10 editions, the annual *NAHC Wild Game Cookbooks* have featured many recipe contributions from North America's greatest hunters and outdoor industry figures. Each of these prominent sportsmen gladly welcomed the chance to share their favorite recipes with the growing number of NAHC members. Imagine enjoying venison ribs prepared just as Fred Bear (above) liked them. Or Bob Allen's pheasant divan. Or Pete Shepley's pit barbecued javelina. Over the years, they and many more have shared their outstanding favorites.

Since publishing their recipes originally, some of the celebrities like Bear and Roy Weatherby have passed away. The entire body of North American hunters mourns their passing, but their favorite recipes are shared again in this chapter.

Fred Bear
(1902-1988)

Fred Bear's nickname even during his lifetime was "Papa Bear"—already a sign that history will recognize him as the father of modern bowhunting. The lean, six-foot archer was an inventor of no mean ability whose contributions to the design of modern archery tackle and manufacturing processes lifted the ancient sport from the home workshop into a world-wide multi-million dollar business. Bear's activities helped in getting special archery hunting seasons passed in every state in our land. While Fred Bear is no longer with us, the company he founded is still a prime force in the archery industry as a member company of Hanson Industries.

Fred Bear's Roast Ribs

Serves: 2-6
Prep Time: 2 hours

Ribs (Mountain sheep, mountain goat, moose, caribou or deer)

Cut 2 green forked stakes and 2 poles about 4 feet long. Make 4 S hooks from coat hangers or baling wire. Break ribs with a hatchet or axe every 4 or 5 inches. Fasten two S hooks top and bottom. In the meantime, start a fire after clearing away leaves and other inflammables. If hardwood is available, it will take some time to burn to a bed of hot coals at which time you drive the forked stakes and hang the meat to roast. A good bed of hardwood coals should be sufficient to roast ribs. If your fuel is coniferous, the coals will not burn as long and wood must be added from time to time. If you have aluminum foil, shape a rectangular pan to catch drippings for basting. Lift the pole from which the ribs are hung and turn from time to time. Turn them upside down occasionally. To do this, the other pole is placed in the bottom S hooks. Lift the ribs up by the top pole and, with the other hand, grasp the bottom pole. Turn them 180 degrees and place back on the forked sticks. These turnings, both front to back and top to bottom, assure a uniformity of cooking and reverses the juice flow, preventing drying out. It will be ready to eat in approximately 2 hours, when the meat turns brown or you can no longer stand the heavenly aroma.

Fred Bear
Gainesville, Florida

Roy E. Weatherby
(1911-1988)

Roy Weatherby's interest in guns and hunting started at age six as a farm boy in Kansas. It led him to become a firearms genius who, many experts claim, accomplished more in the gun industry than any other inventor in generations. At the age of 29, Weatherby wounded a deer. His feelings of regret for that incident spurred his search for powerful, efficient rifles. The results are legendary. But, firearms development was a second career for Weatherby. He had become involved in a lucrative insurance business in California before pursuing his first love in 1945. Since then, Weatherby's products, which bear his name, have gained a reputation of quality and prestige second to none, which they still carry today. The company is now under the direction of his son.

Elk, Venison Or Moose Oven Burgundy

Serves: 6-8
Prep Time: 3 hours, 30 minutes

2 **lbs. venison, elk or**	1 **garlic clove, minced**
moose stew meat	¼ **tsp. pepper**
2 **T. soy sauce**	¼ **tsp. marjoram**
2 **T. flour**	¼ **tsp. thyme**
4 **carrots, chunked**	1 **cup burgundy, or any**
2 **large onions, sliced**	**dry red wine**
1 **cup celery, thinly sliced**	1 **cup sliced mushrooms**

Blend soy sauce with flour in 3-qt. baking dish. Cut meat into 1½-inch cubes. Add meat to soy sauce mixture and toss to coat meat cubes. Add remaining ingredients, except mushrooms, to meat. Stir gently. Cover tightly and oven-simmer 2 hours at 325 degrees. Add mushrooms and stir. Cover tightly and bake 1 hour or until meat and vegetables are tender. Serve with hot wild rice, noodles or mashed potatoes.

Roy E. Weatherby
South Gate, California

Larry Kelly

President, Mag-na-port

Larry Kelly, inventor of the
Mag-na-port recoil reducing process,
is one of the world's foremost handgun
hunters. He has taken a remarkable
number of big game animals with a
handgun, including all types of
dangerous game in North America
and the African Big Five. Among
Larry's most exciting hunting tales is
the story of an Alaskan brown bear
which decided to join him and his
guide *inside* their makeshift cabin!
The Michigan native has been equally
successful with long guns. Kelly,
founder of the Handgun Hunter
Museum and Hall Of Fame, received
1984's Outstanding American
Handgunner award. Also, in 1989, he
was inducted into the Safari Club International's Hall Of Fame—a prestigious
honor which provided worldwide recognition for Kelly.

Cape Buffalo

Serves: 6
Prep Time: 2 hours, 30 minutes

2 **lbs. cape buffalo meat, cut into 1½-inch cubes**	1 **tsp. Worcestershire sauce**
⅓ **cup flour**	4 **celery stalks, sliced**
⅓ **cup fat**	12 **small onions, whole**
dash salt and pepper	6 **medium carrots, cut into**
½ **cup onions, chopped**	**2-inch lengths**
2 **cups hot water or meat stock**	4 **medium potatoes, quartered**
1 **cup canned tomatoes**	

Coat meat with flour. Slowly brown meat in hot fat on all sides.
Add salt, pepper and onions. Slowly stir in hot water or meat
stock and tomatoes. Add Worcestershire sauce. Cover pan and
simmer 2 hours. Add celery, onions, carrots and potatoes. Cover
and simmer 20-30 minutes. If desired, a can of green beans can
be added when ready to serve.

Larry Kelly
Mt. Clemens, Michigan

Bob Allen,

President, The Bob Allen Companies

Bob Allen is the "Wingshooting Columnist for *North American Hunter.* He grew up hunting small game with a BB gun near his home in Fort Dodge, Iowa. Since then, Bob has been a member of the All-American Trapshooting team 11 times. He won the Iowa skeet championship 12 times, and the Iowa trap championship 15 times. He is the only shooter ever to have won both titles in the same year. He was the National Doubles Champion and a runner-up for that title seven times. He has hunted all across North America and in Africa. Though foremost a wingshooter, Bob enjoys big game and turkey hunting as well. Bob is president and owner of the Bob Allen companies, in Des Moines, Iowa, which makes luggage and an exclusive line of top-quality sportswear for hunters.

Pheasant Divan

Serves: 10-12
Prep Time: 1 hour, 30 minutes

3-4 pheasants (mainly breasts), cooked and boned	**2 10-oz. pkgs. frozen broccoli spears**
2 cans cream of chicken soup	**1 cup shredded cheddar cheese**
1 cup mayonnaise	**1 stick butter**
1 tsp. lemon juice	**¾ cup dry bread crumbs**

Mix together soup, mayonnaise and lemon juice. Cook broccoli, drain and arrange in 8x12 baking dish. Place pheasant pieces on top of broccoli. Pour soup mixture on top. Sprinkle shredded cheese over all. Mix butter with bread crumbs in skillet and sprinkle on top of casserole. Bake at 350 degrees for 1 hour.

Bob Allen
Des Moines, Iowa

James H. Glass
President And CEO, WLFA

Jim Glass has dedicated most of his life to the sportsmen's conservation movement. In 1978, the same year in which the North American Hunting Club was founded, Glass co-founded The Wildlife Legislative Fund of America, along with Pittsburgh Pirate's president, and sportsman Daniel M. Galbreath. The WLFA protects the heritage of the American sportsman to hunt, fish and trap. It is an association of America's major national, state and local sportsmen's conservation groups. The WLFA staff features experts in political action, public relations and the law. The WFLA's most prominent work is embodied in the popular "Protect

What's Right" program. Jim serves as president and chief executive officer of WLFA. Jim was an executive of Rockwell International before founding WLFA.

Texas-Style Venison Chili

Serves: 6
Prep Time: 1 hour, 45 minutes

3 **lbs. venison**	**garlic to taste**
1 **15-oz. can tomato sauce**	1 **tsp. cayenne powder**
1 **cup water**	1 **tsp. paprika**
1 **tsp. Tabasco**	12 **red peppers (optional)**
2 **T. (heaping) chili powder or ground chili peppers**	4-5 **chili pods (optional)**
	1 **tsp. salt**
	2 **T. flour**
1 **T. (heaping) cumin or "camino" powder**	
2 **onions, chopped**	

Cut venison into ½-inch cubes and sear until gray. Add tomato sauce and water. Add remaining ingredients, except flour, and simmer for 1 hour and 15 minutes. Add thickening (2 heaping T. flour mixed with water). Simmer 30 minutes.

James H. Glass
Columbus, Ohio

Chuck Saunders

President, Saunders Archery

Chuck Saunders, a lifelong archer and benefactor of the sport, founded the Saunders Archery Company in 1941. The company specializes in archery accessories and slingshots and is among the largest in the world in these two areas. Many of its products are patented. It has received more than 40 patents in these two fields. The company was also active in founding the Bowhunters Who Care organization which champions hunting ethics among North American sportsmen. The company which Saunders heads celebrated its Golden Anniversary with continued production of its Indian-cored fiber matt (target backing) which it pioneered and has proven to be adaptable for wood, aluminum and the new thinner, penetrating carbon arrows.

Venison Casserole

Serves: 2-4
Prep Time: 45 minutes

1 **lb. ground venison**	1 **can tomato soup**
½ **lb. pork sausage**	1 **can corn**
½ **pkg. egg noodles**	1 **can mushrooms**
1 **T. green pepper, chopped**	1 **can tomato sauce**
	salt and pepper
1 **medium onion, thickly chopped**	¼ **tsp. garlic powder**
	pinch of oregano

Boil noodles until tender in salted water and drain. Saute crumbled meat, green pepper and onion in small amount of fat. Add other ingredients. Put noodles in greased casserole dish and pour other mixture into the noodles. Bake at 275 degrees for about 30 minutes.

Chuck Saunders
Columbus, Nebraska

Jim Crumley

President, Bowing Enterprises

Jim Crumley is founder and president of Bowing Enterprises, Inc., and originator of the Trebark Camouflage design. He was a public school teacher, administrator and hunting guide before starting his company in 1980. His favorite pursuits are fall bowhunting and spring gobbler hunting, with a pinch of dove shooting, duck hunting and trout fishing thrown in. Jim's innovative "vertical" camo pattern spawned dozens of other new specialty patterns, yet his original creation is still a favorite of many hunters in-the-know. A bowhunter and former guide, Jim has logged many miles in pursuit of whitetail deer and turkey, as well as bear hunting in Canada, and stalking and shooting boars in Florida and mule deer and elk in Colorado.

Sauteed Venison Or Turkey

Serves: 2-4
Prep Time: 10 minutes

2 lbs. venison tenderloin or turkey breast	**lemon pepper (key ingredient)**
salt	**1 stick butter**

Slice meat ¼-inch thick. Sprinkle slices with salt and lemon pepper. Melt butter in skillet, keeping heat low enough so butter does not burn. Saute meat slices in butter 2 minutes on each side. Serve hot as main course and as sandwiches the following day.

Jim Crumley
Roanoke, Virginia

Bill Harper
Advisor, Lohman Mfg.

Bill Harper, well-known sportsman, game calling expert, past president and current advisor to Lohman Manufacturing Company, Inc., is always working to improve and develop new game calls and accessories. Lohman has produced calls of the finest quality since 1937. Today, Bill is in the process of starting a game call company bearing his name and the reputation for quality which he has established at Lohman. Bill is a nationally-known lecturer and game calling expert and instructor. A winner of numerous championship calling contests, Bill has taught students who have gone on to win State, National and World Championships. Bill has been teaching and writing about game calling since 1968 and sharing his hunting expertise with hunters throughout the nation.

The Bill Harper Special

Serves: 4
Prep Time: 1 hour

2	**lbs. venison, cubed**	¼	**tsp. allspice**
	butter	½	**tsp. garlic powder**
1½	**cups celery stalks and**	¼	**tsp. paprika**
	tops, chopped	½	**cup wine**
1	**medium onion, chopped**	2	**cans cream of chicken**
½	**lb. fresh mushrooms,**		**soup**
	sliced	8	**oz. milk or**
½	**green pepper, chopped**	½	**pint sour cream**
1	**T. Worcestershire sauce**		

Brown meat in butter and simmer until tender. Add vegetables and seasonings. Saute until tender. Add wine, soup and the milk or sour cream. Heat through and serve over wild rice, white rice or noodles.

Bill Harper
Neosho, Missouri

Pete Shepley

President,
Precision Shooting Equipment

Pete Shepley presides over Precision Shooting Equipment, or PSE, manufacturing compound bows, compound crossbows and archery accessories known around the world for their quality and dependability. It's become one of the top manufacturers in the industry. As one of North America's best known bowhunters, he has successfully hunted grizzly, moose, barren ground caribou, black bear, Yellowstone elk, cougar, stone sheep, desert bighorn sheep, whitetail deer and two species of wild turkey. However, javelinas are inhabitants of the Southwest, around Pete's Tucson home, and they continue to be one of Pete's favorite game animals because they are particularly fun to hunt with bow and arrow.

Pit Barbecued Javelina

Serves: several
Prep Time: overnight

1 **whole javelina**	2 **cups barbecue sauce**
1 **onion, chopped**	7 **clove leaves**
7 **garlic cloves, chopped**	**black pepper (healthy**
1 **cup Worcestershire**	**shot)**
sauce	**salt**
2 **cups catsup**	

Soak whole javelina in salt water for a couple of hours before seasoning. Place javelina on ample piece of heavy duty aluminum foil and apply well-mixed ingredients on and around meat. Wrap securely in foil, possibly adding second sheet. Place into damp cloth baking bag. Place javelina in a pit where mesquite coals can be arranged below, around and above meat. Cover with soil and allow to cook overnight or at least 7-9 hours while you tune your bow and get ready for the next javelina hunt. Meat will shred easily and is perfect for tacos and burritos.

Pete Shepley
Tucson, Arizona

Upland Birds

Upland birds have long held a tremendous value in the eyes of the sportsmen who hunt them. Such was the value of the sport that the nobles and gentry of long ago Europe made it a hanging offense for a peasant to kill a pheasant or partridge! Culinary geniuses around the world base some of their most renowned and elegant dishes on the tender, succulent meat of upland birds.

On the whole, upland birds make exquisite table fare. Sure you'll run into a tough old pheasant or a gamey woodcock now and then, but seldom with more frequency than you'll pick a tough T-bone from the butcher's display case. The trick is proper field care.

To this day you'll hear of gourmands who demand that upland birds be "hung" or "aged" for the table. That means the birds are hung in a cool, dry place for as long as two weeks with the innards, skin and feathers still in place!

There's no reason to hang upland birds in this day and age. The roots of this tradition are based in the days before refrigeration. Those folks didn't have any choice for preserving meat that couldn't be eaten fresh. Besides, most of the recipes that call for hanging birds include so much fancy-shmancy sauce and seasoning that the delicate, delicious flavor of the meat is completely lost. If anyone tells you to hang your birds, tell 'em to go fly a kite!

In handling your upland birds in the field, think of them just as a big game hunter thinks of the animals he harvests. The most pressing concerns are getting out the entrails and cooling the carcass.

Field dressing upland birds is simple and quick. It can be accomplished quickly with only a knife, but a gut hook can be handy.

If the bird is not dead when it comes to hand, finish it off quickly and humanely. Most often this is done by wringing the bird's neck. Another method is to insert the point of a knife into the bird's open mouth, up into its brain. Hunting preserve guides who dispatch hundreds of birds in a season often carry a tool that is sort of a specialized pliers/punch which quickly severs the spinal cord from the base of the brain.

When the bird has quieted, pluck the feathers in the area from the base of the breast back around the anus to the base of the tail feathers. Also, pluck the feathers out from the base of the neck to the front edge of the bird's breast.

Slit the length of the rear feather-free area with a knife, working around the anus. In the front, cut or pull out the bird's crop. Reach in the rear slit and pull out all the entrails. You may have to scrape your fingernails along the connection of the ribs to the backbone a couple of times to remove as many particles of the lungs as possible. Use caution when inserting your hand into the bird to avoid cutting fingers on sharp, broken bones. Running a fine rib bone under your fingernail makes a less than enjoyable job absolutely miserable.

With all entrails removed, you now have a field dressed bird. If the law permits, you can also remove the head at this stage if you wish. Even on the largest pheasant you shouldn't have blood much above your wrist. If you think of it, carry along paper towels to wipe your hands; but if you forget, grass, leaves, cornstalks and a handy pond or puddle have worked before and will again. With practice you'll be able to dress a bird in 45 seconds or less. A bird so dressed will cool nicely.

The rubberized game bag is still not the best environment to carry even a dressed bird. Cooling air can't circulate in there, especially as more birds are brought to bag. Go ahead and use the game bag on your coat or vest if the duration of your hunt won't be long. But if you'll be out all day, use a bird carrier that attaches to your belt or slings over your shoulder. These will at least keep the birds out in the open where the air is circulating.

Dove hunters on traditional field shoots have it best when it comes to cooling birds. They generally have a cooler of cold soft drinks close at hand and can replace drinks with birds. Even so, the hunter would do his dinner guests well to remove the entrails of the birds during the first lull in the action.

Field dressed birds can be iced and taken home or to camp for cleaning. If you want, and transport regulations allow, you could finish the cleaning process in the field, too. Whenever you dress your kill, take into consideration the sensitivities of anyone who is liable to come across the viscera. Don't leave a pile of guts and feathers and heads and wings lying near a road or public trail. Ask landowners if they mind you dressing birds in the field.

Dove Load Burritos

Serves: 5-6
Prep Time: 1 hour

36	dove breasts, boned and diced		garlic salt
½	lb. butter	1	16-oz. jar salsa
1	large purple onion, diced	4	oz. chile peppers, diced
	lemon pepper	12	large flour tortillas
1½	lbs. potatoes, diced	1	lb. Monterey Jack cheese, shredded
			green taco sauce

In large skillet over medium heat, melt butter and add diced dove meat, onion and lemon pepper. Cook 10 minutes; set aside. In same skillet, melt remaining butter and fry potatoes, adding lemon pepper and garlic salt. Place meat in with potatoes, adding salsa and chile peppers. Simmer 15 minutes stirring frequently. Spoon onto warm tortilla; cover with cheese and taco sauce. Fold and serve.

H.E. Price
Littlerock, California

Dove Breast On Rice

Serves: 2-3
Preparation Time: 1 hour, 25 minutes

10	dove breasts, boned	1	1½-oz. pkg. onion soup
1	can cream of mushroom soup	1	small can mushroom stems and pieces
1	soup can milk	¾	cup uncooked rice

Heat oven to 350 degrees. Mix mushroom soup with milk; save ½ cup and half the onion soup mix. Pour into 2½-qt. baking dish. Place dove breasts on top. Pour remaining soup mixture on top; sprinkle with remaining onion soup mix. Add mushroom stems and pieces. Cover and bake 1 hour; uncover and bake 15-25 minutes more. Serve over rice.

Duane Lee
Colorado Springs, Colorado

The Gray Ghost Casserole (Dove)

Serves: 6
Prep Time: 2 hours, 30 minutes

12 doves	**2 cups frozen green peas**
1 cup flour	**1 medium onion, chopped**
1 T. salt	**2 celery stalks, diced**
1 T. pepper	**4 cups chicken stock**
1 T. thyme	**½ cup white wine**
butter	**(optional)**
2 cups carrots, sliced	

Heat oven to 375 degrees. Shake whole doves in mixture of flour, salt, pepper and thyme in a sack until well covered. Saute birds in butter until well browned. Place birds in 1 layer in a casserole, Dutch oven or flat roasting pan with cover. Add carrots, peas, onion and celery. Saute until lightly colored, add chicken stock and put on low heat. Pour vegetables and chicken stock over doves, almost covering meat. Cover pan and place in oven. Cook 1-2 hours. Add chicken stock if needed. When tender, remove meat and keep warm. Salt and pepper vegetables; add white wine. Thicken with 2 T. butter mixed with 2 T. flour. Cover birds with warm vegetables and sauce.

Bill Gold
Seven Fountains, Virginia

Mexican Fried Dove

Serves: 4
Prep Time: 1 hour

10 doves	**1 egg**
salt and pepper	**2 cups pancake flour**
1 cup milk	**vegetable oil**

Clean doves, singe, split down the back and flatten. Season with salt and pepper. Soak in milk and egg mixture. Dip in pancake flour and drop in vegetable oil heated to 375 degrees. When brown, remove and drain. Should cook about 10 minutes.

Junior Bukaske
River Ridge, Louisiana

Barras Jambalaya

Serves: 10
Prep Time: varies

2 lbs. dove or quail meat
1½ lbs. smoked sausage
2 cans stewed tomatoes
1 bell pepper, diced
1 medium onion, chopped
1 tsp. salt, pepper

¼ cup cooking oil
1 cup green onion, diced
¼ tsp. garlic salt
2 banana peppers, diced 1
  lb. shrimp
2 lbs. rice

Cook dove or quail until done. Cook sausage separately and dice when done. Bone meat and cut into 1-inch pieces. Put tomatoes and other ingredients except shrimp and rice into Dutch oven. Add wild game and sausage. Add 1-qt. water and bring to a boil. Cook for 15 minutes. Add shrimp and cook for an additional 20 minutes. Add washed rice and water to pot, covering ingredients by 1 inch. Boil for 5 minutes. Cover pot and steam cook for 40 minutes at 250 degrees.

Dr. Donald Barras
Troy, Alabama

Tomatoed Doves

Serves: 4
Prep Time: 2 hours, 30 minutes

10 dove breasts
   salt and pepper
½ cup flour
½ cup vegetable oil
1 medium onion, chopped
1 cup celery, chopped
1 cup long-grain rice

1 16-oz. can stewed
   tomatoes
   poultry seasoning
1 cup water
½ lb. fresh mushrooms,
   sliced (optional)

Salt and pepper doves to taste. Dust with flour and brown in hot oil in large skillet. Remove and place in 2-qt. casserole. Combine remaining ingredients and uncooked rice and pour over doves. Cover with foil. Bake 2 hours at 350 degrees.

Cheryl Buster
Fort Collins, Colorado

Dove And Oyster Pie

Serves: 6-8
Prep Time: 2 hours

16 doves	**cayenne pepper**
2 cups celery, chopped	**1 qt. water**
1 cup onion, chopped	**4 dozen oysters**
3 bacon slices, chopped	**4 T. flour**
salt	**¼ cup water**

Place cleaned, whole doves in pot. Add celery, onion and bacon and cover with water. Bring to a boil, then simmer until doves are tender. Cool doves enough to handle. Drain oysters. Stuff oysters into each dove. Mix flour with ¼ cup water to make paste. Add enough liquid from pot to blend well. Add this to pot in which doves were cooked, put on low heat and stir until thickened. Add remaining oysters and remove from heat. Line casserole with flaky pastry and bake for 10 minutes at 350 degrees. Let cool. Put in layer of doves, then liquid with oysters. Repeat within ½ inch of top. Cover with pastry. Bake at 350 degrees.

Tom Michelson
Roanoke, Virginia

Baked Mourning Or White-Winged Dove

Serves: varies
Prep Time: 1 hour, 30 minutes

2 or 3 doves per serving	**cooking oil**
salt and pepper	**½ cup applesauce per**
oregano	**serving**
marjoram	

Sprinkle doves lightly with salt, pepper, oregano and marjoram. Place in skillet and brown oil. Prepare cornbread dressing, using applesauce. Spread layer of dressing in baking dish and place birds on top. Place rest of dressing around birds. Cover dish with foil and bake in a preheated oven at 300 degrees for 45 minutes.

Kathleen Milkey Frame
Sutton, West Virginia

Crock Of Doves

Serves: 4-5
Prep Time: 10 hours

20 doves	**12 oz. fresh mushrooms**
4 cups water	**2 T. parsley**
2 bay leaves	**1 tsp. sage**
1 pt. red wine	**1 tsp. salt**
1 large onion, chopped	**½ tsp. black pepper**

Bone breasts and set aside. Put bony bird parts into kettle with water and bay leaves. Bring to boil, cover tightly, reduce heat and simmer for 1 hour, or until meat can be pulled from bones. Discard bay leaves, but save broth. Pick meat from bones and add to pot. Discard bones. Strain broth and add to kettle. Turn heat to low. Add wine, breasts, onion, mushrooms, parsley, sage, salt and pepper. Cook for 8 hours on low, adding more sage, salt and pepper 30 minutes before serving, if needed. Serve over a bed of rice.

"Wild" Bill Rought, Jr.
Owega, New York

Dove In A Blanket

Serves: 4
Prep Time: 30-45 minutes

16 doves, cleaned	**8 bacon strips, cut in half**
8 jalapeno peppers	**Worcestershire sauce**
salt and pepper	**butter**

Line 3-inch baking pan with foil to retain juices. Place ½ jalapeno pepper inside each bird cavity. Season tops of birds with salt and pepper. Wrap each bird with bacon strips and secure with toothpicks. Shake tops of birds with Worcestershire sauce and brush lightly with butter. Bake uncovered at 350 degrees until birds are done, about 20 minutes. Serve with wild rice cooked with mushrooms. A burgundy or dry rose wine goes well with this dinner.

Jennie Crowder
Johnson City, Texas

Grouse-Au-Chanterelle Pilaf

Serves: 6-8
Prep Time: 1 hour, 30 minutes

2 grouse	**1 cup mushrooms**
1 T. salt	**3 T. cornstarch**
1 tsp. pepper	**2 cups brown rice,**
1 small onion, chopped	**steamed (measured**
2 chicken bouillon cubes	**before cooking)**
1 cup celery, chopped	

Place birds in large covered sauce pan and add enough water to
¾ cover them. Add salt, pepper, onion and bouillon cubes and
bring to a boil. Remove meat from bones. Cube meat into ½-inch
pieces and return to broth, discarding bones. Add celery and
mushrooms and simmer for approximately 1 hour. Add
cornstarch mixed with water, stirring frequently until cornstarch
has thickened the mixture to a thin gravy consistency. Serve
while piping hot over a bed of steamed brown rice.

Robert Mason
Pierce, Idaho

Turtle Creek Grouse

Serves: 2
Prep Time: 45 minutes

2 grouse	**2 T. water**
¼ cup port wine	**½ tsp. orange rind, grated**
¼ cup butter	**parsley**
¼ cup orange juice	

Grouse should be at room temperature. Preheat oven to 450
degrees. In sauce pan, bring port wine, butter, orange juice,
water and rind to a boil. Place birds in roasting pan and pour
liquid over birds equally. Bake for 30 minutes, basting frequently.
Take scrapings from roasting pan, mix with water and heat for
sauce. Garnish with parsley.

Stephen Kaminski
Derry, New Hampshire

Grouse And Dumplings

Serves: 2
Prep Time: 1 hour

1 **grouse and giblets**	1½ **cups flour**
1 **potato, cubed**	2 **tsp. baking powder**
2 **carrots, sliced**	¾ **tsp. salt**
3 **T. shortening (bacon grease is best)**	¾ **cup milk (half & half is best)**

Put grouse in kettle, cover with water. Add potatoes and carrots. Boil 10 minutes. Mix shortening, flour, baking powder and salt. Stir in milk. Drop spoonfuls of dough into boiling grouse. Cook uncovered for 10 minutes. Cover and cook 10 minutes more or until dumplings are done.

Matt Olson
Toutle, Washington

Jana's Savory Sauteed Grouse

Serves: 2
Prep Time: 3 hours

2 **grouse**	2 **tsp. seasoned salt**
	1 **T. oregano**
Flour Mixture:	3 **T. oil**
flour	1 **medium onion, chopped**
½ **T. celery salt**	¼ **cup celery, chopped**
½ **T. garlic salt**	1 **cup water**
1 **T. onion salt**	3 **T. Worcestershire sauce**

Cut grouse from bone into pieces (easiest if bird is semi-frozen) and roll in flour mixture. Brown in oil. After browning, sprinkle any remaining seasoned flour on top. Cover with onions and celery. Add water mixture and simmer until tender, approximately 2 hours. It makes a thick gravy so more water may be needed as it cooks. Serve over noodles. If more water is needed, check seasoning.

Jana Kytchak
Greenville, Pennsylvania

Wild Grouse Deluxe

Serves: 4-6
Prep Time: 1 hour, 30 minutes

3 grouse	**1 cup flour**
1 egg, slightly beaten	**¼ cup butter**
½ cup milk	**½ cup oil**
1 tsp. salt	**1 can golden mushroom**
1 tsp. pepper	**soup**
garlic salt	**1 cup water**

Clean grouse and cut into serving pieces. Dip pieces in mixture of egg, milk, salt, pepper, garlic salt, and roll in flour. Put butter and oil in skillet and heat. Brown grouse on all sides. Remove from skillet and place in a single layer in pan. Add drippings from skillet to mushroom soup and mix well. Spoon over pieces of grouse. Add water to bottom of pan. Cover with foil and bake at 350 degrees for 1 hour until tender.

"Sweet Sue"
Narraway River Outfitting
Goodfare, Alberta

Oven Stewed Grouse

Serves: 4
Prep Time: 2 hours

2 large grouse, quartered	**½ cup carrots, ¼-inch**
salt and pepper	**slices**
½ stick butter/margarine	**½ cup sliced mushrooms**
2 onions, thinly sliced	**¼ tsp. sage**
2 celery stalks, cut ½-inch	**6 pork sausages**
thick	**2 cups chicken bouillon**

Sprinkle bird parts with salt and pepper. Melt butter in large skillet and brown birds over medium heat. In covered pan, make a layer of onions, celery, carrots and mushrooms. Sprinkle with sage. Place sausage in ring around outer edge of layered vegetables and place grouse quarters in center. Pour on chicken broth and cover. Bake at 325 degrees for 1-2 hours.

Anonymous

Oyster Stuffed Grouse

Serves: 2-4
Prep Time: 1 hour, 30 minutes

2 whole grouse or 4 breasts	**4-6 whole grain bread slices**
½ cup butter	**¼ tsp. garlic powder**
1 8-oz. can oysters	**¼ tsp. pepper**
1 large onion	**½ tsp. poultry seasoning**
	1 tsp. crumbled parsley

Melt butter over low heat in liquid drained from can of oysters. Dice oysters, onion and bread slices. Add seasoning and mix. Pour butter mixture over all and mix well. Cut a large piece of aluminum foil to cover bottom of 13x9-inch pan and leave plenty of extra on all ends to fold up over grouse. Lay stuffed birds on foil or put dressing on foil and place breasts on top. Rub butter on birds or breasts. Cover and seal foil edges well. Bake 1 hour at 350 degrees.

Judy Bean
Grangeville, Idaho

Blue Grouse With Wild Rice

Serves: 4
Prep Time: 1 hour

1 blue grouse	**½ cup onions, chopped**
1 cup flour	**1 cup cooking wine**
salt and pepper	**½ pt. whipping cream**
½ cup butter	**wild rice**
1 cup mushrooms	**parsley (optional)**

Combine flour, salt and pepper. Roll grouse in mixture and brown in butter. Remove grouse. Add mushrooms and onions and cook until done. Return grouse to pan, add wine and simmer 30 minutes. Remove grouse and add whipping cream to drippings. Stir until smooth. Arrange over wild rice on warm platter, adding parsley if desired.

Jeff Wolaver
Colorado Springs, Colorado

Moist Grouse With Rice

Serves: 4
Prep Time: 1 hour, 15 minutes

4 grouse breasts	**sliced mushrooms**
1 can peas	**salt and pepper**
1 can chicken broth	**poultry seasoning**
water	**parsley**
1 cup cooked rice (not	
Minute Rice)	

Preheat oven to 350 degrees. In shallow baking dish, place peas, including juice from can. Add chicken broth with enough water to make 2 cups. Spread rice across evenly, topping with sliced mushrooms. Season grouse breasts with salt, pepper, poultry seasoning and place across mixture in baking dish. Sprinkle entire thing with a little more salt, pepper and poultry seasoning and some dry parsley. Cover with foil and bake for 1 hour.

John Robinson
Coopersburg, Pennsylvania

Grouse Casserole

Serves: 4
Prep Time: 45 minutes

2 whole grouse, skinned,	**4 fresh mushrooms, diced**
cut into ½-inch pieces	**salt and pepper**
butter	**1 can cream of mushroom**
1 celery stalk, diced	**soup**
1 medium onion, sliced	**½ cup white wine**
4 water chestnuts, diced	

Saute grouse in butter with celery, onion, water chestnuts and mushrooms. Season with salt and pepper to taste. Remove from heat. Dilute mushroom soup with white wine and add to grouse mixture. Put all ingredients in covered casserole. Bake at 350 degrees for 45 minutes. Serve over wild rice.

Bob Keller
Edina, Minnesota

Roast Partridge

Serves: 2-3
Prep Time: 1 hour

2 **partridges**	8 **mushrooms, chopped**
salt and pepper	1 **small onion, chopped**
1½ **cups cooked wild rice or**	1 **cup chicken bouillon**
wild and brown rice	**poultry seasonings**
mixed	¼ **cup water**

Sprinkle birds with salt and pepper. Mix rice, mushrooms, onion and broth. Add poultry seasoning, salt and pepper to taste. Spoon mixture into each bird, closing cavities with small skewers. Place birds in roaster with water. Bake 25-30 minutes at 400 degrees.

Anonymous

Phineas' Partridge Pie

Serves: 3-4
Prep Time: 2-3 hours

3 **partridge**	3 **T. flour**
½ **lb. veal, cut ½-inch**	2 **cups bouillon**
thick	2 **whole cloves**
1¼ **tsp. salt**	1 **cup mushrooms, sliced**
⅛ **tsp. pepper**	2 **T. butter or margarine**
6 **bacon slices**	1 **T. parsley, chopped**
¼ **cup bacon fat**	**sherry**
1 **T. salad oil**	**flaky pastry**

Cut partridge in half lengthwise. Slice veal into 6 strips. Sprinkle partridge and veal with 1 tsp. salt and ⅛ tsp. pepper. Cut bacon slices in half. Saute until golden brown. Put partridge in 2-qt. casserole. Cover with veal and bacon. Add salad oil and flour to bacon fat in skillet. Stir in bouillon. Cook until thick. Add cloves, remaining salt. Pour over meat. Cover and bake at 350 degrees 1 hour. Saute mushrooms in butter and place with parsley over ingredients in casserole. Pour sherry over all. Top with dough ⅛-inch thick. Bake at 450 degrees uncovered.

Phineas Lea
Auburn, Georgia

Partridge Or Quail In A Basket With Lemon Butter

Serves: 4
Prep Time: 2 hours

8 quail or partridge	**2 lemons, use juice**
4 large russet potatoes	**½ cup dry white wine**
salt and black pepper	**2 T. parsley, chopped**
¼ lb. butter	**¼ lb. butter**

Bake potatoes and hollow out top portion large enough for bird to fit in; set aside. Season birds with salt and pepper and fry in ¼ lb. butter until brown. Squeeze lemons over birds. Put birds in potato nests, legs pointing outward. In same pan, add wine and chopped parsley. Swirl in ¼ lb. butter to make creamy. Pour over bird and potato.

Scott Eckenberg
Eden Prairie, Minnesota

Poulet Aux Fines Herbes

Serves: 4
Prep Time: 1 hour

3 lbs. pheasant or partridge	**2½ cups dry white wine**
3 T. butter	**3 garlic cloves, chopped**
3 T. oil	**2 bay leaves**
2 onions, chopped	**¼ cup parsley, minced**
4 cloves	**¼ tsp. thyme**
1 10-oz. jar sliced mushrooms	

Melt butter in oil. Saute birds over medium heat. Remove. Slice root ends off onions; stick in cloves. Chop rest of onions; saute. Slice mushrooms and add to pan. Saute until golden brown. Add birds, wine, garlic (stuck into onion slices), bay leaves, parsley and thyme. Cover. Cook over low heat for 30-40 minutes or until tender. Remove garlic cloves and bay leaves.

Herb Scharff
Evanston, Illinois

Pheasant En Creme

Serves: 8
Prep Time: 2-3 hours

4 **pheasants**	2 **cups light cream**
flour	1 **cup dry sherry**
salt and pepper	2 **tsp. tarragon leaves**
butter	2 **T. Worcestershire sauce**
cooking oil	**paprika**
4 **cans cream of**	
mushroom soup	

Cut pheasants in half or section; wash and pat dry. Shake pieces in bag with seasoned flour to coat. Brown lightly in butter and oil. Arrange in shallow baking pan, cut side down. Combine undiluted soup with remaining ingredients, except paprika, in skillet used for browning. Heat and stir until smooth. Pour over pheasant. Sprinkle with paprika. Bake uncovered at 350 degrees for 1-2 hours. Baste several times with sauce during baking. Sprinkle paprika once more.

Avis Roe
Golden Valley, Minnesota

Pheasant Parisienne

Serves: 3-4
Prep Time: 6-8 hours

1 **pheasant, cut up**	½ **cup dry white wine**
salt and pepper	1 **4-oz. can mushroom**
paprika	**slices**
1 **can cream of mushroom**	1 **cup sour cream**
soup	¼ **cup flour**

Sprinkle pheasant lightly with salt, pepper and paprika. Place in Crockpot. Mix soup, wine and mushrooms and pour over pheasant. Sprinkle with paprika. Cover and cook on low 6-8 hours. Mix sour cream and flour. Remove pheasant while stirring sour cream mixture during last 30 minutes. Serve with rice.

Eugene Fletcher
Lebanon, New Jersey

Joe Martin's Herb Roasted Pheasant

Serves: 4
Prep Time: 1 hour, 30 minutes

1 **pheasant, plucked**	1 **tsp. rosemary**
1½ **cups cooked rice**	½ **tsp. thyme**
¼ **cup onion, chopped**	½ **tsp. garlic powder**
¼ **cup celery, chopped**	**salt and pepper**
⅔ **cup butter or margarine**	

Prepare rice and set aside. Saute onion and celery until tender, about 5 minutes. Stuff pheasant making sure not too full. Stitch closed with poultry skewers. Preheat oven to 350 degrees. Melt butter and add rosemary, thyme and garlic powder. Baste bird several times during cooking. Place bird in roasting pan and cook 60-75 minutes until bird is nicely browned and drumsticks move easily. Salt and pepper to taste.

Joseph Martin
Fremont, California

Pheasant In Red Wine Sauce

Serves: 4
Prep Time: 1 hour, 30 minutes

2 **pheasants, cut up**	2 **chicken bouillon cubes**
½ **cup pancake mix**	1 **cup hot water**
½ **cup butter**	½ **lemon, use juice**
2 **cups fresh mushrooms, sliced**	1 **tsp. pepper**
1 **onion, chopped**	1 **tsp. salt**
	¼ **cup dry red wine**

Roll pheasant in pancake mix. Saute in butter until brown. Remove. Saute mushroom and onion in butter until brown. Dissolve bouillon cubes in 1 cup hot water. Replace pheasant in skillet and add remaining ingredients, except wine. Cover and cook over low heat for 1 hour or until tender. Stir in dry red wine 15 minutes before end of cooking time.

Dave Perkins
Accokeek, Maryland

Smothered Pheasant

Serves: 4
Prep Time: 2 hours

1 pheasant	**salt and pepper**
flour	**1 cup milk**

Cut pheasant into serving-size pieces. Roll in flour seasoned with salt and pepper. Brown slowly on both sides in hot fat, turning only once. Add milk, cover tightly and bake at 325 degrees for 1 hour or until tender. Serve with gravy made from drippings. Old pheasants are best prepared in this manner.

Irene Burke
Edina, Minnesota

Pheasant In Sherry

Serves: 2-4
Prep Time: 4 hours

2 pheasants, boned and cut into bite-size pieces	**1 green onion, cut in julienne-style strips**
sherry	**1 zucchini, sliced**
1 T. teriyaki sauce	**1 carrot, sliced**
2 green onions, chopped (including tops)	**2 T. peanut oil**
1 4-oz. can sliced mushrooms	

Place pheasant meat in glass bowl and add enough sherry to cover. Add teriyaki sauce. Cover and refrigerate 3 hours. Heat peanut oil in large heavy skillet or wok. Take pheasant out of marinade and dry. Be careful if there is any moisture on pheasant as it will splatter. Quickly cook pheasant, remove and set aside. Add remaining ingredients to wok or skillet and stir-fry quickly until tender. Add pheasant and heat through quickly. Remove to plate and serve with hot rice and additional teriyaki sauce.

Donald Gasaway
Mound Prospect, Illinois

Dorsey's Pheasant Divan

Serves: 5-7
Prep Time: 50 minutes

- **3 pheasants, pressure cooked or boiled**
- **2 pkgs. frozen broccoli**
- **butter**
- **2 cans cream of chicken soup**
- **½ cup Miracle Whip**
- **1 tsp. lemon juice**
- **½ cup shredded cheese**
- **1 cup cornflakes**

Boil broccoli 7 minutes and drain. Place in buttered casserole dish. Place pheasant meat on top of broccoli. Combine soup, Miracle Whip and lemon juice and pour over pheasant and broccoli. Spread cheese over all. Bake at 350 degrees for 40 minutes. Add cornflakes and bake uncovered for 10 minutes.

Chris Dorsey
DeForest, Wisconsin

Pheasant Supreme

Serves: 3-4
Prep Time: 2 hours

- **2 pheasants**
- **flour**
- **¼ lb. butter or margarine**
- **salt and pepper**
- **1 8-10-oz. can cream of mushroom soup**
- **1 8-10-oz. can cream of celery or onion soup**
- **1 4-oz. can mushrooms (optional)**
- **¼ cup dry, red or white wine (optional)**

Bone and cut pheasants into ¼-inch thick pieces. Remove remaining buckshot. Roll pheasant pieces in flour. Saute in butter or margarine using deep skillet at medium heat for 20-30 minutes. Salt and pepper to taste. Add remaining ingredients and simmer (covered) over low heat for 1 hour or until tender. Serve over boiled potatoes and carrots as a stew or over noodles, rice, toast or baking powder biscuits.

Donald Portratz
Brooklyn Park, Minnesota

Pheasant Corn Chowder

Serves: 6-8
Prep Time: several hours

2 **pheasants**	2 **cups milk**
1 **cup celery, chopped**	3 **drops Tabasco sauce**
1 **chicken bouillon cube**	4 **T. butter**
1 **potato, cubed**	1 **tsp. pimento, chopped**
1 **pkg. frozen corn**	**paprika**
½ **cup mushrooms,**	**salt and pepper**
chopped	**parsley**

Stew pheasant in 1 qt. water with celery, bouillon and onion until the legs are tender. Cool and strip meat carefully from the bones. Chop into bite-size pieces. Use broth as the base for chowder. Add enough water to make 1 qt. liquid. Add potato and cook for 15 minutes. Add corn and cook 5 minutes. Add meat and mushrooms. Stir in milk slowly. Add Tabasco sauce, butter, pimento, paprika, salt and pepper. Serve garnished with parsley.

E. Jenkins
Elkland, Pennsylvania

Pheasant Patties

Serves: 2-4
Prep Time: 1 hour

ground pheasant meat	**cooking oil**
1 **egg, beaten**	1 **can cream of mushroom**
salt and pepper	**soup**
dried bread crumbs	

Use pheasant meat from legs and breasts which have been torn or shot up too much to keep whole, and grind it. Form meat into patties. Dip patties into beaten egg, season with salt and pepper and roll in bread crumbs. Fry in oil for 20-30 minutes on low heat or pour soup over patties, place in casserole dish and bake at 350 degrees for 1 hour.

Mrs. Ken Reuter
Humboldt, South Dakota

Curried Quail

Serves: 2
Prep Time: 1 hour

4 quail, cut in halves	**parsley**
salt and pepper	**1 can cream of mushroom**
1 medium onion or 8 large	**soup**
shallots	**long grain and wild rice**
4 T. curry powder	

Rub each quail half with salt and pepper and place in roasting pan. Slice onions on top. Sprinkle on curry powder and parsley and pour soup over. Roast at 350 degrees for 50 minutes. Serve with rice mixture.

Theodore Vasilik
Ft. Myers, Florida

Quail Italiano

Serves: several
Prep Time: 4 hours

6-8 quail breasts	**1 #303 can tomatoes,**
cooking oil	**drained**
1 cup milk	**1-2 cans sliced mushrooms,**
1 cup flour	**drained**
½ cup Parmesan cheese	**3 small cans tomato sauce**
1 cup onion, chopped or	**or 2 cans sauce, 1 paste**
sliced	**Italian seasonings**
1 cup green pepper,	**salt and pepper**
chopped or sliced	

Cover bottom of large, deep frying pan with oil. Turn to medium-high heat. Dip quail breasts into milk, roll in flour and then cheese. Fry coated breasts until golden brown. Stir in onions, green pepper, tomatoes and mushrooms. Add tomato sauce and paste. Bring to slight boil, cover and let simmer until onion and pepper are cooked. Add any Italian seasonings to taste. Serve over spaghetti.

Dr. John Woods
Hattiesburg, Mississippi

Lloyd's Quail Delight

Serves: 4-5
Prep Time: 1 hour, 30 minutes

7-9 quail
1 tsp. salt
¼ tsp. pepper
¼ cup flour
butter

⅓ cup white cooking wine
2 large onions, diced
6 celery stalks, sliced
6 carrots, sliced
3 green peppers, sliced

Mix salt, pepper and flour in paper bag. Place 3 quail at a time in bag and shake well. Brown quail in large skillet in butter. Add wine by pouring over quail. Add onions, celery, carrots and green peppers. Cover skillet and simmer 1 hour.

R. Scott Lloyd
Hernando, Mississippi

Dutch Oven Quail

Serves: 4-6
Prep Time: 2 hours

6-8 quail, dressed
⅓ cup olive oil or butter
2 garlic cloves, minced (or garlic salt)
1 medium onion, minced
¾ cup parsley, chopped
½ cup green pepper, chopped

¾ cup sauterne or other white wine
2 8-oz. cans tomato sauce
1 cup (or can) mushrooms
pinch of thyme
pinch rosemary
salt and pepper

Heat oil or butter in hot Dutch oven. Fry birds to red-brown color, turning frequently to assure even heating. Add garlic, onion, parsley and green pepper. Fry until tender and golden. Add wine and cover, lowering heat to simmer. A few minutes later, add tomato sauce, mushrooms and seasoning. Continue simmering for 1 hour, 30 minutes. Serve over rice or noodles.

Chuck Buck
El Cajon, California

King's Quail

Serves: 4
Prep Time: 2 hours, 30 minutes

8 **quail, cut into**	½ **tsp. instant minced onion**
lengthwise halves	½ **tsp. curry powder**
¾ **tsp. seasoned salt**	**dash of pepper**
paprika	2 **T. flour**
1 **chicken bouillon cube**	¼ **cup cold water**
1 **cup boiling water**	1 **3-oz. can sliced**
¼ **cup red wine**	**mushrooms**

Sprinkle quail with seasoned salt and paprika. Place in 11x7x½"
baking pan. Dissolve bouillon cube in boiling water, adding
wine, minced onion, curry powder and pepper. Pour over quail
and cover with foil. Bake at 350 degrees for 30 minutes. Uncover
and bake 35 minutes longer. Remove quail and strain pan juices.
In saucepan, blend flour with water. Stir in slowly with pan juices.
Cook while stirring over low heat until sauce bubbles. Boil 3-4
minutes. Add mushrooms and spoon over quail.

Tony Caligiuri
Tulsa, Oklahoma

Baked Quail

Serves: 4-6
Prep Time: 1 hour, 15 minutes

6 **quail**	¼ **cup butter**
4 **T. Worcestershire sauce**	2 **T. molasses**
½-1 **T. olive oil**	**salt and pepper**
3 **lemons, use juice**	1 **tsp. prepared mustard**

Put quail in roasting pan with water covering bottom of pan.
Cover and bake at 300 degrees. Combine other ingredients and
blend over low heat. When quail have cooked 30 minutes,
remove from oven. Pour sauce over quail, cover and cook 35
minutes, basting frequently. During last 10 minutes of cooking
time, remove cover to brown birds and thicken sauce.

Jeff Hunt
Orange Park, Florida

Sage Hen Spaghetti Sauce

Serves: 6-8
Prep Time: 6-8 hours

**2-3 sage hens—use any
small game or upland
gamebird meat**
2 16-oz. cans tomato sauce
**1 16-oz. can stewed
tomatoes**

4 T. dehydrated onions
**8 oz. sliced pepperoni, cut
in small pieces**

Bone and cut meat into small pieces and brown in large skillet or
pan. Add tomato sauce, stewed tomatoes, onions and pepperoni
and stir the mixture. Simmer 6-8 hours, stirring occasionally.
Serve over spaghetti with French bread smothered with garlic
and butter and warmed in the oven or microwave. A fresh, green
salad goes nice with this dish, also.

Michael D. Ferrin
Lyman, Wyoming

Sage Grouse Appetizers

Serves: 4
Prep Time: 30 minutes

**2 sage grouse breasts,
boned and filleted into
thin slices
cooking oil**
1 egg, beaten

½ cup canned milk
1½ cups flour
**½ tsp. salt
fresh ground pepper
pinch of sage**

Heat an inch or so of oil in a pot or skillet. Mix egg and milk
together. In another dish, mix flour and seasonings together. Dip
slices of breast in egg mixture, then in flour and fry quickly in hot
oil, just until golden brown. Be sure you get a head start on
these—your crew and hunters will eat them faster than you can
turn them out!

Coralee McKee
Pinedale, Wyoming

Turkey

National surveys and information provided by NAHC members show that turkey hunting is one of the fastest growing types of hunting in North America today. The miraculous comeback and expansion of wild turkey flocks across the United States are allowing hunting seasons in parts of the country that never heard a gobble 20 years ago.

In his NAHC *Wild Game Cookbook* contribution titled "Turkey From Field To Table," James R. Davis of the Alabama Department of Commerce says that approximately 245 tons of dressed wild turkey can be expected from the 25,000 or so gobblers harvested in Alabama alone this spring, plus the 10,000 turkeys will be taken during the fall season! This meat will be just as palatable and nutritious, if not more so, as any highly-touted brand bought at a market, if proper care is taken with the butchering and freezing process. Many hunters "show off" their harvest to friends and invariably become engaged in conversations. This delays butchering, so precautions should be taken to insure the quality of the meat is maintained after our vanity has been satisfied.

When butchering (or dressing) is anticipated within three to four hours of the kill, it is usually not necessary to field dress or draw your bird. Field dressed gobblers will be subject to some degree of precooking of the tender tissues inside the body cavity if scalding is used to remove the feathers. Drawn birds are also more likely to attract flies even if you plan to remove the feathers by dry picking.

When more hours or even days will elapse before the gobbler can be butchered, field dressing is necessary. The following directions for drawing a turkey gobbler work well:

Lay the turkey on its back. Locate the vent and, with a small, sharp knife, carefully make a 2-inch incision to either side. Then, still with care not to puncture an intestine, cut all the way around the vent. Remove the intestines and other organs from the body cavity through the incision. Separate the heart, liver and gizzard and lay them aside. If clean water is available, rinse the body cavity and hang the bird by the head in a cool and protected place and allow to drain. Clean the liver, heart and gizzard (for your giblet gravy) and refrigerate.

At first opportunity, the feathers should be removed and final butchering completed. Scalding is a good method to use in removing the feathers from your gobbler. To scald a turkey, a large tub of water (one large enough to immerse the body of the bird) should be heated to approximately 150 degrees.

Immerse the body of the turkey in water for one to two minutes. Remove the turkey and pull the feathers off by hand. When this process is completed, there will be some hair-like feathers remaining. These can be removed by using an open flame (from a butane torch or a crumpled newspaper) to singe them off.

A word of caution—be sure to remove the beard by slicing it off even with the body before scalding so the hot water won't ruin it.

Sever the head and neck about two inches from the body. Remove the crop, esophagus and legs below the drumstick. When the skin is free of feathers, wash the blood from both the inside and outside of the carcass and place it in a position so it can drain thoroughly.

When the skin is dry to the touch, insert the liver, heart and gizzard into the body cavity and carefully wrap in freezer paper and freeze. It is best to place the liver, heart and gizzard in a separate package so they won't freeze to the body tissue. Wild turkeys properly prepared will keep well in the freezer.

If you do not wish to scald your turkey, skinning is another method to try. Skinning is especially useful on young birds which will be fried instead of roasted, baked or smoked.

Make a lateral incision along the breast. Then pull the skin back to each side, work it over the wings and off the back. Preparations for the freezer will be the same as described for the scalding method.

An adult wild gobbler will frequently dress out at 15 pounds or more. Usually, this is more meat than is needed for one meal. To reduce leftovers and prevent waste, you may want to saw the frozen carcass in halves or quarters and only cook a part at a time. There should be no problem in roasting or baking less than a whole turkey by properly adjusting any of the recipes that follow.

Bourbon Wild Turkey

Serves: 3
Prep Time: 15 minutes

12 raw turkey breasts, sliced	**½ cup butter**
salt and white pepper, to taste	**¾ cup bourbon**
1 cup flour	**1 medium onion, thinly sliced**

Season turkey slices with salt and white pepper. Dredge in flour and shake off the excess. Fry in butter. Add bourbon and onion slices. When turkey is golden brown, turn heat to low, cover and finish cooking until breasts fall off fork when pierced. Serve with wild rice or chestnut dressing.

Scott Ekenberg
Eden Prairie, Minnesota

Wild Turkey d'St. Germain

Serves: varies
Prep Time: depends on size of turkey

1 wild turkey	**2 cooking onions, chopped**
4 garlic cloves (or garlic powder)	**½ lb. chopped almonds**
bread stuffing (½ corn bread and ½ regular)	**1½ lb. applesauce**
	poultry spices (optional)
6-8 sweet apples, diced	**salt and pepper, to taste**
	4 lbs. prepared sauerkraut

Slice 2 garlic cloves and rub on turkey. Combine bread stuffing, apples, onions, almonds, 2 garlic cloves and applesauce. Fill cavity of turkey, securing well. (Add poultry spices and salt and pepper to taste.) Mix sauerkraut mixture in bottom of roasting pan (should be at least 1 inch deep). Place stuffed turkey in roaster with breast down on bed of kraut. Roast with lid on (but vented) for 30 minutes to the pound. Remove lid last 30 minutes to brown (more if needed). Serve kraut as a side dish.

Robert d'St. Germain-Iler
Glendale, California

Paul Rankin's Breast Of Wild Turkey

Serves: 6
Prep Time: 2 hours

2 **lbs. breast of wild turkey**	2 **oz. pumpernickel bread**
3 **oz. turkey leg meat, coarsely chopped**	3 **oz. dried pitted prunes, soaked overnight**
3 **oz. pork fat or bacon, coarsely chopped**	1 **bunch caraway thyme (or regular thyme)**
	¼ **cup cream**

Remove breast from turkey carcass with sharp knife and trim.
Carefully make an incision along length of breast to create a
pocket. To make stuffing, lightly saute bacon and leg meat. Add
pumpernickel bread, prunes, half of caraway thyme and cream.
Bring to a boil, check seasoning. Put in food processor and use
pulse action until you have a course ground mixture. Stuff pocket
with mixture. Wrap breast firmly in buttered foil to help keep its
shape. Roast breast at 400 degrees for 15 minutes or until done.
For sauce, loosen any caramelized juices from pan with a little
white wine. Reduce by half. Add 1 cup turkey or chicken stock,
the rest of caraway thyme and ¼ cup cream. Reduce to desired
consistency. Correct seasoning. Slice stuffed breast and serve
with sauce.

Paul Rankin
Calistoga, California

Deep Fried Turkey

Serves: 2
Prep Time: 10 minutes

1 **wild turkey breast fillet, cut into ½-inch thick pieces across grain**	**crushed cracker crumbs**

Dip turkey in cracker crumbs and deep fry in 350-degree
cooking oil. Takes from 5-7 minutes.

James Sanders
Orrtanna, Pennsylvania

Roast Wild Turkey

Serves: 4-6
Prep Time: depends on size of turkey

1 **wild turkey, dressed**	1 **T. pepper**
stuffing (prepared in	4 **strips bacon**
advance)	1 **cup sherry**
½ **T. salt**	

To prepare for roasting, wipe turkey clean inside and out with damp cloth. Stuff with stuffing, truss, salt and pepper. Place 4 bacon strips on breast. Roast uncovered for 1 hour at 325-350 degrees. After first hour, soak heavy paper towel with sherry and place over bird. Baste every 10 minutes with drippings. Most wild turkeys weigh 8-15 pounds dressed. Roast 15-20 minutes per pound. Baste frequently.

Russel Browning
Santa Rosa, California

Jake Slayer's Delight

Serves: 4
Prep Time: 1 hour, 30 minutes

turkey breast fillets	1 **tsp. mustard**
1 **cup lemon juice**	1 **tsp. cayenne pepper**
1 **tsp. cooking oil**	1 **can sliced mushrooms**
½ **cup flour**	½ **cup white wine**
½ **cup cornmeal**	

Fillet and skin breasts from young turkey. Marinate fillets for 1-2 hours in ½ cup lemon juice. Heat oil in skillet. Remove breasts from marinade. Pound breasts with the side of a large knife into slabs ¼- to ⅜-inch thick. Dredge meat in a combination of dry ingredients and fry quickly, about 5 minutes or so, until tender. Place on plate in warm oven. Saute mushrooms quickly. Add remainder of lemon juice and white wine. Simmer mixture until it begins reducing. Ladle mixture over hot fillets as a sauce.

Bill Miller
Chaska, Minnesota

Gobbler A la Mojo

Serves: several
Prep Time: 4 hours

1 **wild turkey**	**black pepper**
1 **stick butter**	**stuffing (your favorite)**
salt	6 **T. flour**

Remove neck and giblets from turkey and set aside. Melt butter and brush on turkey. Sprinkle inside and out with salt and black pepper. Add stuffing to cavity and sew shut. Tuck drumsticks under bird and fold wings to body. If bird is large, (older than a jake), wrap completely with foil before placing in roasting pan to keep bird moist and tender. Cook at 400 degrees, 15-20 minutes per pound. About 45 minutes before done, begin basting with juices or melted butter. If using meat thermometer, bird is done when dial reads 185 degrees. Turkey should cool 20 minutes before carving. While bird is cooking, finely chop giblets and boil in lightly salted water with neck. Simmer until giblets are tender. Add water and flour to stock to make turkey gravy. Add salt and pepper to taste.

Bob Collins
Minneapolis, Minnesota

Barbecued Turkey

Serves: 6-8
Prep Time: 2-3 hours

1 **8-lb. turkey**	1 **T. butter**
olive oil	2 **T. paprika**
5 **T. honey**	2 **T. cayenne pepper**
4 **T. catsup (hot)**	1 **T. lemon juice**
4 **T. brown sugar**	

Brush turkey lightly with olive oil and place on grill. Mix remaining ingredients together to form marinade. Add marinade to bird. Roast until done, basting often.

J.B. Johnson
Washington, Pennsylvania

Dave's Kitchen Sink Smoked Turkey

Serves: 6-8
Prep Time: 8-10 hours

1 **wild turkey**	**salt**
melted butter	**seasoned salt**
honey	**poultry seasoning**
maple syrup	**sweet basil**
soy sauce	**prepared mustard**
cayenne pepper	**garlic powder**
white pepper	**onion powder**
black pepper	

It's easy to see how this recipe got its name. You include everything but the kitchen sink. The actual ingredients you use are up to you, depending on what you like and have got around the kitchen. Combine melted butter, honey, maple syrup and soy sauce to create a thick sauce. Paint turkey liberally inside and out with this mixture. Combine dry ingredients and rub generously all over turkey inside and out. Paint bird one more time with the sauce. Put turkey on smoker or gas grill in smoker mode. For even more unusual flavor use fruit juice, wine or beer in drip pan. Slow cook for 8-10 hours.

Dave VanOrden
Glencoe, Minnesota

Smoked Wild Turkey

Serves: varies
Prep Time: 8-12 hours

1 **turkey**	2 **medium onions,**
1 **T. salt**	**quartered**

Rinse turkey with cold water. Rub inside and out with salt. Quarter onions and put inside bird. Fill water pan underneath bird. Smoke 8-12 hours, until leg moves easily in joint or meat thermometer reaches 180 degrees. Keep pan filled with water.

Rick Ranshaw
Traverse City, Michigan

Seasoned Smoked Wild Turkey

Serves: varies
Prep Time: 8-12 hours

1 **turkey**	2 **T. melted butter**
¼ **cup oil**	1 **T. Worcestershire sauce**
¼ **cup burgundy**	**salt and pepper, to taste**
⅓ **cup lemon juice**	**marjoram**

Clean and rinse turkey with cold water. Rub inside and out with mixture of above ingredients. Put remaining mixture in water pan. Fill water pan beneath bird. Smoke 8-12 hours until leg moves easily in joint or meat thermometer reaches 180 degrees. Keep the pan filled with water throughout the smoking process.

Rick Ranshaw
Traverse City, Michigan

Turkey Patties

Serves: 6
Prep Time: 30 minutes

2 **cups turkey, cubed**	1½ **tsp. dry mustard**
4 **T. butter**	1 **chicken bouillon cube**
2 **green onions, chopped**	2 **cups milk**
2 **T. cornstarch**	1 **T. Worcestershire sauce**
1½ **tsp. salt**	6 **large patty shells**
¼ **tsp. pepper**	2 **tsp. parsley, chopped**

Melt butter and saute green onions. Blend in cornstarch. Remove from heat and coil slightly. Add salt, pepper and dry mustard. Dissolve bouillon cube in milk, and slowly add to pepper mixture. Add Worcestershire sauce, turkey and parsley, and cook over medium heat, stirring constantly until mixture thickens and comes to a boil. Cook another minute, stirring steadily so mixture doesn't stick. Spoon mixture into the patty shells, or use as a filling for crepes.

Darren McClain
O'Fallen, Missouri

Wild Turkey Supreme

Serves: 10-15
Prep Time: 9 hours

1 12-16 lb. wild turkey	**4 bacon strips**
1 onion, peeled	**1 garlic head, unpeeled**
4 parsley sprigs	**and separated**
2 carrots, peeled	

Preheat water smoker or start fire with full pan of charcoal. Pat turkey dry inside and out. Stuff cavity with onion, parsley and carrots. Sew and truss. Place bacon over turkey breast. When fire is ready, add green or pre-soaked hickory chips or chunks. Put filled water pan in place and add garlic cloves to water. Place turkey on food grid and keep temperature constant at about 200-225 degrees. Cook for 6-9 hours, depending on size of turkey, until internal temperature reads 180 degrees.

Anonymous

Savory Turkey Cutlets

Serves: 4
Prep Time: 45 minutes

1 lb. turkey breast, boned	**¼ cup grated Parmesan**
1 egg	**2 T. dried savory**
1 T. milk	**2 T. dried thyme**
1 cup whole wheat bread	**whole wheat flour**
crumbs	**3 T. butter**
½ cup wheat germ	**3 T. oil**

Cut turkey breast into ⅜-inch thick slices. Place each slice between 2 sheets of waxed paper and pound with meat tenderizer or mallet. In shallow dish, beat 1 egg and 1 T. milk. In another dish, combine bread crumbs, wheat germ, Parmesan, savory and thyme. Dredge turkey in flour, and dip into egg mixture. Dredge in crumb mixture. Heat 2 T. each of butter and oil in frying pan. Fry over medium heat until brown on both sides and cooked thoroughly. Add more butter and oil as needed.

Dan Haskell
Springville, Iowa

Wild Turkey Soup

Serves: 8-10
Prep Time: 4 hours

1 **turkey**	½ **tsp. poultry seasoning**
4-5 **qts. water**	**turkey gravy and**
4 **medium carrots**	**stuffing left over from**
1 **small cabbage head**	**roast turkey dinner**
3 **celery stalks**	1 **lb. small macaroni,**
1 **tsp. salt**	**precooked**
½ **tsp. pepper**	

Remove meat from turkey bones. Place bones in 8-qt. pot and cover with water. Simmer 2 hours or long enough to loosen meat from bones, but not long enough for bones to fall apart in broth. While bones are simmering, grind all vegetables in meat grinder. When bones are done, set aside to cool. Add ground vegetables and juice from vegetables and seasonings. Add any stuffing and remaining gravy. Simmer 2 hours. Clean remaining meat from bones, and add to soup. When vegetable bits are tender and broth tastes right, add cooked macaroni. Let stand several hours before serving to allow flavor development.

Rob Keck
Edgefield, South Carolina

Peach Gobbler

Serves: 4
Prep Time: 1 hour

1 **turkey breast, sliced**	2 **cups bread crumbs**
2 **eggs**	**salt and pepper**
3 **T. milk**	½ **cup butter**

Roll turkey breasts in a mixture of eggs and milk. Dip in bread crumbs. Add salt and pepper. Heat butter in frying pan and brown turkey pieces. Reduce heat. Cover pan and let simmer 30 minutes. Cook until meat flakes off with a fork.

Jerome Hinderman
Cuba City, Wisconsin

Mountain State Turkey Stroganoff

Serves: 6
Prep Time: 1 hour

**4 cups white and dark
turkey meat (cooked)**
12 oz. turkey gravy
¾ cup milk
1 can mushroom soup
1 can mixed vegetables
1 tsp. salt
¼ tsp. pepper

½ tsp. celery seed
**½ cup green pepper,
chopped**
½ cup onion, chopped
1 cup water
**1 4-oz. pkg. shredded mild
cheddar cheese**

Preheat oven to 325 degrees. Put turkey meat, gravy, milk and mushroom soup into cooking pan and heat until warm. In another cooking pan add mixed vegetables, salt, pepper, celery seed, green pepper, onion and water; cook 5-10 minutes. Drain water and combine in baking dish. Add cheddar cheese on top. Bake until cheese melts.

Kenneth W. Crummett
Moyers, West Virginia

Wild Turkey Tortellini

Serves: 3-4
Prep Time: 45 minutes

1 lb. ground wild turkey
1 pkg. tortellini noodles
**1 can cream of mushroom
soup**
**1 can cream of celery
soup**

seasoned salt to taste
**½ cup white wine
(optional)**

Brown turkey in frying pan. Boil tortellini in kettle for 20 minutes. While boiling, add soup to turkey and bring to a boil, stirring occasionally. Lower heat, add seasonings and wine. Simmer 10-15 minutes. Drain tortellini and add to turkey combination. Serve with hot buttered dinner rolls and vegetable.

Jon Morem
Hopkins, Minnesota

Basic Cooking Skills

by Bob Collins

*D*o you know what used to really frustrate me about cooking? It wasn't finding good recipes, deciphering the recipes or running around town trying to find all the ingredients. My problem was I hadn't mastered a lot of the basic cooking skills I needed in order to finish some recipes.

The things that used to buffalo me are probably some of the same things that bother you. However, follow the simple instructions in this section and you'll master some of the most important basic cooking techniques. You'll be amazed at how simple some of these tricks really are.

But first, let's establish the importance of two related cooking ideas: time and temperature. Unless you take both into consideration on every meal, your chances of success are greatly reduced.

Of the two, temperature is most important. So, the first order of business is to check the accuracy of the temperature dial on your oven by using an inexpensive oven thermometer. Preheat the oven to 350 degrees (a common temperature in recipes) and, after it stabilizes for a few minutes, read the thermometer. Now you can see how far off your oven is when the temperature dial is set at 350.

It would also be a good idea to have an oil thermometer on hand so your fried creations turn out better.

Stock—The Cooking Necessity

Sometimes I'm amazed at how much insight our ancestors demonstrated. We've all been surprised to learn how some of our most common practices originated. One of those discoveries—meat stock—has contributed to some of our most basic flavor traditions.

Stock is one of the fundamental ingredients in numerous recipes. It is also one of the easiest to make and store. You should keep chicken, beef and fish stock on hand in your freezer at all times to enhance the flavor of almost any dish you are preparing.

Start keeping all the leftover parts when you are cleaning your game. If you're cleaning a chicken, for example, don't throw anything out. Put all the extra parts—gizzards, hearts, neckbones, skin, backbone, whatever—in a plastic bag and save. You might like to keep this bag in the freezer until you're ready to make stock. I generally have the parts of 2-3 chickens in my stock bag.

That's all the prep you'll need to do. To make the stock, put all your parts and pieces in a large pot and cover with water. Throw in a couple of carrots and celery stalks. You can add other seasonings, too—garlic, bay leaf, thyme, etc.—there are no restrictions or strict requirements. Bring to a boil and simmer for 3-4 hours while periodically skimming to keep the surface clear. Water can be added as needed.

Be careful not to add too many seasonings as the stock is cooking. You'll want the stock to maintain the natural flavor of your game. Instead, add seasonings to your recipes that actually use the stock.

The final step is to strain all the chunks. This is best done with a stock strainer, but anything can be used as long as you can get all the pieces and chunks out of the liquid. Let the stock set for a few minutes and then skim the fat off the surface. You now have stock.

You can refrigerate the stock for a few days. But it's best to fill an ice tray and freeze into cubes. These cubes are easy to handle and available for your recipes that call for meat stock. Once you cook with homemade stock, you'll want to have a supply of chicken, beef and fish stock in your freezer at all times.

Boning A Bird

Several years ago, a friend of mine gave me a recipe that required taking bones out of a duck. Even though he swore it was the best duck recipe ever created, I passed on it for a long time because I didn't know how to bone a bird. One day, I decided to learn how. I found out it isn't all that difficult. I now cook boneless chickens, turkeys and other birds all the time.

The most important requirement for boning any bird is a sharp knife. A boning knife works best for most work, but make sure it's sharp all the way to the point. You'll also want to have a cleaver or heavier knife handy for cutting through the bones and tough cartilage.

Go to the store and buy a roasting chicken. They're usually bigger than most and will make your first bird a little easier. After you take the little envelope of parts out of the body cavity, you're ready to start. Be sure to put those parts in your stock bag.

The first step is removing the wishbone from the bird. Lay the bird with the breasts down. The wishbone is in front of the neck cavity and basically holds the back to the breast. All you do is cut around the bone. You'll be able to feel the outline of the bone through the meat around it. After you've cut through the meat, cut through the connecting tissues on both sides, top and bottom. Remove the wishbone and throw it in your stock bag.

Next make a deep cut through the meat on both sides of the backbone, front to back. With your cleaver, cut down through the bones on both sides until you can remove the backbone (stock bag). You should be able to look right into the bird's body cavity.

Take your boning knife again and, starting anywhere, cut between the meat and the ribs all the way around the bird. It will be like scooping the ribs out. This step will take about 10 minutes. Be careful to cut close to the bones but don't worry about getting every little piece of meat off—what's left will help flavor your stock. Avoid cutting through the skin as you go around.

When you've gone as far as you can, you'll want to separate the breast bone from the thigh bone. Do this by cutting through the meat along each side of the thigh bone. At the end of the thigh bone (that's connected to the breast bone), cut the meat completely away. Pull the meat back to the thigh so you can cut through the joint and remove the bone when you pull out the rib cage. Do the same on both sides and remove the rib cage and thigh bones (stock bag).

You now have a bird with its breast and thigh meat intact, skin still attached, and the wings and drumsticks left with the bones in them. You can, if you're a glutton for punishment, continue by taking the wing and leg bones out, but this is where I quit boning and start cooking.

One of the best ways to cook this bird is as follows: Mix your favorite stuffing recipe (make plenty). Lay your bird on its back and fill the body with stuffing. Wrap the skin around it and connect with toothpicks. Put the bird in a roasting pan, breasts down, and arrange the wings and legs next to the body in their natural positions. Bake at 350 degrees for 45 minutes. When carving, cut the wings and legs away and slice the rest of the bird like a loaf of bread. Each diner will get a nice sampling of white and dark meat along with a big slice of dressing.

You'll quickly discover this is the best way to cook any bird and the few minutes it takes to remove the bones is well worth the effort. No matter if you're baking, frying or grilling, this technique results in great eating.

Incidentally, that duck recipe my friend gave me is absolutely delicious ... but that's another story.

Making Breading Stick

There are few things in this world as mysterious as getting breading to stick to the food you're frying. It used to drive me crazy! But after a great deal of trial-and-error, I figured it out. And like most skills, it's easy when you know how.

You'll find a lot of recipes that call for coating your food with bread crumbs before frying. No matter what the food is—meat, fish, potatoes, vegetables or whatever—you bread it the same way. Here's the secret to making breading stick:

1. Start by getting your food into the piece sizes you want to fry.

2. Pat on all sides with paper towels until completely dry. (This is an important step if you want the rest to work.) Let the food continue to air dry while doing the next step.

3. In separate bowls (big enough to lay the largest food piece), put the following ingredients: A nice pile of flour, seasoned with a little pepper; enough beaten eggs to coat all your food pieces; and, a generous portion of bread crumbs. (You can get these at the grocery store in a variety of seasonings or make your own by crushing crackers with a rolling pin and adding seasonings to taste.)

4. Remembering to completely cover the food on each step, take each individual food piece and roll in flour, dip in beaten eggs and roll in bread crumbs.

5. Lay the finished pieces on a plate. It is best if you can allow about 10 minutes per side to air dry.

6. In a skillet, heat oil until it's hot enough to begin sizzling as soon as food is put in. Fill the skillet with the breaded food pieces. Depending on the type of food, the frying time will vary. Your recipe will usually guide you on this. In general, when the breading is golden brown, the food should be ready to eat.

Cooking Over Coals

One of the easiest—and hardest—cooking skills to learn is how to cook over coals. I've seen a lot of people prepare mediocre meals because they didn't know the basics. Whether you're cooking in camp or on the backyard barbecue, a few easy-to-learn steps will put you on your way to consistently well-prepared meals.

The trick is the way you build the fire. Your average backyard hacker will pile charcoal in the middle of the pit, douse with starter and light the bonfire. Then, as the flames subside, he'll give it another shot of starter for a few more blazing minutes. In the end, he'll put the grill on and get ready to start the ceremony.

But he forgot the most important step—he didn't spread the coals.

If you're cooking a large piece of meat or a whole bird, spread the coals out to the edge of the pit so the heat isn't directly under the meat. This produces indirect heat for a more oven-like situation. Your meat will cook a little slower so you may have to add a few briquettes or logs to keep the fire hot. But the advantage is your meat will be cooked in the center without cremating the outside.

If, on the other hand, you're grilling burgers or steaks, you want to be sure the coals are spread evenly under the meat. For these types of foods, you should be sure to keep the grill far enough from the coals to prevent cooking too quickly.

Cooking over coals comes down to two basic rules:

1. Spread the coals

2. Cook slower rather than faster

Gravy Every Time

Did you ever make gravy that turned to lumps or wouldn't thicken no matter how long you heated it? How about the gravy that becomes a thick jell as soon as it begins to cool? I've had every kind of gravy problem you can imagine. But, gravy is easy if you know and execute the following secret.

Cook your meat—either bake or fry—as per your favorite recipe. When finished, pour off all but 2 T. of drippings (to make larger amounts, just double or triple this recipe). Don't bother to scrape the little pieces of meat and other remains from the bottom of the pan.

Add an equal amount of flour—a little at a time—to the heated drippings, stirring constantly. Your goal is to make a smooth paste of flour and drippings and bring to a boil. Stir paste as you slowly add about 2 cups of milk. Salt and pepper to taste. As gravy thickens to suit you, remove from the heat.

You can tell if your gravy is too thick by running your spoon or spatula across the bottom of the pan. If gravy is slow to run back into area you scraped, add some water and stir into gravy. If gravy is too thin, continue to heat while stirring until enough moisture cooks off to get gravy to consistency you desire.

For additional flavor, try adding 1-2 cubes of the frozen meat stock of your choice (see page on making stock).

Remember, you only need three simple ingredients for gravy—2 T. of drippings, 2 T. of flour and 2 cups of milk. You can add a little flavor with salt, pepper and stock.

No matter what kind of meat you're preparing, learn this recipe to consistently make great, flavorful gravy.

Camp Biscuits

Each autumn, for the last 15 years or so, I've been invited to go bird hunting with a group of friends. It's not because I'm such a great wingshooter or know the best ways to flush pheasants. I get to go because those guys love my delicious camp biscuits.

Every morning of pheasant camp, I get up, put on a pot of coffee and start making my camp biscuits—enough for eight hungry men and a couple of youngsters. But the secret of my biscuits isn't in the ingredients. My biscuits are special because of the way I make and cook them.

If you want to make enough biscuits for four people, start with 1 cup of flour. Add about ¼ tsp. of salt and 1½ tsp. of baking powder. If you're going to use buttermilk, add ¼ tsp. of baking soda. Mix all these together. Although many recipes call for it, never add sugar to biscuits (or cornbread).

To your flour mixture, add 1½ T. of shortening and cut it in with a pastry blender or fork until it takes on the consistency of coarse cornmeal. I recommend you moisten with buttermilk, but regular milk works just fine. Add buttermilk a little at a time and mix into flour until your batter becomes "gooey." Remember, if you want moist biscuits you have to start with a moist batter. Let stand for 10 minutes.

Pour some flour onto a board or plate. Spoon an egg-size portion of batter onto the flour. Lightly roll in the flour. Pick up the batter and roll between your hands gently to form a ball. When it starts to feel sticky, flatten slightly and place in a greased pan. Continue until all the batter is gone. The biscuits should be touching each other in the pan.

The secret to good biscuits is that they are wet on the inside and dry on the outside. Bake for 10 minutes at 450 degrees until light brown on top. Biscuits are done when they are the same color on top and bottom.

Small Game

The simplicity of the sport, not of bagging the game, is what makes North American small game hunting so alluring to so many hunters. It is that simplicity which makes rabbit and squirrel hunting an excellent way to start youngsters on a lifelong hunting career. And it is that same virtue which keeps grown hunters coming back to small game hunting.

This "a few shells in the pocket and head for the Back Forty" kind of hunting results in a lot of delicious small game feasts for NAHC Members every season. Over the years they've come up with some great recipes and some clever ways to handle those savory small game delicacies in the field and in the oven.

What To Look For In Rabbits

It's a pretty safe bet that more cottontail rabbits will be taken this fall by NAHC members than any other species of game animal. It is also a pretty safe bet that a lot of these tasty little morsels will be thrown out when the person dressing the carcass discovers white spots on the liver, or numerous little jelly-like cysts in the body cavity. If all such rabbits were discarded, at least 80 percent, and more likely more than 90 percent, of our bunnies would end up in the garbage can.

Fortunately, these two common problems are no cause for concern in eating the meat.

Most small game hunters are aware that white spots on a rabbit's liver are the telltale sign of tularemia. However, not just any spot indicates "rabbit fever". The white spots characteristic of tularemia are fine spots—pinhead sized—and number in the hundreds or thousands.

Some spots you will commonly find on rabbit livers are large ones, about the size of an eraser on the end of a pencil, and will be few in number. All that's necessary when you discover this kind of spot is that you discard the viscera carefully so that it won't be eaten by other animals, especially pets.

More readily seen than white spots on the liver are dog tapeworm cysts. They consist of little white objects about the size of a grain of rice, encased in a clear jelly envelope. Often there are only a few which may go unnoticed when the viscera is removed. At other times they may be very common and scattered throughout the body cavity.

These cysts are the dormant stage of the dog tapeworm, just waiting for some canine to catch and devour the rabbit so they can get on with being a tapeworm in the intestine of a dog, fox or other of the clan. The cottontail is the intermediate host in the life cycle of the tapeworm.

Skin A Squirrel In Two Minutes

by Jim Rupar

When I go squirrel hunting I carry a sharp knife, paper towels and a few plastic bags with me. I also have a five-gallon, plastic pail half full of salt water in the back of my vehicle. With that gear at hand, it's easy to clean any squirrel in two minutes or less:

1. Lay the squirrel on its belly, head facing to your left, if you are right-handed.

2. Grab the tail and bend it back toward the head and keep it tight. Your left hand should grip close to the base of the tail. Take your knife and cut through the tail at the base. Be careful not to cut the tail completely off. After you cut through, pull back the hide and cut it back about one-half to three-fourths of an inch.

3. Take the squirrel and lay it on its back. Place your left foot on top of the tail next to the rear of the squirrel. Grab its hind legs with one or both hands and pull slowly up toward your chest. This process will remove the hide from the squirrel's back and also from the middle of the belly. Pull until the hide is beyond the neck. The front legs should be exposed so you can pull them loose from the hide.

4. Hold the hind legs with your left hand. With your right hand, grab the wedge-shaped hide on its belly and pull up with both hands after you get it started. Do this until the back legs are completely exposed.

5. Cut off the legs and head. Split the crotch and cut down the belly and chest. Take out all the viscera and place the squirrel in a plastic bag. Roll it up and put it in your pocket or game bag. Use the paper towels to wipe your knife and hands. You are ready for your next squirrel. When I get back to the truck I empty my game into the salt water.

By the time I get home and bring my limit in the house, all the blood is removed, and it's a simple procedure to put the squirrels in the frying pan or freezer.

Rabbit Pie

Serves: 12
Prep Time: overnight plus 4 hours

2 **jack rabbits or 4-5 cottontails**	1 **large onion, diced**
	salt and pepper
1 **celery stalk, diced**	1 **tube pkg. biscuit mix**

Gravy:

reserved stock	**flour**
chicken bouillon	**salt**
1 **medium onion, diced**	**pepper**
celery (from above stalk)	**sage**
	poultry seasoning

Soak rabbits in salt water in refrigerator overnight. Dry, cut up and stew rabbits with celery and onions for 2-3 hours. Add salt and pepper to taste. Then strip meat from bones and put in 26-inch pie pan, add stock or gravy for moisture. Cover with biscuits. Bake at 350 degrees for 1 hour. For gravy, take reserved stock, add bouillon, onions and celery. Bring to a boil. Strain. Mix flour with an equal amount of water, add sauce to thickening. Season to taste with spices.

Michael D. Ferrin
Lyman, Wyoming

Raised Rabbits With Prunes

Serves: 2
Prep Time: 45 minutes

1 **rabbit, boned**	¼ **lb. butter**
salt and white pepper, to taste	1 **pkg. prunes**
	1 **small can beef broth**
½ **cup flour**	1 **small can chicken broth**

Season rabbit pieces with salt and white pepper. Dredge in flour and shake off the excess. Fry in moderately heated butter. Add flour and brown slightly. Add prunes, beef broth and chicken broth. Cover and bake at 375 degrees until meat falls away from bones. Serve with wild rice.

Anonymous

Chef's Rabbit

Serves: 2
Prep Time: 45 minutes

1 **rabbit or 2 pheasants** (cut into serving pieces) **salt and white pepper** **flour**	1 **onion, chopped fine** 8-10 **extra large mushrooms** (whole or quartered)
6 **bacon slices, cut into** **large squares**	6-8 **oz. beef stock** 1 **cup sour cream**

Season meat with salt and white pepper and dredge with flour. In hot skillet, cook bacon pieces about half way. Add rabbit and/or pheasant and brown on both sides. Add onions and saute with meat. Add mushrooms. Pour beef stock over all and put in preheated oven at 450 degrees for 30 minutes, or until meat is done. Take meat out. Whip sour cream into remaining pan juices and pour over meat.

Scott Ekenberg
Bloomington, Minnesota

German Style Hasenpfeffer

Serves: 4
Prep Time: 1 hour, 15 minutes

1 **rabbit, cut into pieces**	2 **small carrots, chopped**
2 **T. vegetable oil**	**mushrooms, (optional)**
1 **bay leaf, crumbled**	½ **cup vinegar**
1 **garlic clove, chopped**	1½ **cups water**
1 **spice clove**	1 **cup sour cream or**
2 **T. bacon, diced**	**evaporated milk**

Heat vegetable oil in sauce pan. When hot, add leaf, garlic clove, spice clove, bacon, carrots and mushrooms. Add rabbit and simmer until browned. Pour solution of ½ cup vinegar, mixed with 1-1½ cups water over meat. Cover pan and simmer until tender. Before removing pan from heat, add cream or evaporated milk. Serve hot with dumplings or large noodles.

C. Johnson
Victoria, Minnesota

Sweet And Sour Hasenpfeffer

Serves: 6
Prep Time: 27 hours

1 **rabbit**	2 **T. fat**
1 **qt. vinegar**	2 **T. flour**
2 **T. salt**	1 **cup cold water**
1 **T. pickling spice**	1 **tsp. cinnamon**
1 **T. peppercorns**	½ **tsp. allspice**
2 **large onions, sliced**	

Cut rabbit into serving portions, place in Crockpot and cover with vinegar combined with salt, spices, peppercorns and 1 onion. Let stand in a cool place for 24 hours. Drain, cover with boiling water and simmer until tender (about 1 hour, 30 minutes). Remove meat and strain broth. Melt fat in frying pan, blend in flour and add water, stirring constantly. Cook until thickened. Add rabbit, strained broth, cinnamon, allspice and remaining onion and simmer for 1 hour.

Boyd Miller
Fremont, Louisiana

Sweet And Sour Rabbit

Serves: 4
Prep Time: 1 hour, 30 minutes

2 **rabbits**	1 **cup pineapple chunks**
¼ **cup oil**	1 **green pepper, chopped**
1½ **tsp. salt**	1½ **T. cornstarch**
¼ **tsp. pepper**	¼ **cup sugar**
1 **cup pineapple juice**	½ **cup water**
¼ **cup vinegar**	

Heat oil and brown rabbit over moderate heat. Season with salt and pepper. Add pineapple juice and vinegar. Cover pan and cook over low heat 45 minutes or until tender. Add pineapple and green pepper. Cook a few minutes longer. Mix cornstarch and sugar; stir into water. Stir mixture gradually into liquid in pan. Cook slowly for 5 minutes until sauce thickens.

Anonymous

Roast Jackrabbit

Serves: 4
Prep Time: 2-3 hours

1 **rabbit, 7-8 lbs.**	3 **T. butter**
2 **T. prepared mustard**	1 **pint heavy cream**
4 **bacon slices**	2 **T. cognac or brandy**
salt and pepper	

Preheat oven to 375 degrees. Remove front legs and breast of rabbit. Rub saddle and back legs of rabbit with mustard and cover with bacon. Season. Place in oven in open roasting pan with butter. When well browned on top (about 45 minutes) baste with 3 T. heavy cream. Repeat every 10 minutes until rabbit is done (about 1½ hours). Keep rabbit hot. Skim fat out of roasting pan. Add rest of cream and cognac. Season. Pour sauce over rabbit and serve rest in sauce boat. Surround rabbit with applesauce, watercress, French fries and sauteed mushrooms.

Michael Courtney
Pella, Iowa

Le Lapin (The Rabbit)

Serves: 2
Prep Time: 1 hour

1 **rabbit or squirrel**	**pinch oregano**
flour	1 **beef bouillon cube**
5 **bacon slices**	1 **cup water**
½ **onion, cut into small**	**sprinkling of garlic**
pieces	2 **cloves**
1 **cup red wine**	1 **peppercorn**
1 **bay leaf**	

Fry bacon until done. Remove bacon and cook onions in grease. When onions are soft, dredge rabbit or squirrel in flour and brown. Add remaining ingredients to rabbit or squirrel and simmer 45 minutes or until tender. Serve with riced potatoes and gravy made from drippings.

Cathy Burnett
Minneapolis, Minnesota

Rabbit Casserole

Serves: 2-4
Prep Time: overnight plus 1-18 hours (depending on age
of rabbit)

2 **rabbits, cut into serving-size pieces**	3 **large bay leaves**
½ **tsp. salt**	5 **bacon slices**
fresh ground pepper	1 **cup seasoned bread crumbs**
½ **tsp. ground thyme**	

Soak young rabbits 1-2 hours in salt water—12-18 hours for older rabbits; 1 tsp. salt per qt. water. After soaking, wrap meat in damp cloth and store overnight in cold place. Butter casserole dish and add layer of rabbit pieces. Sprinkle seasonings. Add bacon slices. Repeat layering until ingredients are used up. Pour 1 cup water over casserole, cover and bake at 350 degrees until tender, 1-2 hours depending on age. Remove cover and sprinkle bread crumbs over casserole. Bake 30 minutes and serve.

Ken Cook
Fort Myers, Florida

Louisiana Squirrel

Serves: 4-6
Prep Time: 2 hours

4 **squirrels, quartered**	½ **tsp. seasoned salt**
1 **cup brown rice**	⅛ **tsp. garlic powder**
2 **14½-oz. cans tomatoes, cut up**	⅛ **tsp. black pepper**
	⅛ **tsp. cayenne pepper**
¾ **green pepper, chopped**	**salt and pepper**
¾ **cup onion, chopped**	3 **T. vegetable oil**

Preheat oven to 325 degrees. Line 13x9x2-inch baking pan with heavy duty foil, leaving 1½" foil collar. In pan, combine rice, tomatoes, green pepper, onion and seasonings. Season squirrel pieces with salt and pepper. Saute in oil until lightly browned. To cover, use casserole wrap, bake 1-2 hours.

Richard Orban
Kankakee, Illinois

Brunswick Stew

Serves: 8
Prep Time: 3-4 hours

5 lbs. half squirrel, pork	**1 chili pepper, chopped**
¼ cup shortening	**2 cloves**
½ cup onions, chopped	**3 cups corn, cut from cob**
1½-2 cups tomatoes - skinned,	**2 tsp. Worcestershire**
seeded, quartered	**sauce**
3 cups fresh lima beans	**1 cup toasted bread**
1 cup boiling water	**crumbs**

Cut meat into "stew size" pieces. Saute slowly in shortening until lightly browned. Remove and brown onions in remaining fat. Place meat, onions, tomatoes, lima beans, water, chili pepper and cloves in large stewing pan and simmer covered, until nearly tender. Add water if needed. Add corn. Simmer until tender. Add salt and pepper, Worcestershire, stir in bread crumbs.

Jane Obern
Minneapolis, Minnesota

Warna's Squirrel Stew

Serves: 6
Prep Time: 4 hours, 30 minutes

3-5 squirrels, quartered	**1 can cream of chicken**
2 tsp. salt	**soup**
½ tsp. paprika	**1 can cream of mushroom**
dash of pepper	**soup**
4 T. butter	**2 soup cans of water**
2 cups water	**5 potatoes, cubed**
2 onions, chopped	**3 celery stalks, chopped**
1 tsp. poultry seasoning	**6 carrots, chopped**
1 pkg. dry onion soup mix	

Sprinkle squirrels with salt, paprika and pepper. Set aside. Melt butter in Dutch oven and brown squirrel. Add water, onions, poultry seasoning and onion soup mix. Mix well, cover and simmer 30 minutes. Add other ingredients. Cover and cook 3 hours.

Warna Reed

Chuck's Squirrel Stew

Serves: 4-6
Prep Time: 3-4 hours

1 **squirrel, cut up**	3 **potatoes, diced**
¼ **lb. mild salt pork, cut up**	3 **carrots, diced**
¾ **lb. lean raw pork, cut**	1 **can stewed tomato**
into pieces	**chunks**
salt and pepper	1 **green pepper, sliced**
½ **cup flour**	1 **onion, sliced**
1 **bay leaf**	**paprika**
several whole cloves	

Dice salt pork and fry until crisp. Remove crisp pork if preferred, but keep drippings. Sprinkle cut-up squirrel and raw pork pieces with salt, pepper and flour. Brown in 2-3 T. salt-pork drippings. Add enough water to cover meat, bay leaf and cloves. Cover tightly and cook slowly for 2-3 hours until tender. Add potatoes, carrots, tomatoes, green pepper and onion. Cook until tender. To thicken, mix 1-2 T. flour to a smooth paste with an equal amount of cold water and add to stew. Season with salt, pepper and paprika.

C. Johnson
Victoria, Minnesota

Squirrel Jambalaya

Serves: 4
Prep Time: 2 hours

4 **squirrels**	1 **garlic clove**
1½ **cups water**	⅛ **green pepper**
salt and pepper	4 **T. parsley**
2 **large onions**	1 **cup uncooked rice**
2 **celery stalks**	

Cut squirrel into pieces. Add water, cook with vegetables and spices. Remove meat from bones. Discard bones. Add rice to meat and broth. Cook 20-30 minutes or until rice is done.

Andrew Stevens
Loganberries 4-H

Crockpot Squirrel Stew

Serves: 3-4
Prep Time: overnight plus 8 hours

3 **squirrels**	½ **tsp. rosemary**
marinade (see below)	6 **whole allspice**
12 **small whole onions**	2 **bay leaves**
6 **medium potatoes,**	1 **T. salt**
quartered	¾ **tsp. pepper**
8 **carrots, quartered**	¼ **cup beef consomme**
½ **tsp. thyme**	6 **oz. fresh whole**
¼ **tsp. basil**	**mushrooms**

Marinade:

¼ **cup chianti**	¼ **tsp. paprika**
2 **garlic cloves, minced**	1 **tsp. bacon bits**

Cut squirrel in quarters and marinate overnight, turning squirrel several times. Put onions, potatoes and carrots in Crockpot. Put spices in tea steeper and put steeper in Crockpot. Add squirrel, salt and pepper, beef consomme and all marinade from squirrel. Cover and cook on low 8 hours. Add mushrooms during last hour and stir once. Serve with biscuits or cornbread. To thicken gravy, add creamed mixture of ¼ cup flour and 2 T. butter.

Anonymous

Squirrel With Parsley

Serves: 2
Prep Time: 1 hour

3 **squirrels**	**salt and pepper**
2 **small onions, minced**	4 **T. dandelion greens or**
1 **cup cold mashed**	**watercress, chopped**
potatoes	2 **T. butter**
4 **T. parsley, chopped**	

Cook squirrels in salted water for 30-45 minutes. Remove meat from bones. Blend meat, onions, potatoes and parsley. Season. Form into balls and roll in greens or watercress. Fry in hot butter.

John Lee
Osceola, Wisconsin

Bob Bassett's Braised Squirrel

Serves: 4
Prep Time: 1 hour, 30 minutes

2 squirrels, quartered
½ cup water
½ cup red or white wine
  fresh ground pepper
4 T. margarine or corn oil
2 celery stalks, thinly
  diced

1 can drained mushrooms
1 large onion, sliced
1 chicken bouillon cube
  salt, ground if possible
  pinch of sage
  pinch of thyme

Place water, ¼ cup wine, pepper and squirrels in frying pan on medium-low heat. Cover and cook slowly for 45 minutes to 1 hour. Watch carefully to keep water level up. Keep adding water, also turn meat occasionally. The wine will help tenderize meat and add a nice flavor to the game. After 45 minutes, add remainder of wine, a little water, margarine or oil, celery and onions. Simmer 5 minutes. Add bouillon cube and spices. Simmer until celery and onions are partially cooked. Turn heat up a little to let water boil off. As water disappears, add mushrooms. Just before it starts to fry, remove from heat.

Bob Bassett
Kunkletown, Pennsylvania

Krafty Squirrel

Serves: 3-4
Prep Time: 2 hours

4-5 squirrels
1 bottle Kraft barbecue
  sauce

1 8-oz. can pineapple juice
5 T. Worcestershire sauce

Brown whole squirrels in an iron skillet. Place browned squirrels in baking pan. Mix barbecue sauce, pineapple juice and Worcestershire sauce and pour over squirrel. Bake in covered dish at 375 degrees. Periodically baste squirrels with sauce mixture and bake until tender.

Paul Pierce
Atascadero, California

Tasty Critters

Great tasting wild game meals come wrapped in some pretty unusual packages—namely the hide of a critter like a raccoon, beaver, woodchuck or opossum! The rule around many NAHC households is "if you killed it, you eat it!"

And with that philosophy in mind, NAHC members have come up with some delicious ways to serve "game" animals that might not seem too appetizing at first glance.

As in the preparation of any type of wild meat, there are some tricks that will help make "tasty critters" more appealing at the dinner table. Many are unique to the unusual critter you want to cook! The following recipes should provide the adventuresome family with excellent meals from new sources which you may never have considered before. And many will work on what most NAHC members consider traditional wild game meat as well.

Raccoon
Skin the raccoon and remove glands in the small of the back on both sides of the spine. Also remove the gland under each foreleg. Remove all fat and soak in salted water for eight to 10 hours in the refrigerator. Blanch in water for five minutes with two tablespoons of baking powder. You are now ready to prepare the raccoon in any manner that suits you. Raccoon should be cooked until the meat reaches 190 degrees or until the juice runs clear.

Opossum
Opossum should be cleaned but not skinned. Put in boiling water deep enough to cover it, and take it out when you can pull the hairs off. Scrape while flushing with cold water. Remove small red glands in the small of the back and under each foreleg between the shoulder and ribs. Cook in boiling water for approximately 20 minutes. Then roast like you would pork or rabbit.

Porcupine
Porcupine should be soaked overnight in salted water. Bring to a boil in the same water, then repeat in fresh water. Your porcupine is then ready for any preparation.

Woodchuck
After dressing out the woodchuck, leave it hanging for two days. Make sure to remove the several kernel-like glands under the forelegs. Soak in salted water for 24 hours and cook the woodchuck like you would rabbit or chicken.

Beaver
To cook beaver you should first remove all fat, being careful not to cut into the musk glands. Hang the beaver in the cold for several days and blanch in salt water for one hour before cooking. Braise as beef. Beaver tails should be held over an open flame until skin blisters. When cool, peel off skin and barbecue meat inside until it's tender.

Muskrat
Preparation for cooking can be done much like beaver. It's important to remove the little glands under the hind and forelegs.

Barbecued Coon

Serves: 4-6
Prep Time: 5 hours

1 **young raccoon**	2 **tsp. barbecue spice**
1 **dried red pepper**	1 **tsp. Worcestershire**
1 **bay leaf**	**sauce**
several celery leaves	1 **tsp. vinegar**
Barbecue Sauce:	2 **dashes of liquid smoke**
2 **cups catsup**	1 **tsp. sugar**

Trim fat from coon and cut into pieces. Pressure cook coon and spices for 1-2 hours or until meat falls off bones. (Time depends on the size and age of the coon.) Discard liquid and spices. Tear meat into small pieces and put in roaster. Mix together barbecue sauce, adding spices to taste, and pour over coon. Make sure all is covered. Cover roaster and bake 2-3 hours in slow oven. Serve on buns. If you double or triple ingredients you can make enough to freeze for those days when the whole coon-hunting party stops by unexpectedly.

Harold Stultz
Lawrence, Kansas

Roast Raccoon

Serves: 4
Prep Time: 3 hours

8 **coon legs and 2 backs**	1 **large onion, chopped**
flour	3 **garlic cloves, chopped**
2 **cups tomato juice**	1 **celery stalk, diced**
salt and pepper	2 **tsp. chili powder**

Roll legs and backs in flour. Brown meat. Put in roaster. Pour tomato juice over legs and backs. Salt and pepper. Add onion, garlic, celery and chili powder. Roast at medium heat for 3 hours. Serve with any side dish and bread and butter. Makes an excellent main course when served with a green vegetable and boiled potatoes.

Louis F. Dell
New Riegel, Ohio

Muskrat Minnesota

Serves: 4
Prep Time: 3 hours

1 muskrat
1 qt. water
1 tsp. salt
⅛ tsp. pepper
1 small onion, sliced

½ cup butter or margarine
1 cup catsup
½ tsp. Worcestershire
**   sauce**

Wash and cut muskrat into quarters or slightly smaller pieces. Soak overnight in 1 qt. of water with 1 tsp. salt. When ready to cook, place muskrat pieces in deep pot and add fresh water along with salt, pepper and onion. Cook for 1 hour on medium-high heat. Remove muskrat pieces from water, dry off and brown in butter in a heavy skillet. After browning on one side, turn over and pour catsup and Worcestershire sauce over meat. Cover meat with water. Simmer for 30 minutes or until gravy is thick enough to serve. Serve gravy over mashed potatoes and French green beans as a vegetable on the side.

Judi Smith
Apple Valley, Minnesota

Alligator Stew

Serves: 4-6
Prep Time: 1 hour

2 lbs. alligator meat
½ cup oil
½ cup green onions,
**   chopped**
½ cup bell peppers,
**   chopped**

½ cup onions, chopped
**   (red onions taste best)**
½ cup celery, chopped
2 T. ground parsley
1 10-oz. can tomatoes

Put ½ cup oil in pot and brown alligator meat. Add remaining ingredients, cover pot and cook over medium heat 30-40 minutes. Stir occasionally. Serve over cooked rice.

Chris Yezzi
Greenbelt, Maryland

Alligator Meatballs

1 lb. alligator meat	2 tsp. lemon pepper
1 egg	½ tsp. salt
2 T. onion, finely chopped	¼ cup bread crumbs
2 T. celery, finely chopped	flour
1 T. parsley flakes	1 cup cooking oil
2 T. shallots, chopped	mustard (optional)

Chop or grind alligator meat. Combine the egg, onion, celery, parsley, shallots, bread crumbs and seasonings in a bowl, and allow to set for 1 hour. Form into 1-inch balls, dredge with flour and fry in oil until brown. For added flavor, dredge meatballs in mustard before dredging in flour. Serve hot. It's a perfect entree for dinner with hunting friends.

Thomas Fletcher
Mathews, Louisiana

Beaver Tail A La Denny

Serves: 4-6
Prep Time: 1 hour

4 beaver tails	1 cup sherry
1 onion	dash of Tabasco sauce
1 T. butter	3 cups barbecue sauce
2 T. prepared mustard	grated Parmesan cheese

Place whole beaver tails on barbecue or oven broiler rack until scaly skin blisters. Let cool in freezer compartment. Remove cold blistered skin and discard. Put white meat aside. In shallow roasting pan, saute onion in butter until clear, stir in mustard to coat onions, then stir in sherry, Tabasco and half of barbecue sauce, making sure bottom of pan is covered. Spread out beaver tails in pan, cover with remaining barbecue sauce, sprinkle with cheese, and bake in 450-degree oven for 45 minutes. Serve hot with wild or ordinary rice topped with generous spoonfuls of remaining sauce.

Major E.M.S. Deneumoustier
Barrie, Ontario

Beaver Tail Beans

Serves: 2-4
Prep Time: 45 minutes

1 **beaver tail**	**salt and pepper**
pot of beans	1 **onion, chopped**

Blister tail over fire until skin loosens (or dip into boiling water for a couple minutes). Pull off skin. Cut up meat and boil with a pot of beans. Add salt and pepper to taste. Add chopped onions to enhance flavor. Beaver tail is also good roasted over a campfire or in the oven.

Guides And Outfitters Association
British Columbia

Baked Groundhog In Sour Cream And Mustard

Serves: 2-4
Prep Time: overnight plus 1 hour, 30 minutes

1 **medium groundhog, cut up**	½ **cup carrots, thinly sliced**
flour	½ **cup mushrooms, sliced**
salt and pepper, to taste	3 **T. parsley, chopped**
5 **T. butter**	1 **T. rosemary, chopped (optional)**
spiced mustard	1 **tsp. Kitchen Bouquet**
4 **bacon slices (smoked)**	1 **cup sour cream**
1 **onion, diced**	½ **cup sweet cream**

Soak pieces overnight in salted water, drain and pat dry. Roll in flour, salt and pepper and saute in butter until well browned. Spread spiced mustard on both sides and place bacon strips in a shallow baking dish. Saute onion, carrots and mushrooms. Add parsley, rosemary, Kitchen Bouquet, salt and pepper. Over low heat, stir in sour cream and sweet cream. Pour over meat in baking dish and bake at 350 degrees for 45 minutes or until tender. Add a little cream 15 minutes before removing from oven to keep meat moist.

Tom Squier
Aberdeen, North Carolina

Salisbury Steaks A La Groundhog

Serves: 6
Prep Time: 2 hours, 30 minutes

2 lbs. ground meat from 2 groundhogs	**1 tsp. salt**
½ 10-oz. can flavored bread crumbs	**½ tsp. pepper**
	1 cup cooking oil
	1 qt. tomato juice

Mix together ground meat, bread crumbs, salt and pepper. Form into serving-size portions and press firmly together to form steaks. In heavy skillet, brown on both sides in oil. Remove from skillet and place in roasting pan. Cover the mixture with tomato juice. Cover roaster and bake at 350 degrees for 2 hours. Note: If the steaks seem too soft and mushy, add more bread crumbs.

J. W. Townsend
Masontown, Pennsylvania

Chuck's Famous Crow

Serves: 4
Prep Time: 1 hour

6 crow breasts	**2 cups carrots, sliced**
½ cup flour	**½ cup celery, chopped**
bacon drippings	**1 cup green pepper, chopped**
1 cup onion, chopped	**salt and pepper**
1 garlic clove, chopped	
½ cup dry red wine	

Roll crow breasts in flour and brown in bacon drippings. After browning, add onion and garlic. Saute. Add wine and cook on low heat for 30 minutes with cover on. Add carrots, celery and green pepper. Salt and pepper to taste. Cover and cook for another half hour. Add more water to the pan liquid for making a tasty gravy to complement the entree if gravy is desired. Serve over rice with buttermilk biscuits and a lettuce salad.

R. Hanson
Reno, Nevada

Coyote Soup

Serves: 6
Prep Time: 4 hours

coyote hind quarter	**salt and pepper**
cooking oil	**spices**
2 cups red wine	**2 cabbage heads, chopped**
3 onions, chopped	**8 potatoes, chopped**
1 garlic clove	

Cut meat into chunks and brown in oil. Add wine, onions, garlic, salt and pepper and your other favorite spices. Cook for 30 minutes. Add cabbage and potatoes. Cook until tender. Serve with hot biscuits or corn bread. Makes a hearty meal out on the open range.

Henry Johnson
Trinidad, Colorado

Fox Nuggets

Serves: 2-4
Prep Time: overnight

1 fox	**2 T. sugar**
1 onion, chopped	**⅓ cup Mesquite or Hickory**
3 garlic cloves, minced	**smoke flavor**
½ cup red wine vinegar	**cooking oil**

Skin, bone and cut fox meat into strips, 2-3 inches long, removing most of the fat and tendons. Mix all ingredients except oil in a 1-gallon, zip-lock plastic bag. Close bag and knead contents to cover fox well. Place bag in refrigerator for at least 10 hours or overnight, turning once or twice. The next day, heat oil to 350 degrees while draining meat in a colander, discarding the marinade. Deep fry meat about 3-5 minutes or until well done. Drain well on paper towel. Serve plain or with one of your favorite dipping sauces.

Anthony Vernier
Allegan, Michigan

Roast Opossum

Serves: 3
Prep Time: 1 hour

1 opossum
2½ tsp. salt
black pepper
flour
½ cup water

Trim excess fat from opossum. Wipe with damp cloth to remove hair, and wash inside and out with warm water. Drain thoroughly. Rub opossum inside and out, with salt and pepper. Sprinkle again with flour. Lay opossum on its back in roasting pan. Seal with tinfoil or use a tight-fitting cover. Add water and bake at 350 degrees for 1 hour, 30 minutes. Serve with potatoes and a salad. It is not true that opossum are born dead on the side of the road, but a roadkill will do just fine for this recipe. Just trim off the fat and any damaged meat before fixing.

Clinton Johnson, Sr.
Conowingo, Maryland

Breaded Lion Loin

Serves: 8
Prep Time: 2 hours

2 lion backstraps
4 eggs
1 tsp. garlic salt
1 tsp. salt
1 tsp. pepper
2 cups flour
cooking oil

Cut meat into ½-inch slices. Whip eggs until smooth. Add seasonings. Dip meat in eggs, then in flour. Fry in medium-hot skillet until batter is crisp on both sides. If meat is tough, pound it with a knife first. Serve with a green vegetable and your favorite red wine.

Bryce Pinning
Delta, Utah

Lion Supreme

Serves: 8
Prep Time: 1 hour, 45 minutes

1 **lion hindquarter or 8 steaks**	1 **tsp. garlic salt**
½ **cup margarine**	2 **T. dried onion, minced**
½ **tsp. salt**	**wine**

Put meat in casserole dish and pour ½ cup margarine over. Add salt, garlic salt and onion. Bake 1 hour at 350 degrees. Remove from oven, marinate for 45 minutes in wine.

Jane Smith
Trout Creek, Montana

Mixed Bag Soup

Serves: 4-6
Prep Time: 10 hours, 30 minutes

game animal/bird parts	1 **large tomato**
1 **large beef soup bone**	3 **large carrots, chopped**
water to cover	2 **small potatoes, chopped**
salt and pepper	1 **cup peas**
1 **large onion, chopped**	1 **cup lima beans**
3 **celery ribs, chopped**	1 **cup string beans, cut**
1 **2-inch cabbage wedge, chopped**	1 **cup corn**

Place bone in large pan and cover with water. Add salt and pepper. Cover and simmer 8 hours. Remove bone and refrigerate broth until fat congeals. Remove fat, add game parts, cover and simmer 2-3 hours until all ingredients are tender. Strain broth, removing bone chips. Add onion, celery, cabbage, tomatoes, salt and pepper to taste. Cover and simmer until vegetables are done. Cut meat from cooled bones into small pieces. Add carrots to broth, cook 10 minutes. Add rest of vegetables. Cook until tender. Add meat and heat to serve.

E. Jenkins
Elkland, Pennsylvania

Appetizer To Casserole In One

Serves: varies
Prep Time: 30 minutes

any game meat
bacon slices
1 tsp. black pepper

2 cups water
½ cup Worcestershire
sauce

Cut meat into cubes and wrap each in ½ bacon slice. Secure with toothpicks. Mix remaining ingredients in cast iron skillet. Broil meat in mixture until tender and most of the liquid is gone. Brown meat by stirring in hot grease left in pan. Makes great hors d'oeuvres. For casserole, cut meat, chop bacon and cook as indicated above. Then, stir in a can of sliced potatoes and a can of any vegetable. Heat thoroughly and serve.

Shelly Amys
Poplar, Wisconsin

Pipikaula (Hawaiian Jerky)

Serves: 10 as "pupu" (hors d'oeuvres)
Prep Time: 10 hours

2 lbs. meat (aged wild
game)
1½ cups water (boiled and
cooled)

⅛ cup table salt
½ tsp. monosodium
glutamate (MSG)
1 tsp. Tabasco sauce

Age meat by leaving it unwrapped in refrigerator for 5 days. Cut meat with the grain into long strips, about ½-inch thick and 2-2½ inches wide. Combine all ingredients except meat, stir well and let mixture stand 30 minutes. Marinate meat in covered container in refrigerator for 12 hours. Drain meat and spread strips on oven rack. Form a shallow pan out of aluminum foil and place foil on rack below to catch drippings. Leave meat in 150-degree oven for 8 hours. After 4 hours, remove foil with drippings and turn meat strips over. Cut strips into thin slices to serve.

W. T. Yoshimoto
Honolulu, Hawaii

Index